RESCALING URBAN GOVERNANCE

I0222939

Urban Policy, Planning and the Built Environment

Series Editors:

Nick Gallent, Bartlett School of Planning, University College London, UK

Pierre Filion, University of Waterloo, Canada

Nicole Gurran, University of Sydney, Australia

This international series embraces the interdisciplinary dimensions of urbanism and the built environment – extending from urban policy and governance to urban planning, management, housing, transport, infrastructure, landscape, heritage and design. It aims to provide critical analyses of the challenges confronting cities around the world at the intersection between markets, public policy and the built environment, as well as the responses emerging from these challenges.

The series looks in particular at the contested nature of government intervention in the urban land and housing market and how urban governance, planning and design processes respond to increasing social complexity, social-spatial diversity and the goal of democratic renewal.

Urban Policy, Planning and the Built Environment

Editorial Board:

Karen Chapple, University of California, Berkeley, US

Marco Cremaschi, Sciences Po, Paris, France

Robyn Dowling, University of Sydney, Australia

Jill L. Grant, Dalhousie University, Canada

Umberto Janin Rivolin, Politecnico di Torino, Italy

Markus Moos, University of Waterloo, Canada

Libby Porter, RMIT University, Australia

Mike Raco, University College London, UK

Mark Scott, University College Dublin, Ireland

Quentin Stevens, RMIT University, Australia

Igor Vojnovic, Michigan State University, US

Laura Wolf-Powers, City University of New York, US

Forthcoming in the series:

The Self-Build Experience: Institutionalization, Place-making and City Building, edited by William Salet, Camilla D'Ottaviano, Stan Majoor and Daniel Bossuyt

The New Urban Ruins: Vacancy, Urban Politics and International Experiments in the Post-Crisis City, edited by Cian O'Callaghan and Cesere Di Feliciantonio

Find out more at
policy.bristoluniversitypress.co.uk

RESCALING URBAN GOVERNANCE

Planning, Localism and Institutional Change

John Sturzaker and Alexander Nurse

P

First published in Great Britain in 2021 by

Policy Press, an imprint of
Bristol University Press
University of Bristol
1-9 Old Park Hill
Bristol
BS2 8BB
UK
t: +44 (0)117 954 5940
e: bup-info@bristol.ac.uk

Details of international sales and distribution partners are available at
policy.bristoluniversitypress.co.uk

© Bristol University Press 2021

British Library Cataloguing in Publication Data
A catalogue record for this book is available from the British Library

978-1-4473-5079-8 paperback
978-1-4473-5077-4 hardback
978-1-4473-5080-4 ePub
978-1-4473-5078-1 ePdf

The rights of John Sturzaker and Alexander Nurse to be identified as authors of this work has
been asserted by them in accordance with the Copyright, Designs and Patents Act 1988.

All rights reserved: no part of this publication may be reproduced, stored in a retrieval system,
or transmitted in any form or by any means, electronic, mechanical, photocopying, recording,
or otherwise without the prior permission of Bristol University Press.

Every reasonable effort has been made to obtain permission to reproduce copyrighted
material. If, however, anyone knows of an oversight, please contact the publisher.

The statements and opinions contained within this publication are solely those of the authors
and not of the University of Bristol or Bristol University Press. The University of Bristol and
Bristol University Press disclaim responsibility for any injury to persons or property resulting
from any material published in this publication.

Bristol University Press and Policy Press work to counter discrimination on grounds of
gender, race, disability, age and sexuality.

Cover design: Andrew Corbett
Front cover image: Getty

This book is dedicated to Jenifer and Sarah.

Contents

List of tables, figures and boxes

Notes on authors

John Sturzaker is a Senior Lecturer in Planning at the University of Liverpool, UK. He has had a varied career as a planner in both practice and research, and aims through his work to bring both areas closer together. His teaching and research interests include community planning, planning and housing and sustainable urban development. In recent years he has closely followed the localism agenda in the UK and its implementation, with a particular focus on Neighbourhood Planning.

Alexander Nurse is a Lecturer in Urban Planning at the University of Liverpool, UK. His teaching and research interests primarily focus on sub-national governance, particularly at the city and city-regional scales. In recent years this work has centred on the city-regional devolution agenda in the UK, with a particular focus on the Northern Powerhouse.

Glossary

Barnett Formula   The means by which the budgets to be devolved from the UK to the devolved nations of Scotland, Wales and Northern Ireland are calculated.

Brexit   The portmanteau used to refer to the UK leaving the European Union (*British exit*).

(Statutory) Development plan   The documents that carry legal weight in the determination of planning applications for development proposals.

General power of competence   Introduced by the Localism Act 2011, this, in theory, gave local authorities the power to do anything they were not explicitly forbidden by legislation from doing as opposed to only being able to do things they were explicitly permitted to do by legislation.

Governance   The concept that the delivery of the aims of government is not done purely through the state but by a range of actors, some state and some non-state.

IMD (Index of Multiple Deprivation)   The measure used to quantify relative deprivation at various scales across England.

LEP (Local Enterprise Partnership)   A series of economic development agencies instigated in 2011, spanning multiple local authorities and premised on travel-to-work areas – these LEPs would be led by business leaders.

Local Planning Authority   The body with the legal powers to produce a local plan and determine planning applications for development proposals in accordance with that plan.

Localism Act 2011   A landmark piece of legislation by the UK Parliament that purports to deliver on the 2010–15 UK coalition government's pledges to decentralise power within the UK.

Midlands Engine   The equivalent of the Northern Powerhouse (see below) for the Midlands region of England.

Neighbourhood Planning   A specific part of the English planning system introduced by the Localism Act 2011, operative at the community scale.

New Homes Bonus   A payment to English local authorities from the UK government for each house granted planning permission.

Northern Powerhouse   The initiative, first introduced by George Osborne in 2014, which came to encompass the programme of devolution and infrastructure spending towards the cities and regions of Northern England.

Northern Way A collaboration between the North East, North West and Yorkshire and Humber regions, active from 2004 to 2011.

PCC (police and crime commissioner) Elected posts introduced in 2012 to supervise activities of the spatially bounded police forces in the UK.

Preston Model A term to describe a mode of operation of local government whereby large local institutions spend more of their money locally, focused where possible on cooperatives and other community-led institutions. Derived from the city of Preston in the North West of England that has utilised this approach since 2012.

West Lothian Question As a consequence of devolution to Scotland, Wales and Northern Ireland but not equivalently to England, English MPs in the UK Parliament can no longer vote on devolved matters whereas MPs from the devolved nations can vote on matters that only pertain to England.

Acknowledgements

We would like to thank all those who have directly assisted us with writing this book, including an anonymous reviewer who had the thankless task of reading the entire draft manuscript and made wholly positive and helpful comments.

We have been grateful for the help and support of many colleagues and friends who have helped and supported us over many years in the work this book draws on. These are too many to name, but it would be remiss not to specifically mention Ian Mell, Olivier Sykes, Michael Parkinson, Alex Lord and Andy Plater.

Finally, and most importantly, our thanks go to our families for their enduring support.

Introduction: Planning reform and state spatial rescaling

In a time of political upheaval around the world, many jurisdictions are making changes to how they govern their cities in an attempt to redistribute (or appear to redistribute) power within those cities. Such changes can occur at a range of scales, with various aims, explicit or implicit. The UK is one such place, having experienced a particularly rapid series of changes over the last 10 years, at every scale, from national to community levels. This book provides, for the first time, comprehensive analysis of this period, looking in detail at the UK but situated within the broader international context.

The overall aim of the book is to analyse the overall effects of these recent reforms to city governance, explicitly considering whether they can be said to be progressive in nature. We do this through three objectives. The first is to present in one easily accessible volume comprehensive yet concise analysis of results of the changes to city governance that have been seen in the UK since 2010 (chosen as the latest in the series of 'epochal' years of substantial shift in approach – 1979 and 1997 being previous loci of change, as we discuss in subsequent chapters), at a range of scales. This is important for two reasons: (a) many of the changes that have been made provide important lessons for other jurisdictions which are making changes to their own city governance practices; and (b) UK governance has undergone extensive change over that period and no single point of reference exists which deals with that change in a comprehensive manner. The second objective is to consolidate and disseminate research in this field, and to disseminate new thinking about the overall implications of this research, to facilitate informed discussion and debate about changes to governance practices and the outcomes of those changes. The final objective is to challenge policy and practice in the field of city governance in the UK and internationally, to strengthen the evidence base for policy-makers to take decisions regarding reforms to governance practices.

By looking 'from top to bottom', that is, starting with the changing relationship between cities and their national governments, and moving from regional to local to community scales, this book deals with the totality of reforms to city governance that are variously badged as *devolution, decentralisation* and *localism*. Our central analytical theme is to explore how moving power away from a centralised space improves prospects for the people who live in today's cities. The rhetorical aims often espoused for reforms of this nature include that the quality of decision-making will be improved, that democracy will be 'deepened' in some way, and that thorny contemporary issues (the type dubbed 'wicked problems' by Rittel and Webber, 1973) will be more easily resolved. Reflecting this, we are particularly interested in the redistributive effects of localism in terms of both the processes of governance and the outcomes of decisions taken in cities.

The book interrogates the results of changes to governance practices as a means to explore the extent to which power is genuinely being redistributed and spatial inequalities are being addressed. The UK provides the basis for much of this analysis, because to understand the nature, scope and variegated results of changing governance practices in a particular context requires such focused study, and also because the UK is perhaps unique in the extent to which its city governance agenda has changed so significantly in the last decade. Thus it provides an unusual opportunity to explore the effects of changes in such practices at a range of scales. It is clearly important, however, to situate this exploration within the experience elsewhere, so each chapter includes a discussion of international examples.

The book is therefore highly topical, given the ongoing imperative for those in power to at least appear that they are interested in 'empowering' their citizens to take (back) control of the places in which they live and work, and the need for the rest of us to interrogate the claims of those in power, to challenge assumptions about any automatic correlation between devolution and decentralisation and positive outcomes, and to try to make changes to governance practices work in the best interests of all in society.

This chapter sets the context for the book. It first considers the pressures and drivers for change facing cities around the world, and specifically in the UK, including globalisation and the consequent structural changes to cities' economies, the 2008 financial crisis, and climate change. It then defines what we mean by city governance and identifies the range of governance approaches adopted to confront these issues at the various scales discussed in subsequent chapters: national, sub-national, regional to city-regional, local and neighbourhood and community. It then discusses the major policy preoccupations of politicians in the UK that the various approaches must deliver against: housing, transport and jobs provision. The chapter situates the discussion in subsequent chapters within the wider frameworks of urban governance, including the theoretical and analytical tools that we use to explore the processes and outcomes of these governance practices.

Drivers for change in cities

As we face down the global challenges of the 21st century, the nation-state finds its position as the natural place in which those solutions are found increasingly challenged (Dasgupta, 2018). Instead, it is argued that levels below the nation-state (that is, cities and regions) now offer productive ways forward to meet the challenges of this century (Barber, 2013).

The major policy challenges facing cities are profound, and have deep roots in the increasingly globalised world brought about in the latter half of the 20th century. Increasingly, and ironically, it is the interconnections that define globalisation – whereby individual actors (for example, economies and consumers) are reliant on goods, services and interactions outside of their immediate vicinity – which simultaneously define its shortcomings (Sassen, 1999; Giddens, 2003). Although papered over for some time as an inconvenience, those shortcomings have had a knock-on effect to manifest as fundamental policy issues. They are: the growth of 'global' cities and simultaneous de-industrialisation, (unequal) responses to the 2008 global financial crisis, and the emergence of a populism and political crisis that has taken hold in many Western democracies. We argue that these issues cannot be treated individually: they are inextricably connected.

One of the major themes of the globalising world was the shift away from traditional industrial economic activity as the major driver of the global economy towards cities specialising in other forms of economic activity (for example, banking). Recognising this shift, Sassen (1991, 1994) made the case for a new breed of 'global cities' that embodied these shifts – often identified by the headquartering of major transnational corporations, as well as a unique mix of 'centrality and networks' (Sassen, 2001, p 79) or, in other words, access to national governance networks. The result was that cities which embodied those characteristics – often capitals – became increasingly dominant players in this globalising economy to the extent that over time their national economies became increasingly reliant on their success, while other smaller city-economies were increasingly pushed to the fringes. In this book, we frequently explore this through the lens of the UK's 'North–South divide' (Dorling and Thomas, 2004; Dorling, 2010; McCann,

2016), arguing that London is emblematic of this type of growth, and has benefited from a specific and prolonged policy focus over the last two decades (something we discuss in Chapter 2), often to the detriment of other cities in the UK. However, the UK is far from the only place where these effects can be observed. Indeed, the same can be observed in France (Nurse et al, 2017), South Korea (Park, 2008; Lee, 2009), and, per Sassen's original arguments (1991, 1994), the USA.

In 2008 many of those issues relating to the global cities were brought to a head by one event: the financial crisis. Although the causes of the financial crisis are well documented (Coffee Jr, 2009; Foster and Magdoff, 2009), it is the responses to it – and particularly 'austerity' urbanism (the dramatic reduction in state spending on and in cities, observed by Peck, 2012) – which provides a key context for this book. The resultant cuts to public expenditure were largely loaded onto municipalities. In doing so, and certainly in the UK, there remains widespread consensus that the effects of this austerity were distributed unequally, with poorer places being forced to bear a greater burden (Lowndes and Pratchett, 2012; Lowndes and McCaughie, 2013; Lowndes and Gardner, 2016). The result was that, often, the same places already facing significant periods of de-industrialisation, and largely perceived as the 'losers' during the period of advancing globalisation, would be further penalised.

This feeds into a third interconnected issue – the rise of populist political unrest, seen by many as a pushback against the issues discussed earlier. Although the drivers of these protests are contested, at face value each appears to be driven by a revolt against a political status quo which supports the practices that underpin the broader success brought about by globalisation. Ultimately, the potential solutions to those problems (in broad terms, either a retrenchment from transnational organisations or a revisiting or reformation of their core principles) and their efficacy are equally contested.

Beyond these overarching and deeply interconnected debates, cities also find themselves at the forefront of action in other global agendas. The most prominent example of this is climate change in which, as a consensus is increasingly being reached around limits to both emissions and global temperature rises, cities are recognised as a 'Goldilocks Zone' for climate action. Although we visit some examples of action in this area later in this book, such as New York's PlaNYC and sustainable transport initiatives in one of the UK's city-regions, in broad terms what we can observe is how global issues are increasingly being played out at the urban scale – requiring innovative, and sometimes contested, solutions.

Ultimately, the urban scale remains a melting pot of both policy innovation and modernisation, while increasingly serving as the site of responses to many 'wicked' issues that plague today's policy-makers. Across the following chapters, these drivers for change run through the entire debate. In our analysis, we don't necessarily suggest straightforward solutions to complex problems but rather, seek to examine the UK's post-2010 responses to explore how policy-makers are attempting to deal with those issues and the extent to which they are enjoying success. To achieve this, we now turn to some of the conceptual questions and considerations that similarly underpin our discussion.

Conceptual questions

Who governs, and where?

It is questionable whether this text needs to discuss the difference between the terms *governance* and *government*. It is now probably taken as read by most scholars in the field that when we speak of governance, we don't (just) mean the literal process by which the government delivers its aims, but rather the activities of 'a whole range of actors who are involved in the delivery of policy' (Jones and Evans, 2008, p 31). This is certainly the interpretation we adopt in this book – regardless of our normative position over whether the state *should* be more directly involved with the delivery of policy, we cannot avoid the reality that in the UK, and most other countries, the state *is* reliant on a range of other public, private and third sector agencies to achieve its ambitions.

This, of course, raises a further series of questions, perhaps best encapsulated by Robert Dahl in 1961: 'In a political system where nearly every adult may vote but where knowledge, wealth, social position, access to officials, and other resources are unequally distributed, who actually governs?' (Dahl, 1961, p 1). Dahl's answer, based on his case study of the US city of New Haven, Connecticut in the late 1950s, was that political power was actually quite widely dispersed through a 'pluralism' of interest groups. Dahl's concept of pluralism has been contested since its introduction, with many authors observing that despite a theoretical dispersal of power, decisions tend to favour certain groups and individuals. The dominance of neoliberal governance has heightened this tendency, resulting in dramatic economic and political changes in the USA since Dahl was writing (Bartels, 2008). Those changes, resulting in, among other things, a huge increase in inequality, have been mirrored in the UK, so when the question of 'who governs' is explored empirically (for example, in Wilks-Heeg and Clayton, 2006; Wilks-Heeg et al, 2012), the answer is an increasingly narrow elite.

When one adds in the interweaving of multiple scales of urban governance (Brenner, 2004), the complexity deepens, so that the initial question of 'who governs' must be broadened to ask at what level of government or governance they govern (MacLeod and Jones, 2011). It is here we should acknowledge the 'relational' perspective, which argues that 'places and localities are formed mutually in the context of relations between them and not through relations of a vertical sort' (Cox, 2013, p 49), and thus challenges the use of categories such as national, regional and local to analyse governance, because these impose false boundaries that do not reflect the connections formed across them. A practical example would be that we might live in a particular territory, but work in a different territory, shop in another, take our leisure in yet another, and so on. In that case, what is the relevance of the lines on a map that denote the boundaries of those territories? Further, these territories are not 'ontologically pre-given' (MacLeod and Jones, 2011, p 2446) – they are the result of decisions made, perhaps after conflict and political struggle. This is particularly pertinent in Chapter 2, where we discuss the policies adopted in the 'devolved nations' of Scotland, Wales and Northern Ireland.

Territories and tiers of governance

While we fully accept the relational vs territorial argument as an important component of urban theory, this book is also about what is happening in particular places *empirically*. It is an inescapable fact that territorial boundaries, artificial as they may be, are central to how a state such as the UK is governed. Different laws and policies apply, in some fields at least, in Scotland but not in England, for example. Territorial boundaries can also carry considerable discursive power. Jones and MacLeod (2004) use the example of Cornwall, in the South West of England, which is viewed by the UK state as an administrative unit (a county council) but by Cornish nationalists as 'a separate Celtic nation akin to Scotland and Wales' (Trowler et al, 2003, p 441).

As a glance at the 'Contents' page of this volume would suggest, we have therefore chosen to make use of a series of territorial boundaries to structure our arguments, but remain mindful throughout of their contested nature and the increasing use within urban governance of 'soft spaces' and 'fuzzy boundaries' (Haughton et al, 2010). Such fuzziness is an integral part of the focus of Chapter 3, sub-national governance. Since at least the 19th century, the problems of a nation dominated by one city have been of concern to some (Cobbett, 1885), and these concerns were highlighted during the Second World War, when the strategic risks of concentrating the population in and around London were highlighted (Barlow, 1940). This has led to a series of initiatives to address the dominance of London, including the *Northern Way* in 2004 (González, 2006; Goodchild and Hickman, 2006; Liddle, 2009) and, most recently, the *Northern Powerhouse* (Nurse, 2015b; Haughton et al, 2016), the boundaries of which are typically defined in a deliberately fuzzy way to reflect the reality of how people live their lives (Harvey, 1989), in contrast to the regional government offices (in place from 1994 to 2011), which Chapter 3 also discusses.

In Chapter 4 we move 'down' a tier to the city-regional scale. The metropolitan scale, that is, one which acknowledges that cities have hinterlands and decision-making should reflect that (Clapp, 1971), is one that has moved in and out of political 'fashion' in the UK numerous times, partly in accordance with changes in the political control of national government. For example, metropolitan county councils were created in 1974 and abolished only 12 years later by Prime Minister Margaret Thatcher in an 'act of political spite' (Jones and Stewart, 2012, p 351). City-regions are now back on the agenda, and the complexities involved in defining them and their relationships with local authorities are discussed in Chapter 4.

Chapter 5 focuses on a tier of local governance that has, despite persistent reform, existed in a broadly unaltered state for over 100 years (John, 2014) – local government. From the high points of 'municipal socialism' in the late 19th and early 20th centuries, through the years of nationalisation (and hence centralism) after the Second World War, Chapter 5 charts these various periods of growth and reduction in local powers before analysing the contemporary position. Local authorities in England are, in many cases, in a parlous state, with bankruptcy threatened for some (Butler, 2018) amid widespread concerns about delivery of services (Hastings et al, 2015). Yet others see cause for optimism, for example, in the 'Preston model' of a re-born municipal socialism (Hanna et al, 2018).

In Chapter 6 we reach the bottom of the ladder in terms of tiers of urban governance – the community. Featuring both the oldest and newest forms of urban governance in England, the community scale has been the focus of much statutory attention in the years since 2010. Chapter 6 contextualises this attention within the history of community activism in the UK and elsewhere, and presents the latest empirical research on *Neighbourhood Planning*, a new tier of the English planning system.

Policy preoccupations

In some respects there is a great deal of innovation in urban governance in the UK – as we discuss in detail in subsequent chapters. In other respects, however, there is a deep conservatism to thinking about cities, as reflected in an enduring focus on a small number of thematic areas that have remained core to the goals of urban policy for many years. These are transport, jobs and, above all else, housing. A succession of UK governments has been preoccupied with these issues, attempting to address (perceived) problems of quantity and quality in relation to all three. An obsession with these issues reflects their importance to the electorate, and their dominance in relation to conversation about UK cities reflects the fact that they are three key areas for which solutions could be applied at the urban scale. In the following brief sections we highlight how the three issues dominate the discourse.

Transport

Halfway through the 2010–15 coalition government's tenure, one minister admitted that the UK's transport infrastructure was 'poor' (Dominiczak, 2013). This is not a controversial opinion, with others describing it as 'dirty and over-crowded' (RIBA, 2018, p 5) and 'well below average' (Aghion et al, 2013, p 22). Governments have been aware of problems in relation to transport infrastructure for some time, with various reviews (see, for example, Eddington, 2006) urging increased investment in key parts of the transport network. Under-investment in public transport is a common theme, with the UK's rail infrastructure – little updated since the 19th century (University of Southampton, 2018) – frequently labelled as 'Victorian'.

Conversely, the billions of pounds invested in the road network has done little to reduce congestion or increase travel time, perhaps reflecting the opinion that investing in roads and other infrastructure for the private car simply generates more demand for that infrastructure (Newman and Kenworthy, 1989). However, the Conservative-led UK governments since 2010 in particular have committed to 'ending the war on motorists' (DCLG, 2011a), suggesting that a more sustainable approach is not likely in the short to medium term. This is reflected in the latest multibillion pound transport strategy produced by the current government (DfT, 2017), which maintains an approach of 'funding on a massive scale' directed towards car-based transport (Davis and Tapp, 2017, p 313) while sustainable options such as cycling continue to be sidelined (Aldred, 2012).

Jobs

One of the key justifications for investing in transport is that it helps support the economy: 'By maintaining and upgrading our transport infrastructure ... we can connect communities and businesses and help deliver balanced growth across the country' (DfT, 2017, p 6). As with transport, economic growth is a recurring obsession of governments. 'The economy, stupid' proved core to Bill Clinton's US presidential campaign in 1992, and retains its relevance today (Hart, 2017), not least in the UK where, after the 2017 General Election, the government launched an 'Industrial Strategy' to 'help businesses to create high quality, well paid jobs right across the country' (HM Government, 2017, p 4).

Economic growth is often measured in terms of growth in the number of jobs (DWP, 2018), but this headline figure can be misleading, concealing as it does underemployment, insecurity and wage stagnation (*The Guardian*, 2018). There are also significant spatial differences in the number and quality of jobs, with places that have not benefited from economic growth feeling 'left behind' (Jennings et al, 2017), feeding into some of the issues of political unrest discussed previously.

Housing

Since 2010 there has been a bewildering array of policies designed to increase housing supply and to deal with what politicians across the political spectrum now seem comfortable calling the 'housing crisis' (Newton Dunn, 2017; Press Association, 2017; Watts, 2017). One of the first acts of the 2010–15 coalition government was to abolish regional planning and the housing targets contained within them (DCLG, 2010a). As we discuss in Chapter 5, housing targets have now effectively been reintroduced via a different route, but in the interim various other approaches were tried. Some related to planning, including the *New Homes Bonus*, a payment to English local authorities from the UK government for each house granted planning permission (Wilson et al, 2017), and the requirement that local authorities demonstrate a five-year supply of 'deliverable' land (LGA, 2017). Others were tenure-related, with preference for so-called 'intermediate' (now known as 'affordable') renting to traditional social housing and public funding allocated accordingly (W. Wilson,

2018), and the promotion of 'starter' homes, to be available at a 20% discount on market prices for first-time buyers (Cromarty, 2018). The latter has, apparently, been spectacularly unsuccessful (Wallis, 2018), and some have similarly argued that another initiative, 'Help to Buy', which offers buyers of new-build homes interest-free loans, has done little to increase housing supply, instead favouring housebuilders and a small number of individuals by pushing up house prices (Shelter, 2015; Collinson, 2017).

Combined, the ongoing shortcomings of central government policies in relation to transport, jobs and housing to address problems such as the North–South divide and continuing inequality (Belfield et al, 2016) have led to ever-increasing calls for localism, decentralisation and devolution.

Localism, decentralisation and devolution

Definitions and discourses

Rodriguez-Pose and Gill (2003) use the terms *decentralisation* and *devolution* interchangeably. As we have discussed elsewhere (Sturzaker and Gordon, 2017), there is likewise a tendency to treat *localism* and *decentralisation* as synonyms. These three terms, in fact, have subtly different meanings, but to avoid a lengthy semantic discussion, our general approach in this book is to use the terms interchangeably except where they refer to something specific. For example, the Localism Act 2011 is a piece of legislation, and the generally used term to refer collectively to Scotland, Wales and Northern Ireland is *the devolved nations*.

Nomenclature aside, there is a 'global trend towards devolution' (Rodriguez-Pose and Gill, 2003, p 336), whether in the broadly defined 'north' or 'south'. In the years following the Second World War, central government was the dominant source of power. This changed around the start of the 21st century, best illustrated through the break-up of the Soviet Union into smaller nation-states and the widespread devolution of power within nation-states (Rodriguez-Pose and Gill, 2003). The nature and extent of this devolution varies dramatically from place to place, of course, but there are common trends, including the rhetoric used to promote and justify the devolution of power. Here, Rodriguez-Pose and Sandall (2008) identify three main forms of decentralising discourse: identity, good governance and efficiency. *Identity* is often used by those seeking independence on the basis of ethnic identity in opposition to a homogenising national project. *Good governance* is unusual in that it is mobilised by those on both the left and right of politics, either in terms of empowering the poor or reducing the influence of the state. Finally, *efficiency* assumes that decentralising power allows more flexibility and adaptability in economic development (Tomaney, 2015).

In the UK, all three of these discourses feature in relation to the devolution debate. The identity discourse, while not always prominent, plays a role in how devolution to Wales, Scotland and Northern Ireland is discussed, and in relation to some of the regional and sub-regional arguments (Jones and MacLeod, 2004). The most prominent is perhaps the democracy/good governance discourse, with control being passed back to people from a somehow sinister central state, featuring heavily in the 'Coalition Agreement' of 2010 (HM Government, 2010a), and perhaps reaching its nadir with the 'taking back control' rhetoric of the 2016 referendum on leaving the European Union (EU) (Taylor, 2017). The efficiency/economic discourse is also commonly used, both by central government (DCLG, 2011b) and by local advocates of devolution (Leese, 2014).

Localism in the UK

As noted earlier, the democracy/good governance decentralisation discourse is particularly interesting because it is used by those on both the left and right of politics – suggesting that localism is in itself ideologically neutral (Brownill, 2017). However, the form it takes has the capacity to be regressive, and there are arguments that the approach taken by the UK government towards localism in England, from the Localism Act 2011 onwards, is explicitly so. There are several specific elements to these critiques.

The first is that the UK governments' move towards decentralisation and localism represents the latest front in the neoliberal attack on the state that has been in play since the 1970s (see, among many others, Featherstone et al, 2012; Hickson, 2013; Tait and Inch, 2016). Writing in 2012 in relation to the approach taken by the 2010–15 Conservative-Liberal Democrat coalition government, Lowndes and Pratchett (2012, p 21) observed that the reforms instituted 'do show traces of an ideological commitment to localism' but concluded that radical change was unlikely due to conflicts within the Conservative Party (Tait and Inch, 2016), the dominance of the Conservative Party within that coalition (Hayton, 2014), and the overwhelming constraints imposed by 'austerity', that is, the large cuts to public expenditure seen since 2010. It is a fact that, as we discuss in more detail in Chapter 2, reforms enacted under the localism banner in England since 2010 have accompanied extreme cuts to public services under the auspices of 'austerity', and the potential for localism to deliver greater 'efficiency' in public service delivery feature strongly in various government publications from 2010 onwards (HM Government, 2010b; DCLG, 2011b). While the government argued that localism would ameliorate the impacts of budget cuts by enabling the move to a 'smarter state' (Lowndes and Gardner, 2016), there remains widespread scepticism about the feasibility of this (Newman, 2014).

The second key area of criticism is that, despite government rhetoric, real power is not actually being devolved, but rather those in receipt of devolution 'are expected to be the mere servants of Whitehall' (Hambleton, 2015, p 18), because ministers (or probably in reality, civil servants) define and control key details. At the local authority scale, commentators have observed that, despite the introduction of a so-called *general power of competence* that was portrayed as radically loosening central controls on local authority activity, in reality, local authorities remain dependent on parliamentary authority for everything they do (Stanton, 2018). In relation to the community level, the new Neighbourhood Planning powers are similarly constrained by national policy and framed by the ability for top-down intervention in what communities do throughout the process (Sturzaker and Gordon, 2017).

The third area of criticism we wish to discuss here is that localism continues to privilege the powerful in society, and the individual over the collective (Lowndes and Pratchett, 2012; Newman, 2014; Crisp, 2015), enabling more powerful individuals and groups within communities to use localism to cement their power (Haughton et al, 2013; Jacobs and Manzi, 2013; Catney et al, 2014; Coelho, 2015; Bradley, 2017a). There are a number of studies that illustrate how the powerful are able to use the planning system to further their own ends (see, for example, Sturzaker, 2010), and it has been suggested that localism will only reinforce this position (Hastings and Matthews, 2015).

This is only the briefest summary of the rich literature on this topic, and we expand on these issues and others in the rest of this book. What we have demonstrated, however, are a number of fundamental issues from which one might draw the conclusion that localism is 'part of an attack on the very notion of the public/public sector' (Featherstone et al, 2012, p 178), and that to explore how it is working in practice is to, in some way, buy in to this attack. We disagree. We do not, fundamentally, disagree with any of the criticisms of localism – the Localism Act 2011 was initiated by a government led by the right-wing Conservative Party and the powers it introduced have been perpetuated by the (thus far) three Conservative-led governments that have followed. It has been accompanied by extreme cuts to public spending, particularly targeted in many cases at more deprived areas. However, we would argue that none of this renders localism as an unacceptable topic of study. Indeed, we would argue the reverse, for several reasons.

First, the system has been in place since 2011 and there is no evidence it will not remain in place for some time to come. The number of areas taking up the powers available to them is growing, with, for example, more than 500 areas having produced a new Neighbourhood Plan (MHCLG, 2018g), and more than 30 City Deals between the UK government and local actors having been signed (Ward, 2018). So, if the reforms are going to remain part of English governance, it is a legitimate area of research interest to explore how they are being used.

We also wish to join others who have taken issue with the 'hegemonic' (Williams et al, 2014, p 2798) neoliberal critique of localism and suggested that there is a need for research that explores the progressive potential therein (Newman, 2014; Williams et al, 2014; Crisp, 2015) – or to seek a 'hermeneutics of faith' within localism (Levitas, 2012). We wish to explore whether the reforms are being used in a progressive way, and/or how they could be used to have more progressive outcomes.

Finally, we wish to make a contribution that looks beyond and across the various tiers of government or governance that have been the subject of reform. There are an ever-growing number of perceptive analyses of the 'localist' reforms at the sub-national and city-regional, local authority and neighbourhood scales. What there have been relatively little of, however, are attempts to look across these scales and analyse the aggregate impact from what is an incoherent and poorly coordinated set of policies and decisions made by the UK government. In short, and pending the final outcome of the tortuous process of the UK leaving the EU, how has the rescaling of urban governance in England affected its citizens? In the final section of this chapter we explain how we will seek to answer this question.

Analytical tools and theories

Rodriguez-Pose and Gill (2003, p 334) argued that in analysing any example of devolution, researchers should consider three factors: 'subnational legitimacy ... decentralisation of authority and resources'. These three factors are key to our analysis. We explore whether these are present in the different forms of devolution we discuss in the subsequent five chapters, and assess both how effective devolution and localism have been in those terms; we use a range of theoretical lenses to underpin this analysis. This book brings together much of our own work on the topics of planning, localism and institutional change as they pertain to urban governance, and many key contributions from other scholars, using various theoretical approaches. Those we find most significant are briefly summarised here.

Power

The word *power* features frequently in discussions of urban governance, localism and planning. Shifting power to local people is a recurring rhetorical trope in government discourse relating to localism (Cameron, 2010; DCLG, 2010c, 2012a; Osborne and Pickles, 2011; DCLG and Lewis, 2015), and the very name *Northern Powerhouse* emphasises it. But what do we mean when we talk about power? There is no 'single, unified concept of power' (Pansardi, 2012, p 73) – theorists sometimes talk of 'power over' and 'power to', that is, someone or something might have *power over* another and use that to control them, or someone or something might have *power to* do something. The former is often cited as being more relevant in UK politics (Hickson, 2013), but the latter is important when we reflect on approaches to democratising planning (Forester, 1989; Healey, 2006). Planning theorists are also cognisant that power is complicated and multidimensional, and can be used in different ways (Flyvbjerg, 1998, 2002). We have used power in our own research (Sturzaker, 2010, 2011; Sturzaker and Shucksmith, 2011; Sturzaker and Gordon, 2017), drawing particularly on the interpretations of sociologists Steven Lukes (2005) and Pierre Bourdieu (1973, 1977, 2005). That work, in common with others (cf Hastings and Matthews, 2015; Brownill and Bradley, 2017), has illustrated how certain individuals and groups – specifically the middle classes and elites – have been able to use the planning system to their own ends. We are therefore particularly interested in whether the reforms we discuss in this book are likewise empowering those who are already well served by governance institutions, or whether they are playing a more progressive role.

Strategic relational approach

In step with those themes of power, we also frequently refer to concepts regarding *strategic-relational approaches* (SRAs), as brought forward by Jessop (1990). At its heart, this requires acknowledging the long-standing, deep-seated and persistent trend towards centralisation within the UK state that has left it in a position of clear power. In conceptualising this, Brenner (2004 p 74) suggests that this power is held and exercised in different ways – most often 'through regulatory projects and socio-political struggles articulated in diverse institutional sites and at a range of geographical scales', although, as Davies and Imbroscio (2009) argue, the state maintains a number of unique power bases (for example, central budget allocation). In this light, Jessop (1990) recognises that there has been a period of state 'rescaling' in which state-related activity has been carried out at different levels (for example, the programmes of devolution and localism discussed in this book). In turn, this rescaling brings about what Gerber and Kollman (2004) term *authority migration*, in which power is transferred away from those actors traditionally seen as the arbiters of state power. However, Somerville and Haines (2008) caution against taking this devolution at face value as often the result can be a further increase in the power of the central state – in large part because those responsible for the delivery of those procedures still owe their loyalties to the state (Goodwin et al, 2006). As such, we are drawn to questions not about 'the extent to which the national state has somehow become "less" powerful in the process, but how it has become differently powerful' (Peck, 2001, p 447).

Building on this premise, the SRA recognises that, as policy changes its focus over time (that is, as a result of the party political process), in exercising its power the state cannot, and does not, remain neutral, and as such does not arbitrate policy decisions in a wholly neutral way. Instead, any policy enacted by the state can be seen as favouring one party over another: a 'strategic selectivity' (Jessop, 1990, p 9). In effect, there are always winners and losers, something known as 'privileging'.

Ultimately, therefore, alongside considering the extent to which the reforms discussed in this book do 'what they say on the tin', we are interested in examining who the 'winners' and 'losers' are in those processes. In doing so, we seek to critically comment on the extent to which the post-2010 devolution and localism reforms either break from the expectations of the literature, or uphold them.

The entrepreneurial turn

David Harvey (1989) is commonly credited with conceptualising the shift from 'managerial' to 'entrepreneurial' urban governance. The former involves local authorities focusing on the delivery of key services to their citizens, the latter a change in approach emphasising the exploration of various ways to effectively increase their income in order to better provide for those citizens – a perhaps pragmatic response to ongoing financial problems. Particularly in the USA, this was not a new phenomenon, but by 1989, Harvey observes that this approach was generally the norm in local government.

At the centre of the entrepreneurial approach is a partnership between the public and private sector. However, this partnership is not equally balanced – reflecting the increasingly mobile nature of capital in the global economy (Feenstra, 1998) and the attempts by local authorities to make their area more attractive to this mobile capital. In order to do so they must invest in a range of strategies in the hope that businesses (and indeed, central government functions, as we return to shortly) will (re)locate to their jurisdiction. This might not pay off, as many places deploy similar strategies to compete with each other so businesses can pick the locations that suit themselves, and 'losing' local authorities effectively waste their time and money: 'the public sector assumes the risk and the private sector takes the benefits' (Harvey, 1989, p 7).

A key difference that Harvey highlights between the managerial and entrepreneurial approaches is that the former is focused on improving the conditions of particular 'territories' (local authorities) specifically to benefit the people living and working there, whereas the latter is more interested in 'place' – for example, industrial parks or flagship buildings. Any benefits that accrue from place-focused approaches may be larger or smaller in scale than the territory within which the place is located. Further, such projects can absorb a great deal of public and political attention. In Chapter 5 we will see evidence about these issues in practice.

Conclusion

In this introductory chapter we have set out the basic 'terms of reference' for this book. We began by identifying some of the major challenges facing cities internationally and in the UK, recognising the key role cities play in dealing with some of these challenges. We then discussed the conceptual questions that, for us, frame how we consider the future of cities, such as the oft-quoted distinction between *government* and *governance*. While these and other theoretical concerns are writ large throughout this book, it is also rooted in the realities of urban life in the 21st century and what we have called the 'policy preoccupations' of those attempting to shape that urban life in the UK

– housing, jobs and transport provision. We suggest that an ongoing concern with those issues indicates a long-term failure to satisfactorily deal with them, and in part explains the emergence of the new kid on the block – *localism*.

Those promoting a shifting of power outwards or downwards from central governments cite a range of potential benefits, many of which feature as justifications for the programme of reforms deployed in the UK, specifically England, since 2010. There is, however, scepticism that those benefits will be realised – both reflecting the form of localism that is being implemented and the wider context within which it sits – specifically, a regime of neoliberalism, perhaps exemplified by the 'austerity' to which we return in Chapter 2.

Hence we return to the opening words of this book, the need for analysis of the outcomes of 'localism' at a range of scales. In the substantive chapters that follow we provide such an analysis. The range of topics – from sub-national governance to Neighbourhood Planning – all draw to some degree on the themes discussed thus far. In covering the period from 2010, inevitably we will not discuss every minutiae but rather, in each chapter, we attempt to discuss the main thrust of policy development and its broader implications. At this point we also acknowledge a frequent elephant in the room throughout this book – *Brexit*. While we do not engage with the advantages and disadvantages of Brexit directly – that is not the purpose of the book – we note that this book has been written during a period of extraordinary political tumult in the UK, which has cast uncertainty across much of the political agenda. Localism is no exception to this. As such, we have attempted to chronicle developments across this period as best we can, and in turn, to comment on the potential implications for policy-making. It is beyond doubt that Brexit will come to define popular accounts of the UK in the 2010s, but as we will see, there is much more to it than that.

2

Devolution: A patchwork quilt of planning reform

We draw much of the evidence in this book from evidence relating to England, as this is the jurisdiction we are most familiar with, the site of most rapid and intense reform in the UK, and perhaps as a consequence of this, the subject of a great deal of attention from scholars. In this chapter, however, we compare England to the other parts of the UK – illustrating both the opportunities and constraints offered by the UK's lack of a written constitution, and how urban governance in England is at the same time similar and very different to Wales, Scotland and Northern Ireland.

City governance is an area that offers a great deal of scope for variation at the national level. The structures put in place by national governments can act to give a great amount of flexibility to the approach taken by others tiers of governance, or they can constrain and frame those tiers in various ways. In the UK the devolution agreements with Wales, Scotland and Northern Ireland allow this variability, and this chapter considers their respective developments with regards to city governance. This includes how the UK government, responsible for England, has changed its regime of funding and policy for cities. Key aspects that will be discussed are the introduction and implications of urban austerity measures, and an overview of the other funding arrangements that have been made available for cities. The chapter then explores how the devolved administrations of Wales, Scotland and Northern Ireland are proceeding in different and similar ways. Key differential factors including the scope of devolved powers and contextual differences are discussed, along with how the political contexts of the different nations have led to a variety of policy choices. Finally, the chapter reflects on how the latter developments in the devolved administrations have affected English governance arrangements.

The United Kingdom

The ways in which the UK are governed can be complex and often difficult to follow. Across the following chapters the ultimate aim of this book is to discuss the UK focusing specifically on the sub-national scale, that is, everything from regional development (Chapter 3), to cities and local authorities (Chapters 4 and 5), and neighbourhoods (Chapter 6). However, and acknowledging that the UK is commonly regarded as one of the most centralised Western democracies, a persistent theme of this book is that this work is both heavily reliant on policy that is brought forward by the central UK state and contingent on an ongoing relationship with those structures. It is therefore important to provide some context in the form of an overview of governance at the scale of the UK. Here we briefly discuss some of the UK's main institutions and their functions.

The UK is a constitutional monarchy. The Monarch (currently Queen Elizabeth II) serves as head of state, and has three core functions: appointing the Prime Minister to lead the government on the Monarch's behalf in the House of Commons, announcing the government's legislative agenda through the Queen (or King's) Speech, and exercising the Royal Prerogative, that is, signing laws into effect.

In practice, UK policy-making is done through the House of Commons and its 650 Members of Parliament (MPs), each of whom is elected for a five-year period. The UK's government is formed by the political party capable of commanding a majority – currently a threshold of 320 MPs. Although there are consistent political themes, the period covered by this book relates to three distinct governments, albeit linked by political party. Briefly, those three governments are as follows:

Coalition government, 2010–15: Following the 2010 General Election the Conservative Party, led by David Cameron, won 306 seats. Failing to secure an outright parliamentary majority, the Conservatives entered into coalition government with the third largest party, the Liberal Democrats. Cameron would become Prime Minister, while the leader of the Liberal Democrats, Nick Clegg, would serve as Deputy Prime Minister. This was the first time the UK had seen a coalition government since the end of the Second World War. The programme for government, dubbed the 'Coalition Agreement' (HM Government, 2010a), set out a mixture of policies, including proposals for the abolition of regional governance, the early stages of city-level reform and attempts to position the concept of the 'Big Society' (discussed further in Chapter 6) as a central theme of Cameron's vision for localism.

David Cameron's Conservative government, 2015–16: Leading the Conservatives into the 2015 General Election Cameron defied opinion polls and secured 330 seats – enough for a working majority. This success was, at least partially, attributed to the electoral implosion of the Liberal Democrats, whom the public blamed for many of the unpopular elements of the 2010–15 coalition (Cutts and Russell, 2015). Although this period did not see a substantive shift in many policy agendas, the 2015–16 government will forever be associated with the 2016 referendum on the UK's membership of the EU. The UK's vote to leave the EU caused Cameron to resign as Prime Minister, and immediately ushered in the third major phase of government.

Theresa May's Conservative government, 2016–19: After winning the Conservative Party leadership election in 2016, Theresa May became Prime Minister with, thanks to the Fixed Term Parliament Act 2011 introduced by her predecessor, the option of staying in office until 2020. Almost inevitably, May's time in office became dominated by attempts to implement the results of the 2016 referendum and, in doing so, navigate the UK's departure from the EU. Buoyed by favourable opinion polling, and in an attempt to grow her working majority, in 2017 May called a snap general election. However, May's majority was reduced, and while the Conservative Party remained the largest group in Westminster, their 312 seats meant they were forced to enter into a 'confidence and supply agreement', a form of loose coalition, with Northern Ireland's Democratic Unionist Party (DUP). On 27 May 2019 Theresa May announced she was to resign after failing to deliver Brexit, with Boris Johnson announced as her successor on 23 July 2019 and taking office the following day. Brexit dominated the early months of Johnson's tenure, with a general election called by the Prime Minister for 12 December 2019 after Parliament frustrated his 'do or die' bid to leave the EU on 31 October 2019.

Across this book we argue that while these three periods of government are unified by the (comparative) electoral success of the Conservative Party, they are frequently heavily influenced by the effects of those general elections.

Beyond this, we do at times refer to previous governments – not least in order to contextualise post-2010 policy developments. For clarity, Table 2.1 sets out the timespan, political party and Prime Ministers of the governments to which we frequently refer.

One of the chief areas of focus for this chapter is devolution to three of the UK's nations: Scotland, Wales and Northern Ireland. This is a process that has developed over the previous two decades, and has seen a number of powers transferred away from the UK parliament

Table 2.1: Recent governments of the UK

Date (to–from)	Political party	Prime minister
1979–90	Conservative	Margaret Thatcher
1990–97	Conservative	John Major
1997–2007	Labour	Tony Blair
2007–10	Labour	Gordon Brown
2010–16	Conservative-Liberal Democrats (2010–15) Conservative (2015–16)	David Cameron
2016–19	Conservative	Theresa May
2019–	Conservative	Boris Johnson

in London towards legislatures in Edinburgh, Cardiff and Belfast respectively. However, this devolution has limits, and across this period, the UK government has consistently retained elements of control over significant elements of policy – not least military and foreign policy, as well as significant elements of financial policy.

The idea that the UK is a heavily centralised country is a common trope, but one that is exemplified by its budgeting arrangements in which, with few exceptions, financial allocations are made annually by the UK government's ministry for economy and finance – the 'Treasury' – through an annual budget. For the devolved nations, a calculation – known as the *Barnett formula* (discussed in more detail later) – ensures that the money they receive from the Treasury remains in line with England. This, in essence, means that the Treasury controls the purse strings. Taking this further, this also means that all parts of the UK are fundamentally tied to the overall success of the UK economy. This has significant implications, and sets the scene for one of the themes that permeates this book: the 2008 financial crisis and austerity as a response to it.

Austerity

The UK 2010 General Election took place in the aftermath of the 2008 financial crisis, and the increase in public spending that was adopted by the 1997–2010 Labour government as its strategy to deal with this (Hodson and Mabbett, 2009). Gordon Brown, Prime Minister between 2007 and 2010, portrayed the election as a choice between growth and deep cuts in public spending – or 'austerity', as the latter became known (Porter and Riddell, 2009). Interestingly, the Conservative manifesto for the election (The Conservative Party, 2010a) makes no mention of the term that was subsequently enthusiastically adopted when the party became the leaders of a coalition government after the election (Pautz, 2018). That coalition swiftly decided that austerity was the solution to the budget deficit it had inherited, and committed itself to eliminating that deficit within one five-year parliament (ConservativeHome, 2010) – something it subsequently failed to do.

Deep cuts in public spending began within weeks of the coalition government taking office, in large part blamed on the outgoing 'New' Labour government of Gordon Brown and the higher levels of public spending that characterised both his and Tony Blair's tenure (see, for example, Summers, 2009). To opponents, however, the austerity programme was ideologically driven, with the financial crisis merely serving as a political foil for swingeing cuts to institutions seen as anathema to the principles of Conservatism (O'Hara, 2015).

Regardless, in practical terms almost all Whitehall departments – with the exception of Health, International Development and Work and Pensions (HM Treasury, 2010) – were instructed by the incoming Chancellor of the Exchequer, George Osborne, to find budget cuts, with an average of 19% cut from each department. Crucially, for this discussion, the Department for Communities and Local Government (DCLG) – responsible for the significant majority of local government budgets – received disproportionately large cuts, with £2.4 billion removed from its operating budget in 2010 alone ahead of a forecasted 27% cut in the overall budget by 2014/15 (HM Treasury, 2010; Lowndes and Pratchett, 2012) and a further 30% cut following the Conservatives' re-election in 2015 (Johnstone, 2015).

The result was that local authorities, characterised by their reliance on central government funding for their budgets, would be among the hardest hit during this period. Going further, it became clear that the extent of those funding cuts would be unequally distributed and, partially as a result of larger populations and resulting fiscal responsibilities (for example, welfare, social care and education), larger urban authorities and the core cities in particular would be particularly heavily affected (Lowndes and Pratchett, 2012; Lowndes and McCaughie, 2013) – something that the leaders of those authorities were quick to point out (Forbes et al, 2012). Research in subsequent years has illustrated the degree of difference, consistently showing that poorer places and people have been disproportionately affected by cuts in local government spending and the welfare budget (Hastings et al, 2015; Beatty and Fothergill, 2016).

Dealing with the effects of those budget cuts gave rise to what Peck (2012) termed 'austerity urbanism', in which fiscal priorities were recalibrated, often prioritising legally mandated functions while cutting others heavily, or entirely. Examples of cuts included the removal of senior local bureaucrats through redundancy, while arts budgets, upkeep of public parks and road maintenance were among the early casualties. Simultaneously, local authorities were also affected by cuts to budgets beyond their control, but on which they were reliant. In planning terms, this included the scrapping of the Housing Market Renewal Initiative (a multibillion programme of housing demolition and construction in deprived parts of the North of England) shortly after the coalition government came to office, even though many authorities were midway through implementing the programme (Turcu, 2012; Leather and Nevin, 2013). In effect this meant that many authorities had a double-hit as they were then forced to either take up the slack as funding ended, or abandon projects midway, regardless of the sunken costs.

As we will see, central government austerity permeates this period – it appears with regularity, colouring the choices that are made and the potential outcomes that are at stake. Therefore, in considering how cities were the locus of many of the post-2010 reforms, the ways in which they managed these intertwining agendas should not be overlooked. This chapter is primarily dedicated to discussing the UK's four nations, the ways in which, post-2010, the devolution agenda has developed, and the implications this has had on their sub-national governance.

England

Ultimately, at present, there is no English parliament, and all legislation relating to England is brought forward at Westminster through the UK parliament. While the broader nature of this book is to discuss the developments as they relate to England, it is important to acknowledge that England as an entity is itself no stranger to devolution debates.

For some, the attitudes associated to the United Kingdom are in reality those of England – particularly during the period of the British Empire in which the British 'values' and institutions exported and left behind were explicitly *English* in their nature (Ashkanasy et al, 2002). Others have pointed to the role played by Scotland, in particular, in the British Empire (MacKenzie and Devine, 2011). Either way, as the British Empire fell away in the first half of the 20th century, more attention was given to the British Isles. Across the following period, and as devolution agendas gathered pace throughout the latter half of the century, there was an irony in that while the Home Nations were increasingly exploring their own identities, England and Englishness was increasingly given less prominence. This fall of English identity was, perhaps, best encapsulated in the period immediately following the election of Tony Blair's New Labour government. Here, and while capitalising on a 'Cool Britannia' movement that increasingly used the Union Flag as a cultural icon, Blair's government accelerated processes of devolution (discussed in more depth later in this chapter) to Scotland, Wales and Northern Ireland.

Throughout this period England received no such high-level provision, and its laws and legislation would continue to be delivered through the UK parliament in Westminster. That said, English policy-making did not remain in stasis during this period, and in lieu of an English parliament, New Labour pursued a regional agenda for England – something we discuss at length in Chapter 3. This took the regional architecture formalised under the Major government (eight regions and London), and developed it, establishing Regional Development Agencies (RDAs) that focused on economic development. These were supported by Regional Assemblies that drew membership from across the counties, districts and authorities within each region (Mawson, 2007), serving as a means to counterbalance any democratic deficit within a business-led/focused organisation.

From an early stage London provided an indication of what the Blair government, in practice driven by Deputy Prime Minister, John Prescott, had in mind for England. Indeed, in July 2000 – some 14 years after the abolition of the Greater London Council – the establishment of the Greater London Authority led by the newly elected Mayor of London alongside the directly elected London Assembly would foreshadow many of the debates of the following two decades. London's new Mayor, Ken Livingstone, would provide clear examples of the strategic leadership a mayor might achieve, including establishing a congestion charge and winning the right to host the 2012 Olympic Games (Tonne et al, 2008; Worthy et al, 2018). However, as we will see, the planned Assemblies for the remaining eight regions never emerged, leaving London as the only region (and in practice, a metropolitan area) with devolved powers. This leadership, supported by specific investment (for example, in transport infrastructure) from central government that far outstripped funds given to other parts of the country (Raikes, 2018), undoubtedly played a role in London's explosive growth throughout the 2000s, and opened up a growth gap to the rest of the UK (McCann 2016). However, in considering England's North–South divide and how to close it, we must keep in mind Martin et al's (2016) conundrum of English growth – do we view London's growth as bad, and if not, how do we secure growth in other places without undermining success elsewhere? These are themes that are central to Chapters 3 and 4.

As the seat of government for the UK, Westminster has retained numerous powers and throughout devolution the devolved nations still send MPs to sit in the House of Commons as part of the UK's broader democratic structures. However, the consequence of this is while English MPs can no longer vote on devolved matters, MPs from the devolved nations can vote on matters that now only pertain to England. This is known as the *West Lothian question* (Bogdanor, 2010), but has also been called the *English question* (Hazell, 2006). This has been a historic issue in British politics, with the then-Prime Minister William Gladstone wrestling with this idea during the period of Irish Home Rule in the late 1800s (Gallagher, 2012), but gained wider prominence – and its name – after being posed by Tam Dalyell, then MP for West Lothian, in a debate ahead of Labour's devolution proposals for Scotland and Wales in the late 1970s (Bowers, 2012).

This *West Lothian question* is far from a thought experiment, and there is a comparatively consistent record of governments using MPs from the devolved nations to push through policies for England. This includes New Labour who had many Scottish and Welsh MPs and, importantly within the context of this book, both the 2010–15 coalition for whom 14 Liberal Democrats were drawn from Scotland and Wales and Theresa May's 2017–onwards government that was reliant on support from Northern Ireland's DUP.

Importantly, as Hazell (2006, p 37) suggests, 'The English Question is not a single question, but a portmanteau heading for a whole series of questions about the government of England'. Accordingly, and while this chapter will momentarily turn to the post-2010 attempts to speak to this issue, it is important to acknowledge that previous governments have approached this issue in different ways – not least New Labour who, through an agenda pushed by Deputy Prime Minister John Prescott, sought to create devolved and directly elected Regional Assemblies in the mid-2000s, before the proposals were ultimately rejected by the public (Shaw and Robinson, 2007). Nevertheless, the Conservatives were undeterred and, having previously made it a campaign issue in both 2001 and 2005 (Hazell, 2006), in the wake of the Scottish independence referendum began to explore proposals for 'English Votes for English Laws' (EVEL) in more detail (Jeffery, 2015; Colomb and Tomaney, 2016). In doing so however, the Conservatives' ambitions, like Prescott's, have been constrained by the underlying irony within this agenda in that, while there is broad underlying public support for English devolution in principle, it is also characterised by little public appetite for it to be put into practice (Hazell, 2006; Henderson et al, 2015). As such, the plans were quietly shelved.

In practice, since 2010, national-scale devolution in England has been little more than a distraction, and as we shall see in Chapters 3 and 4, where this issue is discussed at length, the post-2010 devolution agenda has instead focused on the transfer of power to cities and city regions. Here the city regions that have engaged with the government's reform agenda have been afforded greater control over a variety of issues including strategic planning, housing and, in some cases, health budgeting (Nurse, 2015b). However, these attempts at sub-national devolution in England have been heavily criticised as a poor substitute for devolution at the nation scale (Colomb and Tomaney, 2016), being too narrow in focus, too susceptible to changes in political priorities (Shaw et al, 2014) and, to some, serving as a vehicle to entrench centralised control (Hambleton, 2017). The approach taken in Scotland, Wales and Northern Ireland, or the 'devolved nations', as they are collectively known, has been very different.

Devolved nations

Scotland, Wales and Northern Ireland have a history of being governed differently to England which can be traced back to the union of 1707 that brought Scotland together with England and Wales (Anderson and Gallagher, 2018). The Acts of Union of 1706 (in England) and 1707 (in Scotland) combined the two parliaments, but systems of education and law remained different, and the Scottish church likewise remained distinct from the Church of England. Wales had a longer history of association with England and therefore greater commonalities in governance terms. The situation in Northern Ireland is, of course, tied to the ongoing political and sectarian tensions in that territory, but a specific Northern Irish administration can be traced back to the partition of Ireland in 1921 and the creation of a Northern Irish government. That government was suspended in 1972 and 'direct rule' imposed from London – a situation that has occurred periodically since then.

In the case of all three devolved nations, until devolution in 1998 senior ministers of the UK government (Secretaries of State), and associated civil servants in their Scottish, Welsh and Northern Irish offices, played significant roles in implementing domestic policy (Anderson and Gallagher, 2018). This was changed by the Scotland,

Northern Ireland and Government of Wales Acts of 1998 that devolved a range of powers to the three nations (Birrell, 2009). These powers included various policy areas related to urban governance, including planning, local government, housing and health (for comprehensive lists, see Birrell, 2009, p 11), although there was some asymmetry in that the extent of devolution differed between the three nations (Pemberton et al, 2015). As we will return to shortly, the devolved powers have increased, again asymmetrically, in recent years, which may have consequences for governance in England.

An important point to note in relation to devolution is that powers are merely 'lent' to the devolved nations, and the UK parliament in Westminster retains the right to legislate in relation to the areas of policy that have been devolved, and indeed to take back the powers if it wishes (Keating and Laforest, 2018). Given the politically contentious nature of such activity, the former is done only rarely and the latter never. This reluctance on the part of the UK has been tested to its limit in recent years, in relation to the referendums in 2014 on Scottish independence and 2016 on the UK leaving the EU – a topic we return to later.

Funding

Historically, spending per head in Scotland, Wales and Northern Ireland on matters such as health, education and housing has been higher than in England. This was the case before devolution, and continues to be so (Birrell, 2009). This is partly because on some measures need is higher in the devolved nations than in England – life expectancy is lower and the preponderance of illnesses such as heart disease and cancer is higher (Birrell, 2009). It is also due to the 'Barnett formula', the means by which the budgets to be devolved from the UK are calculated. This formula uses the different sizes of the populations of the devolved nations to calculate their 'share' of UK government spending – so Scotland, which has a population around 10% the size of England, will receive 10% of the spending for England. The devolved nations then have discretion about how to spend their grants (Anderson and Gallagher, 2018). In the first 10 years of devolution, the 'benign fiscal climate' led to a doubling of the grants that each nation received (Banting and McEwen, 2018, p 126). The UK government's austerity regime, discussed previously, has led to smaller increases in recent years, and some cuts in grants. This, allied to the agreements reached around the time of the Scottish independence referendum, have led to the devolution of some tax-raising powers, which we again return to shortly.

Areas of policy change under devolution

As noted previously, social and urban policy is one of the areas with a significant degree of devolution to Scotland, Wales and Northern Ireland. There is a range of policies that the devolved nations have chosen to focus their new powers on. One of these is the provision of pre-existing services but on a 'universalist basis, free at the point of uptake' (Birrell, 2009, p 43). Examples of this include free personal and nursing care in Scotland and free prescriptions for medicines under the National Health Service (NHS) in all three – in all cases different to the approach in England.

Of more relevance to the theme of this book, planning reform has been an area that has received attention across the devolved nations. The systems of planning across the UK were, and indeed remain, broadly similar in that they all rely on the 'discretionary system', that is, a 'development plan' is produced that sets out the policies guiding development in a specific territory, and this plan is used to guide decisions on development proposals, known as 'planning applications'. The decision-making body has the right to deviate from the plan if it can demonstrate good reasons for doing so – hence the 'discretionary' nature of the system (Cullingworth et al, 2015). Under the 'New' Labour government of 1997–2010, the English planning system was reformed in a bid to promote economic development, to speed up decision-making and to 'democratise' the system (Doak and Parker, 2005; Allmendinger and Haughton, 2007; Shaw and Lord, 2009). Similar reforms were instituted in Scotland (Lloyd and Peel, 2009), Wales (Harris and Hooper, 2006) and Northern Ireland (Lloyd and Peel, 2012a). This commonality of reform in part reflected the fact that the Welsh and Scottish administrations were initially also led by New Labour. This commonality is no longer the case, so the reforms brought in from 2010 onwards by the Conservative-led UK governments have been much less widely mirrored in the devolved nations. But even before the UK 2010 General Election there were differences in how aspects of planning and governance were approached.

National and sub-national planning and governance

As we discuss in Chapter 4, a key innovation introduced by the New Labour UK government was that of regional governance in England, which brought with it statutory regional planning. The regions ranged from 2.5 to 8.5 million in population size, which were comparable to the populations of Scotland (5.4 million), Wales (3.1 million) and

Northern Ireland (1.8 million) in 2019. Perhaps unsurprisingly, then, the devolved nations chose to produce nation-level strategic plans in the form of the Scottish National Planning Framework, the Welsh Spatial Plan and the Northern Irish Regional Development Strategy (Winter et al, 2016). This leaves England as the only nation without a strategic plan at the national level (Morphet, 2015).

At the sub-national scale, the greater size in population and area of Scotland meant that city-regional governance was developed in parallel with the national plan (Lloyd and Peel, 2012b). The four main city regions of Aberdeen, Dundee, Edinburgh and Glasgow now have statutory Strategic Development Plans (SDPs) produced by Joint Committees, comprising the local authorities that constitute those areas (Winter et al, 2016). The Planning (Scotland) Act, which was passed by Scottish ministers in late June 2019, abolished SDPs and replaced them with non-statutory regional plans. The latter is similar to the system in Wales, where local authorities can choose to come together to produce SDPs. Frustrated that none had done so, and at the pace of local plan production in Wales, the Welsh Cabinet Secretary for Energy, Planning and Rural Affairs 'invited' local authorities to do so in December 2017, threatening that if they did not she would compel them to (Griffiths, 2017). In Northern Ireland a plan covering the Belfast city region has been the subject of a lengthy process of legal challenge that has, as yet, been unresolved (Planning Portal, 2017).

The 'City Deals' that have categorised devolution in England in recent years are also offered to city regions in Wales, Scotland and Northern Ireland (see Chapter 4 for more details).

Local government

Local government in Scotland comprises 32 unitary authorities introduced in 1996. At the time of devolution there was concern that local government would be undermined, but this has not been borne out in practice (Birrell, 2009). A similar regime of audits and inspections as instituted in England (see Chapter 5) was brought in in Scotland (and Wales) under the New Labour-led administrations. Similarly to Scotland, since 1996, Wales has been organised into 22 unitary authorities. The Welsh government has twice proposed to reduce this number to between 8 and 10, first in 2015 (Winter et al, 2016), and again in 2018 (BBC News, 2018). The last round of boundary reforms in Wales prompted significant political manoeuvring and changing of priorities (Pemberton and Goodwin, 2010), so it seems reasonable to assume that any new reorganisation will do likewise.

The system in Northern Ireland has, until recently, been very different. Unlike in Scotland, Wales and England local authorities have not historically had responsibility for planning. This has been held by the Northern Irish Executive, most recently in the Department for Infrastructure. Local authorities (then 26 of them) were designated as 'statutory consultees' rather than decision-makers in this system, with a centralised planning service producing development plans and making decisions on planning applications (Lloyd and Peel, 2012a). The Local Government (Boundaries) Act (Northern Ireland) 2008 and Planning Act (Northern Ireland) 2011 reformed this system, moving to a framework of 11 local authorities that have responsibility for local planning and local economic development. These 11 local authorities took on their new responsibilities in 2015. The Northern Irish Executive retains control over major decisions, but since the collapse in the power-sharing agreement in Northern Ireland, it has been unable to exercise this control, leading to an 'impasse' (Marrs, 2018).

Beyond planning, there are other key differences between England and the devolved nations in terms of local governance. Social housing is one of these, with the Conservative-led governments since 2010 continuing to pursue the policy of 'Right to Buy' (the option for social housing tenants to buy their home at a discounted rate), which has now been abandoned in Scotland and Wales. The latter have also been more supportive of the construction of new social housing (Birch, 2018), and have allowed local authorities to make much more limited use of powers to transfer council housing to housing associations (Birrell, 2009).

One tier of urban governance that has been very different in the devolved nations than in England has been that of the neighbourhood or community.

Neighbourhood or community planning

As we will discuss in Chapter 6, the Localism Act 2011 saw the creation of a new tier of the statutory planning system in England, Neighbourhood Plans. These have effectively replaced the non-statutory community strategies produced under the previous Labour governments. That system of community strategies was introduced in England and Wales in 2003, in Scotland in 2006 and in Northern Ireland in 2015 (Pemberton, 2017). In the three devolved nations, the old system remains in place and they have not pursued statutory Neighbourhood Planning. Pemberton contrasts the focus in England on land use and economic development with an approach in the devolved nations that sees community planning as a way of delivering more integrated services.

In Scotland, Wales and Northern Ireland community planning does appear to genuinely involve 'reaching out' (Pemberton et al, 2015, p 12) to different communities and strengthening the relationship between local residents and service providers, so it could be seen as being more reflective of a genuine localism than the system adopted in England, which has been criticised for potentially closing down and 'framing' community aspirations as much as opening them up (Gallent and Robinson, 2012). This marked difference in approach between the devolved nations and England arguably reflects a difference in ideologies or values – some have argued that a trend since devolution has been a 'rejection of neoliberalism' (Birrell, 2009, p 157), initially as perceived to be underpinning the New Labour governments (Davies, 2012) and recently, more closely associated with the Conservative-led governments (Williams et al, 2014). The changing ideologies and values that have guided the approaches taken by the devolved nations are one of the drivers of the policy convergence and divergence that we can observe.

Convergence vs divergence

There are differences of opinion as to the extent to which the values and ideology of governance in the devolved nations have varied from the approach in England, led by the UK government. Birrell (2009) contrasts the central role played in Scotland and Wales of three 'values' of 'social justice, equality and collectivism' (2009, p 143) and four 'principles' of 'public involvement, mutualism and co-production, partnership working and localism' (p 148) with the 'neoliberalism ... exemplified in many New Labour policies' (p 157). In contrast, Lloyd and Peel (2009) point out that the Labour–Liberal Democrat coalition that was in power between 1999 and 2007 in Scotland, 'carried with it many of the prevailing and dominant political and economic ideas associated broadly with New Labour in Westminster' (Lloyd and Peel, 2009, p 106), questioning the extent of any ideological difference.

Other factors that create pressure for policy convergence include the influence of civil servants and advisory, pressure and policy groups, many of which are UK-wide (Birrell, 2009). Most important is the dominant role of England within the UK, in population and spatial size terms and in relation to the location of both the Westminster parliament and Whitehall Civil Service in London. As noted earlier, the UK government is only 'lending' powers to the devolved nations, and remains the sovereign authority over Scotland, Wales and Northern Ireland.

Despite these constraints, in recent years policy has perhaps begun to diverge more widely as the devolved nations are taking the opportunity to experiment and assert their national identities (Peel and Lloyd, 2012; Pemberton et al, 2015). In practical terms, the devolved governments have built their capacity and legitimacy to develop policy (Birrell, 2009). In political terms, Labour lost power to the Scottish National Party (SNP) in Scotland in 2007 and the Conservative Party has led the UK government since 2010, leading to a clearer gap in political ideology. The Labour Party has led the Welsh Assembly since its inception, but the Welsh Labour Party is increasingly trying to portray itself as separate and distinct from the main UK party (Morris, 2017), which may contribute to policy divergence. The domination of Northern Irish politics by parties with no equivalence in the rest of the UK, and the specific political and policy issues at play in that territory, makes comparison harder.

Outcomes

The key question, in terms of the theme of this book, is whether all the time and money spent on devolution in the UK over recent years has had any material impact on the lives of people living in Scotland, Wales and Northern Ireland. The starting point for such an analysis is that the UK is, in general, one of the most unequal countries in the developed world (Dorling, 2018). Statistics from the Organisation for Economic Co-operation and Development (OECD) show that in terms of the Gini coefficient, which measures income inequality, the UK is exceeded in its inequality within Europe only by Lithuania (OECD, 2018). For example, in the UK the best-off 10% of households have an income 17 times that of the worse-off 10% – compared to 10 times in Germany or 7 times in France (Dorling, 2017). Inequality increased dramatically during the 1980s, and has 'tended to fluctuate around a similar level since 1990' (Belfield et al, 2016, p 23).

Banting and McEwen (2018) plotted the Gini coefficient for the four UK nations between 2002 and 2014, and found a very similar pattern across all four. They concluded that 'Devolution appears to have had little obvious impact on reducing overall inequality' (Banting and McEwen, 2018, p 125). England has a slightly higher level of inequality, although Banting and McEwen point out that this is not due to policy interventions, but rather, the higher preponderance of higher earners in England than the other three nations. From this we could conclude that devolution does little to help the poorest in society. The converse view would be that the limitations placed on devolution, including the lack of direct tax-raising powers, have correspondingly limited the influence that the devolved administrations can have. It is in this context that we come to the 2014 referendum on Scottish independence and the consequences thereof.

The butterfly effect: Implications for England and the broader UK

Up until the mid-2010s, policy developments within the devolved nations largely took place alongside developments in Westminster, for whom governance issues were increasingly limited to England, with the two rarely overlapping. As we have seen in the previous discussion, while devolution did afford a greater deal of flexibility to Scotland and Wales in particular, in many cases their policies did not depart that drastically from those in England, particularly in the early years. In many ways, the referendum on Scottish independence that took place in 2014 is a key marker in the UK's development – with repercussions that went far beyond the original vote.

Set against the backdrop of a keenly contested and, crucially, tightening race in which the 'yes' pro-independence vote was perceived as gaining ground, two days before the vote the leaders of the three main parties in Westminster (David Cameron, Nick Clegg and Ed Miliband) made an intervention known as 'the vow' in which they promised greater devolution of power to Scotland if the country voted 'no' (Mullen, 2014). Whether this intervention played a decisive role is up for debate. Nevertheless, shortly after and in honouring this pledge, David Cameron announced *The Smith Commission for Further Devolution of Powers to the Scottish Parliament*. Although criticised in some quarters for being a retreat from the popular politics of the referendum (Tierney, 2015), and simply shoring up any post-referendum 'no' sentiment (Henderson et al, 2015), for its part, when it reported in late-2014 (The Smith Commission, 2014), the Commission made wide-ranging recommendations including that Scotland be allowed to control its Income Tax rates (Anderson and Gallagher, 2018), as well as re-committing to the Barnett formula.

The concessions extracted as a result of the independence referendum and implemented through the Scotland and Wales Acts of 2016 and 2017, respectively, gave those devolved nations 'much greater control over their fiscal affairs compared with the regions of

England, many of which are larger than either Scotland or Wales' (Bell and Vaillancourt, 2018, p 101). As such, this did suggest to others that agitating for change might represent a viable strategy, and while some Northern cities did publicly, if not seriously, ruminate about their own independence from Whitehall (Williams, 2014; Brown, 2015), others began to turn greater focus to the proposition (Shaw et al, 2014). In doing so, politicians were working in a variable environment in which, while there was a broad consensus in favour of regional autonomy, the extent to which that autonomy should include policy-making power varied, not least in England (Henderson et al, 2015). As well as suggesting that English attitudes towards regional autonomy had not dramatically shifted since their rejection of Regional Assemblies 10 years earlier (Shaw and Robinson, 2007), English policy-makers were presented with another headache in the rise of English nationalist parties (for example, the United Kingdom Independence Party, UKIP) and their effect on traditional Labour and Conservative voting bases (Jeffery, 2015; Kenny, 2016). While the coalition did toy with EVEL legislation (Jeffery, 2015; Colomb and Tomaney, 2016), the entire city-regional devolution agenda – and particularly that relating to the Northern Powerhouse, discussed across Chapters 3 and 4 – can be seen through the prism of this issue.

In mid–2015 David Cameron was, arguably, at the peak of his political power. After granting, and winning, the Scottish independence referendum, to the surprise of many (Fisher and Lewis-Beck, 2016) he had secured an increased majority in that year's general election – jettisoning the Liberal Democrats as coalition partners and commanding a clear parliamentary majority. In doing so, Cameron benefited from one of the major consequences of the independence referendum, whereby the SNP, buoyed by their 2014 referendum campaign, won 56 out of a possible 59 seats in Scotland (Green and Prosser, 2016), costing the Labour Party and Liberal Democrats all but one of their 41 and 11 Scottish seats held in 2010, respectively. Yet few would have suspected that on entering Downing Street on 8 May 2015, Cameron would have little over a year left in office.

The reason for Cameron's decline came through his delivery of a Conservative manifesto pledge to hold a referendum on Britain's continued membership of the EU (The Conservative Party, 2015). The reasons behind this are multitudinous and contested – but the desire to face down the Eurosceptic and frequently rebellious wing of the Conservative Party, once dubbed 'The Bastards' by ex-Prime Minister John Major, is often seen as the primary motivator (Bale, 2016). This, too, can be seen through the lens of a post-election swagger in which, with the hard Eurosceptic wing of the Conservative Party reduced to a rump (Heppell, 2013) and opinion polls on his side, Cameron could be seen operating in line with a widely held political rule: only hold a referendum when you know you can win (Gamble, 2012).

Cameron lost the referendum.

On 23 June 2018, the UK voted 52:48 to leave the EU. Here the UK was similarly split: England and Wales voted to leave, Scotland and Northern Ireland voted to remain. Shortly after 8am the next morning, Cameron announced his intention to resign as prime minister. The implications of the issues set in train by these two events would be profound, and continue to reverberate across British politics for years to come.

In the immediate aftermath, attention turned to who would succeed Cameron as prime minister and, after a short leadership race in which some ambitions were thwarted, Theresa May emerged as the new prime minister and took office on 13 July. As is discussed throughout this book – principally in Chapter 3 – while May did attempt to rhetorically shift away from Cameron and towards a 'one nation' brand of Conservatism (Quinn, 2016), as well as putting clear ideological ground between her and her predecessor by sacking Chancellor George Osborne, in practice, her administration did not stray that far from the policy principles set out between 2010 and 2016.

Brexit, as it became known, however, transfixed and near-paralysed the government as it set out to implement the EU referendum result. Nevertheless, across her first year in office May ruthlessly maintained and exploited Cameron and Osborne's strategy against the English nationalists – rather than seeking to stop parties like UKIP hiving off Conservative votes, she instead sought to capture those UKIP votes as they fell into disarray and their electoral support dissipated (Ford and Goodwin, 2017; Heath and Goodwin, 2017). Accordingly, and to the surprise of many, on 18 April 2017, May announced a snap general election, to be held on 8 June. With the intent of consolidating her hold over the House of Commons while gaining a clear electoral mandate for her Brexit strategy, the rout in Labour heartlands at the hands of the Conservative Party in scheduled local government elections held a month before the general election made this seem like a sound approach.

Few, therefore, would have predicted the result of the general election. Instead of consolidating her grip on power, while still the biggest party, May's Conservatives saw the majority won by Cameron two years earlier completely wiped out – going from a working majority of 17 to being 9 seats short of overall power.

As the dust settled, it became clear that the principles underpinning May's election strategy, namely, going after the collapsing UKIP vote, did appear sound – even if it didn't go far enough in terms of delivering the required outcome. For their part the Conservatives did win seats in the traditional Labour heartlands – most notably in Middlesbrough and South Cleveland and Copeland and, more broadly, alongside those seat gains, the Conservative inroads would correspond closely to the EU referendum results (see Figure 2.1). Here, the 61 largest Conservative vote gains in England all occurred in seats that voted to leave the EU and of those, all but one could be attributed directly to the UKIP vote collapsing.

At the time of writing (November 2019), the EU withdrawal remains before parliament, a general election is imminent and the course for the UK remains unclear. Acknowledging the sheer unpredictability of this agenda, this book does not seek to make any forecasts as to the outcome – particularly as Theresa May's own words – 'A deal, no deal or no Brexit at all' – suggests that all outcomes remain on the table.

Although it may still be far from over, the years since 2014 have seen a period of enormous tumult that has at one point or another affected every corner of British politics. Moreover, we suggest that although a multitude of factors have influenced this process along the way, the chain of events that has led the UK to the point that it finds itself in is indelibly linked to David Cameron's decision to face down calls for Scottish independence. Across this time, as the consequences of this political decision unfurled, often in unexpected ways, there has been one constant: sovereignty. From Scottish independence through to debates on EVEL and ultimately, a Brexit that 'was promoted in England as a way of bringing back sovereignty and ultimate authority to one place' (Laforest and Keating, 2018, p 183) yet has resulted in all manner of options including a United Ireland re-entering public debate, it appears that Cameron, perhaps unwittingly, opened a Pandora's box of independence sentiment. Here, and while his short-term actions in 2014 may have saved the Union, the longer-term legacy may be far less generous.

Conclusion

This chapter has attempted to provide an introduction to the complex governance structures of the UK. As noted in Chapter 1, devolution, decentralisation and localism are collectively a 'global trend' (Rodriguez-Pose and Gill, 2003). While the UK has started to follow this trend, it is fair to say it has done so slowly and perhaps

Figure 2.1: The EU referendum vote 2016, and Conservative vote change 2015–17

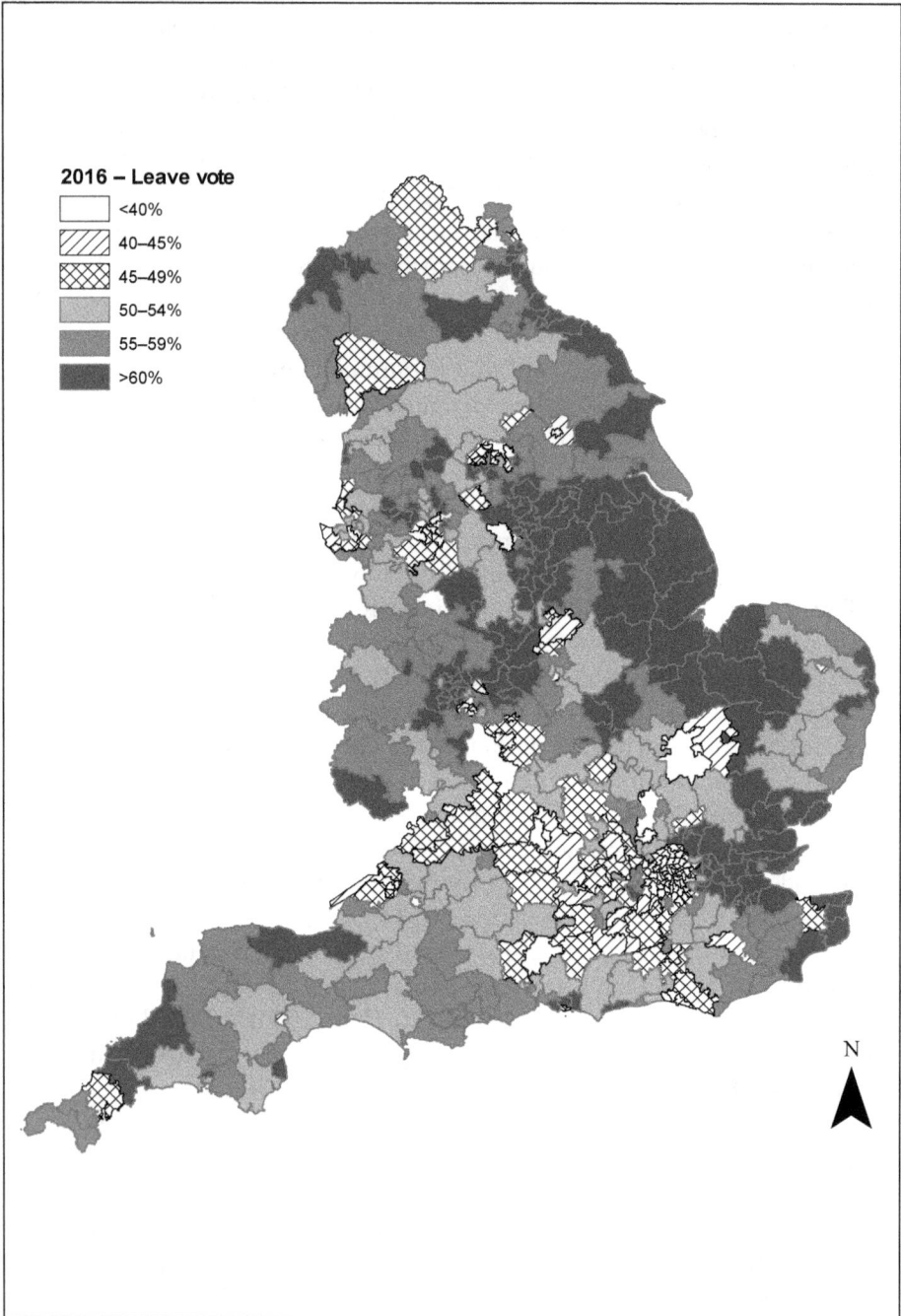

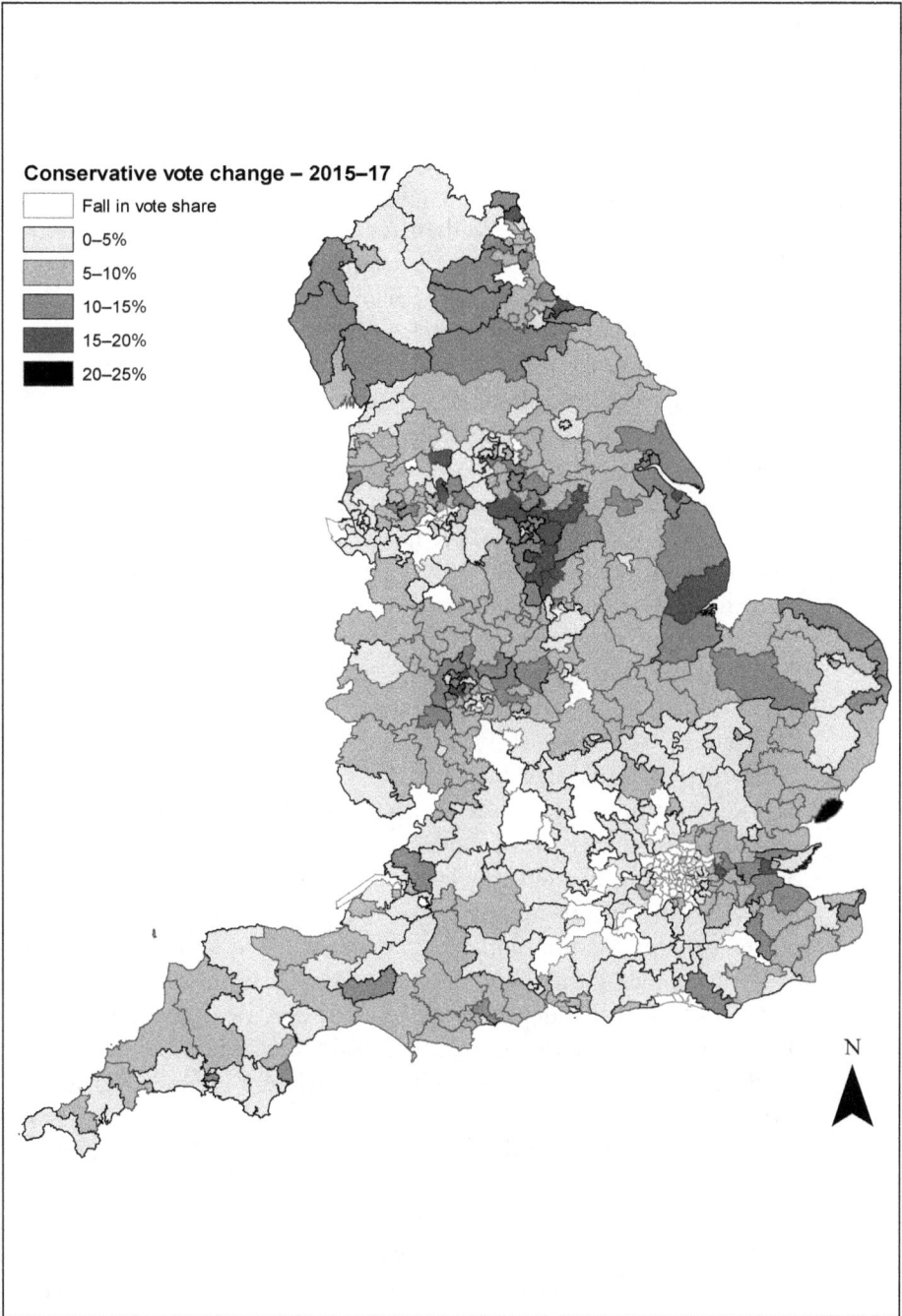

Conservative vote change – 2015–17

- Fall in vote share
- 0–5%
- 5–10%
- 10–15%
- 15–20%
- 20–25%

reluctantly, with the UK frequently being characterised as one of the most centralised countries in Europe (Ferry et al, 2015). The UK parliament retains sovereignty over a range of policy areas, including most tax-levying powers. This means that the programme of 'austerity', that is, massive cuts in public spending that have been the dominant feature of UK government policy since 2010, is of very great significance to devolution debates. We therefore discussed the scale and briefly, the impact of these cuts, and return to them frequently in the rest of this book. We then turned to the 'English question', noting the discrepancy between England and the other nations of the UK in that there is no English parliament and very little in the way of national-level urban governance in England. So the legislation and policy in relation to urban governance that we discuss in subsequent chapters emerges from the UK parliament itself.

Urban governance is one of the policy areas that has, since 1998, been devolved from the UK to the governments of Scotland, Wales and Northern Ireland, for example in relation to planning and housing policy. The devolved nations have national-level spatial plans, indicating how those nations envisage population, housing, employment, and so on will be distributed over the coming years. England has no such plan. There are other areas of difference between the devolved nations and England, and indeed, between Scotland, Wales and Northern Ireland, including as regards their approach to community planning, the focus of Chapter 6 of this book.

In terms of outcomes, however, for example, whether devolution has done anything to address the long-standing levels of social and economic inequality in the devolved nations, the jury is for now still out. Some have blamed this lack of radical change on the limited nature of devolution, including the retention in Westminster of the power to alter Income Tax rates. Since 2016, as a consequence of the 'vow' made by the three main party leaders in the UK just before the 2014 Scottish independence referendum, this power has been devolved to the Scottish government, and 'Scotland is now moving in a different direction to the rest of the UK when it comes to tax' (Sim, 2018) as the current Scottish administration seeks to raise Income Tax. Some have suggested that the 2014 referendum had other, more significant, consequences, arguably playing a role in the rise of UKIP and consequent calls for the UK to leave the EU.

Brexit, assuming it happens (at the time of writing, in late 2019, this is still far from clear) will, of course, have major ramifications for many aspects of life in the UK. One of the many uncertainties is how it will affect devolution in Scotland, Wales and Northern Ireland. Some of the areas of devolved policy, including agricultural and environmental policy, are constrained by membership of the EU. When the UK leaves the EU, this constraint will be removed, so the devolved nations (and England, through the UK government) could adopt different policies, which, in turn, could have impacts on the rest of the UK – for example, in relation to fisheries, a contentious topic for many coastal communities. Because devolved powers are only 'lent' to those nations from the UK, they can consequently be withdrawn. The UK government has never done this, and has been reluctant to legislate in areas of policy that have been devolved, but it has the ability to do so. Such an intervention would no doubt be extremely contentious, perhaps being viewed by the devolved nations as 'constitutionally illegitimate' (Brouillet and Mullen, 2018, p 73), and could, in turn, lead us back to renewed demands for Scottish independence.

Whatever happens in terms of Brexit, the UK has been irrevocably changed, and it seems that the 'cat is out of the bag' in terms of devolution for Scotland, Wales and Northern Ireland. In England the picture is more mixed – as we have observed, in the absence of any form of cohesive nation-level governance structures, the levels 'below' this, from the sub-national to the community, assume greater importance. It is to those levels this book now turns.

3

Replacing the regions: The evolution of English subnational reform

Introduction

Today, London enjoys a hegemonic dominance over UK policy-making – both politically, and economically. London dwarfs the other UK cities in almost every major marker of economic development, while enjoying planning projects and levels of investment that other UK cities could only dream of. Yet this was not always the case. Historically, during the height of the British Empire, other cities such as Liverpool far outstripped London in terms of economic contribution (Sykes et al, 2013; Wilks-Heeg, 2003), and other research suggests that London only really began to grow in the levels taken for granted today as a result of policy in the 1980s while remaining insulated from comparative downturn in the 1990s (Robson et al, 2000). In addition, and as discussed in Chapter 2, it can be argued that in the last 20 years, London's growth has been driven by a level of political autonomy and investment hitherto unseen by other UK cities. Combined, this has deepened the so-called 'North–South' divide, a planning issue that enjoys the same ubiquity as the green belt in terms of public recognition.

It is the most recent attempts to address this 'growth gap' (Dorling and Thomas, 2004; McCann, 2016) – made a priority by the post-2010 coalition – to which this chapter turns. To achieve this, the government rolled out a programme of sub-national reform over the course of four years. Labelled as devolution (although different in form and nature to the national-scale devolution discussed in Chapter 2), the government's basic premise was comparatively simple: move decision-making and nominal levels of spending control to the UK cities as a means to encourage economic growth. This began with a focus on cities and their wider regions, developing into something larger as, driven by Chancellor George Osborne, the government tried to foster urban agglomerations, dubbed the 'Northern Powerhouse' and the 'Midlands Engine'. As we will see, this agenda did not appear overnight, but rather coalesced over several years as a series of policy reforms aligned with a common thread.

As we argue in this chapter, the reality of delivering this agenda presented numerous challenges. For one, as the post-2010 devolution agenda progressed from cities to urban agglomerations, it became clear that the local authorities subject to the reforms, and which have been long-standing economic competitors, would now be expected to abandon their zero-sum entrepreneurial game (Peck and Tickell, 1994) and collaborate. We examine both if, and how, that process has been managed through a discussion of who the key actors are in bringing such collaboration to bear, the challenges they faced, and how they were overcome. As we will see, this work has been taken forward formally and publicly, through a variety of government-endorsed structures, but also through third sector and private endeavour. Similarly, we consider the extent to which any economic success has spread, acknowledging research which suggests that, beyond London, much of the UK's success has been isolated within the core cities, with the surrounding regions being left to wither (Dorling and Thomas, 2004). As such we examine the extent to which post-2010 reforms make any attempt to address this pervasive gap and ask: will a rising tide lift all boats?

Like many aspects of UK policy reform, the course of sub-national governance can be charted by broader patterns of political change. From the technocratic post-war period to the neoliberal reforms of the 1980s and 1990s, to 'New' Labour's 'third way', each remoulded the regions within their political vision. In this chapter we will argue that in attempting to understand the nature of post-2010 reform, there are lessons to be learned from these eras – both recognising the worst policy pitfalls of those periods, and also how best practice from those periods might be of relevance today.

Ultimately, the aim of this chapter is to provide an overview of the strategic policy changes made since 2010 in the sub-national (that is, regional) space, and their implications. However, in this chapter we purposefully stop short of the specifics of governance in the city-regional space, as we discuss this in depth in Chapter 4. Consequently, to gain the fullest understanding of the issues at play, we suggest that both this chapter and Chapter 4 should be considered in tandem.

Of course, this agenda is not one that is solely or merely applicable to a UK audience. London is far from the only context in which a major (often capital) city enjoys such a hegemony over its neighbours, and other countries including France and South Korea (the latter being discussed further later) have attempted to address their growth gap in ways that are of interest here. This chapter draws on these examples as a means to drive the discussion, and to serve as comparators that both challenge and refine the UK approach.

English regionalism: A brief overview

The current regional policy landscape in England has had a tumultuous and non-linear evolution over the previous century with policy responses driven by political winds as much as they have been affected by the times (Sykes and Nurse, 2017). In this section, we discuss some of the major milestones during this period, and highlight their relevance to the themes we discuss as the chapter develops.

Throughout this period, regional policy changes share one consistency – the growth gap. With varying rates of recovery in the aftermath of the Great Depression, and what could be seen as the first inklings of post-industrial decline, the mid-1930s brought forward two issues that persist in British planning: the North–South divide, in which recovery from the Depression was unequally spread, and where London and the South East emerged from the Depression more quickly while other areas, particularly in Northern England, stalled (Couch, 2016), and the attempts to respond to these issues through policy.

The commonly regarded beginnings of the UK's attempts at regional policy can be traced to the Royal Commission on the Distribution of the Industrial Population – better known as the Barlow Report (Barlow, 1940). The Commission recognised this North–South imbalance and subsequent negative effects on the UK economy (Couch, 2016), and recommended restrictions on growth in London in order to capitalise on under-used resources in Northern England. Although the outbreak of the Second World War meant that the Barlow Report was not feted as it might have been in peacetime, its legacy was clear – with its influence evident in Abercrombie's (1944) work in London as well as the post-war New Town movement.

While earlier thinkers clearly recognised that there was an increasing spatial disparity between growth and prosperity within the regions of the UK, and their legacies do include policies that clearly attempted to address this, for much of the early-mid 20th century, the UK did not have any significant regional policy. Rather, outside of bespoke interventions, the significant majority of planning was still undertaken through the auspices of the Town and Country Planning Act 1947 and a two-tier planning system comprising county plans and local development plans. This included the introduction of *Industrial Development Certificates* for 'all new manufacturing establishments and extensions over 5,000sq ft' (Hall, 1999, p 78), which effectively acted as a 'carrot and stick' approach for the marshalling of economic development around the country. Reflecting themes that still persist today, this activity was explicitly redistributive in its intent – moving economic opportunities from the prosperous South East to more depressed areas of the country in a form of spatial Keynesianism (Pike et al, 2016).

The first significant challenge to this – and thus the first real move towards an explicit regional policy – came in 1969 with the publication of the Redcliffe-Maude report (Wise, 1969). Recognising the changing role of central government in issues including urban and economic regeneration, alongside scrapping this two-tier system the report advocated the creation of higher-tier 'provinces'. In doing so, the Redcliffe-Maud report would set in train a slow-burn expansion of regional activity, culminating in the creation of Government Offices for the Regions in 1994 along highly similar geographical lines (of which more shortly).

In the interim, the late 1970s and 1980s saw a period in British sub-national governance which, in hindsight, took the UK further away from what, until this point, more closely resembled the stable long-term governance structures of other 'Western' democracies. In policy terms, the biggest change during this period came in 1986 with the abolition of England's metropolitan counties and the Greater London Authority (Flynn et al, 1985). This abolition – and their replacement with smaller districts – was largely seen as an attempt to dilute the powers of metropolitan areas that were increasingly challenging central government on the scale and nature of local government reform (Parkinson, 1985; Frost and North, 2013).

After a significant period in the policy wilderness, the mid-1990s saw regional thinking return to the mainstream when, in 1994, the Major government announced the creation of Government Offices for the Regions (GORs). During this time, and building on the steady but piecemeal progression of regional thinking stemming from Redcliffe-Maud, the government formalised the eight English regions (see Figure 3.1), and committed to channelling the work of Whitehall departments through GORs based on the rationale that by working locally, civil servants would be better placed to understand, and respond to, local concerns – and thus be better placed to deliver government programmes more effectively (Nurse, 2015a). This move was, in part, also inspired by the broader shift within the EU towards a 'Europe of the Regions' (Amin and Thrift, 1995; Loughlin, 1996), and the new GORs also served as a platform through which EU Structural Funds could flow. This had a profound effect on the UK regions which, as discussed earlier in Chapter 2, were often overlooked in terms of capital investment, and deployed these EU funds to redevelop critical infrastructure and to bolster their economic development (Nurse and Fulton, 2017; Raikes, 2018).

On taking office in 1997, Deputy Prime Minister John Prescott, who held the planning brief for 'New' Labour, was clearly enthused by this regional thinking. Such was this enthusiasm the government brought forward planning policies for the regions in line with national level policy – first through Regional Planning Guidance, and latterly through Regional Spatial Strategies (RSSs) – as well as RDAs tasked with fostering economic development. Going further, while the Blair government instigated proposals for devolved government in the three Home Nations (see Chapter 2), in England they held broadly similar ambitions – with Prescott championing proposals for *Regional Assemblies* as devolved legislatures, adding a level of democratic accountability to the incoming RSSs, and extending the government's broader localism agenda. London was the first English region to experience this reform, with elected members of the London Assembly taking their seats in July 2000, alongside the newly elected Mayor of London (of which more in Chapter 4). However, following a rejected referendum in the North East in 2004 (Shaw and Robinson, 2007), plans to expand the Regional Assemblies to the rest of England were shelved.

During this period, the prominence of the regional agenda also spurred opportunities for some strategic initiatives, the most prominent being plans for the 'Northern Way', a collaboration between the North East, North West and Yorkshire and Humber regions, focusing on transport and economic growth (González, 2006; Goodchild and Hickman, 2006; Liddle, 2009). In doing so, the Northern Way would be the first meaningful attempt to address policy in this way and, importantly, would foreshadow initiatives brought forward under the coalition some 10 years later.

Although the 'New' Labour government, now led in its death throes by Gordon Brown, signalled its commitment to the regional agenda with the promise of creating regional ministers if re-elected (Labour Party, 2010), those proposals would never come to pass. However, during this time Brown's administration would introduce one largely unheralded reform that would carry longer-term significance – through the Local Democracy, Economic Development and Construction Act 2009, the government provided for the creation of 'combined authorities', a mechanism for contiguous local authorities to collaborate on economic, regeneration and transport-related issues

(Sandford, 2017b). This legislation would go on to underpin much of the coalition's agenda towards the end of its first term.

In the period since the Second World War, sub-national governance in the UK has seen regions and metropolitan city regions varyingly holding prominence at one point or another in a policy environment in which trends are revisited and never, truly, cast out. As we will see in this chapter, the post-2010 period continues this pattern, in which some views are sent into the wilderness, and others return to mainstream thinking.

The dawn of a new era

There is a clear starting point to post-2010 sub-national reform: 6 July 2010, the date on which Eric Pickles announced the abolition of the structures of regional governance. Critical of regional governance in opposition, decrying it as 'unwanted and unaccountable regional bureaucracy' which imposed 'Soviet tractor style top-down planning targets' (DCLG, 2010a), Pickles argued that the regional governance project had failed to live up to its purpose (Stratton, 2010). In doing so, Pickles was the first to substantially engage with the policies set out in the 'Coalition Agreement' (HM Government, 2010a), the principles and understandings underpinning the Conservative–Liberal Democrat coalition.

Pickles did not, however, advocate that there was no role for sub-national governance in the UK's policy architecture, and his proposed replacement was quick to follow when, on 29 June 2010, the government announced the formation of Local Enterprise Partnerships (LEPS). In their letter inviting participation in these LEPs, Pickles, along with Business Minister Vince Cable, set out the remit of the new organisations, saying:

> Partnerships will therefore want to create the right environment for business and growth in their areas, by tackling issues such as planning and housing, local transport and infrastructure priorities, employment and enterprise and the transition to the low carbon economy. Supporting small business start-ups will therefore be important. They will want to work closely with universities and further education colleges, in view of their importance to local economies, and with other relevant stakeholders. In some areas, tourism will also be an important economic driver. (Cable and Pickles, 2010)

The new LEPs would also be premised on more concise geographies based on functional economic areas – reasoning that travel-to-work areas would be a much more fruitful venue for decision-making to take place. Perhaps reflecting the guiding principles of the 1980s (such as Development Corporations), the Pickles and Cable letter mandated that while these LEPs would be defined by participating local authorities, they would be led by local businesses who, in the government's view, would be better placed to know what local economic priorities should be. Perhaps attempting to deflect criticism of democratic unaccountability, local authority leaders would be invited to sit on LEP boards (Pugalis et al, 2012).

The 38 LEPs (see Figure 3.1) that came forward in the weeks that followed took a variety of forms. Some were city regions, centred on one of England's eight 'core' cities, and of those, many bore a striking resemblance to the former metropolitan authorities that were abolished in the mid-1980s. In areas where a major economic core was lacking, different kinds of collaboration occurred – often based on strategic interaction between multiple large towns. Where LEPs did reflect former metropolitan boundaries, the government appeared at least somewhat sensitive to the optics of this, going so far as to prevent Liverpool City Region (as it became known) from naming their LEP 'Merseyside' despite widespread agreement among local partners that this was the name they wished to adopt. As such, this was localism, but one that existed within the parameters of national oversight (Hambleton, 2017). This presented an early warning – if a local area cannot even decide its own name, what other limitations might it then have?

In inviting local areas to form their own areas, the formation of the LEPs provided an early indication of one of the main weaknesses that would characterise much of the government's sub-national devolution agenda: collaboration between economic competitors. Since the Industrial Revolution, many of the UK's major urban areas have been economic competitors, which has seen this competition shift from trying to out-mode each other in industrial innovation, to competing in line with urban entrepreneurial agendas in which those cities are classified as either winners or losers (Harvey, 1989; Peck and Tickell, 1994). This was brought to the fore in the West Midlands, where two LEPs formed within the area – Greater Birmingham and Solihull, and the Black Country, each reflecting broader economic tensions within the area. The West Midlands also highlighted another issue, whereby some local authorities were party to both LEPs, something seen elsewhere as local authorities attempted to game the system by being

Figure 3.1: Eight regions to 38 LEPs

Note: Isles of Scilly not shown.

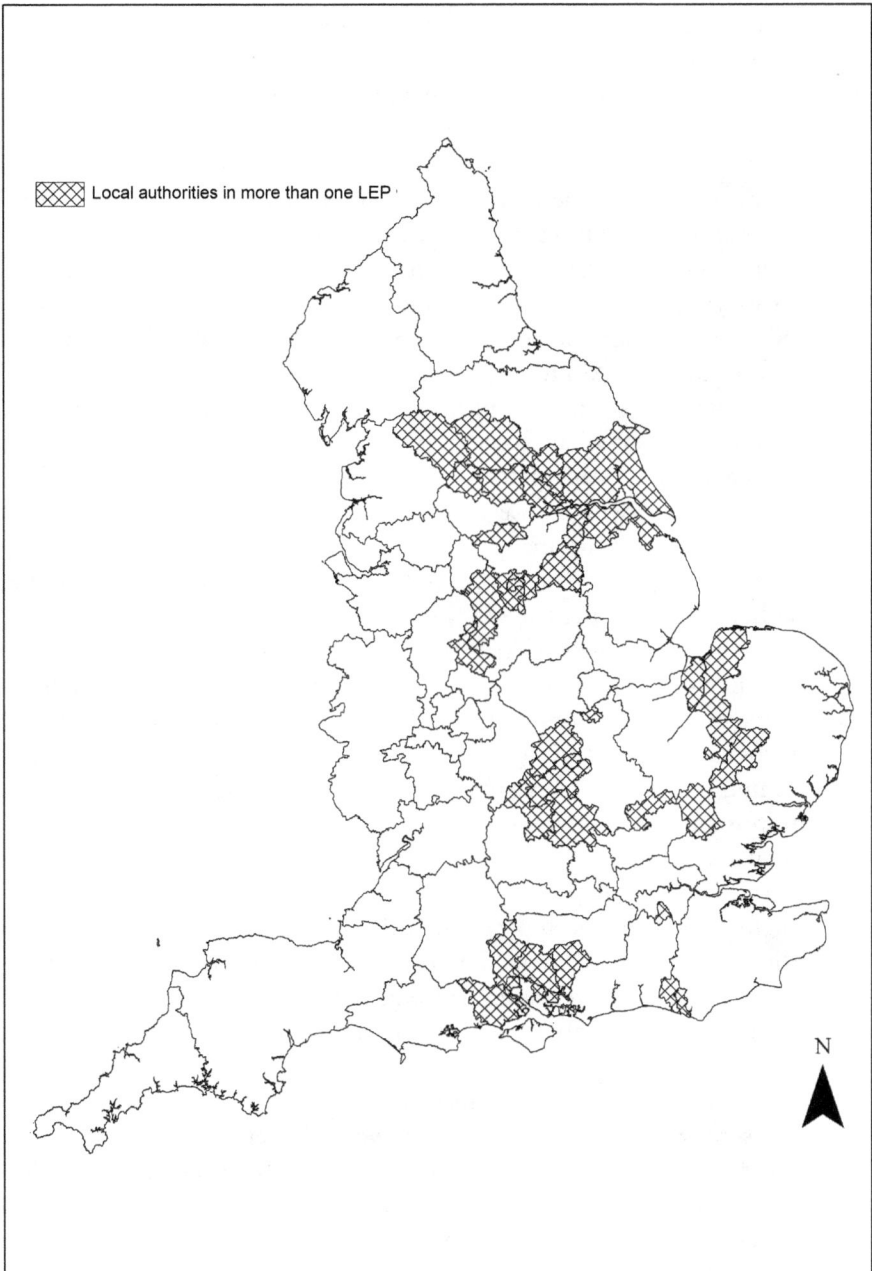

Local authorities in more than one LEP

N

party to multiple LEPS (see Figure 3.1), arguing that their interests were best served by collaborating with more than one functional economic area. This overlap was something that wouldn't explicitly be addressed until 2018 (MHCLG, 2018b).

In practical terms, the LEPs would receive little guidance as to how they might achieve their aims (Pugalis et al, 2012), meaning many LEPs were slow to find their feet, and those with a history of working at this scale found themselves at an advantage (Deas et al, 2013). With limited resources from central government, most nascent LEPs were reliant on buy-in from existing local actors (Pike et al, 2015), leading to varying scales of formality, and meaning that within a few years of their initiation, while well-resourced LEPs that could secure this buy-in became akin to economic development agencies (Pugalis and Bentley, 2013), others languished. Thus, the early stages of LEPs gave an indication of what would go on to be one of the major themes of the coalition's localist reforms – spatially uneven development (Beel et al, 2018) in which areas that were better resourced, less affected by austerity or institutionally more capable simply began to pull away (Pike et al, 2015), and in doing so, left a greater risk of deepening rather than reducing the spatial imbalance.

In the early stages of LEP development, Liddle (2012) recognised another emerging theme of the developing city-regional agenda: managing relationships within and without the region. Liddle not only recognised the vitality of the relationship with central government, something seen as a key factor with GORs (Nurse, 2015a), but more importantly, also recognised that successful LEPs would be able to manage the pressures from lower jurisdictions (that is, their local authorities). This bottom-up pressure would emerge across two themes: the relationship between the core and the peripheries, and the relationship between the core city – as the principal economic driver that, for some time, had enjoyed large amounts of autonomy – and the city region itself. Both are themes discussed in this chapter, and in Chapter 4.

In reality, while in some areas LEPs would play a key role in setting out strategic economic policy, they would largely go on to be sideline players in the broader devolution agenda. However, their creation would be important in setting some of the initial themes that would characterise subsequent reforms. Crucially, the broad strategic focus was now firmly on city region scale thinking and, with those constructs largely left to stand or fall based on the strength of their own networks (Pike et al, 2015), it was clear that underlying neoliberal principles of self-reliance remained at play.

Combining agendas: Combined authorities

The next significant change in the coalition's sub-national devolution agenda came in late 2013 with the revival of the combined authority programme, having largely laid dormant since its genesis in 2009. By this point it was clear that the coalition, with an agenda now largely fronted by Chancellor George Osborne, had increasingly come to view the city regions, as opposed to stand-alone cities, as central to the delivery of its economic ambitions relating to the UK's growth gap. Although little heralded at the time, this shift would be a significant landmark in England's post-2010 landscape, and would establish much of the framework that we can recognise today.

Joining Greater Manchester Combined Authority, which was formed in 2011, the mark II combined authorities were in large part an amalgamation of the LEP and City Deal processes (for more on City Deals, see Chapter 4). As opposed to the LEPs, forming a combined authority was not a mandatory expectation. Instead, authorities seeking to form a combined authority were invited to step forward after satisfying two initial conditions: first, that all participants form a contiguous area and second, that all members of the putative combined authority would be there voluntarily. Responding directly to criticism regarding the LEPs' lack of democratic accountability, and perhaps mirroring the Regional Assemblies of the mid-2000s (Mawson, 2007), the combined authorities would be governed by a board or cabinet comprising the leaders of each of its constituent authorities, led by a chair elected from that number. They would be joined by other key actors including representatives from the LEP.

In forming the combined authorities, and to ensure decision-making did not simply divert attention to the major economic centres, in agreeing the chair, there was an implicit understanding that the chairperson would represent an authority from outside of the central/core city. In most cases this did occur, although not every core city subscribed to this vision. Most notably, the Liverpool City Region Combined Authority risked implosion during its first meeting after Liverpool's leader, Joe Anderson, expressed his desire to lead the new organisation – arguing that his position as mayor of a core city would leave him better placed to get the best of the opportunities on the table (Nurse, 2015a). Although Anderson would be talked down, this would not be the first, or the last, example of in-fighting within the Liverpool City Region, and flagged a number of important issues.

First, the voluntary nature of the combined authorities betrays an element of fragility – that is, if there is any major disagreement of this nature, there is little to prevent things breaking down. Moreover, it demonstrates that such agreements between constituent authorities, each with their own electorates, plans and priorities, will inevitably result in a greater or lesser degree of tension when releasing control upwards to a larger construct (Lupton et al, 2018). Second, and building on this, the formation of the combined authorities highlighted many issues of core versus periphery (Dembski et al, 2017), and how both the decisions, and their benefits and consequences, are equitably and consensually distributed. Although outlined here, this discussion forms a major theme of Chapter 4.

Reflecting the more voluntary nature of the combined authorities, not every LEP sought combined authority status, and within a year only four mark II combined authorities had been agreed. Alongside Greater Manchester, they were: Liverpool City Region, Sheffield City Region, the North East (including Newcastle) and West Yorkshire (including Leeds).

To the casual observer in April 2014, that all the combined authorities were located in Northern England would be of passing consequence, perhaps indicative of a chancellor who was interested in closing the North–South divide, but most likely a reflection of areas that were proactively seeking out (and capable of securing) new funding opportunities,. Yet, less than two months later, George Osborne would give a speech demonstrating that this focus on Northern England was not coincidence but rather, the early running on arguably the most serious attempt to untie English planning's Gordian Knot in a generation.

In his speech of June 2014, Osborne set out his rationale:

> The cities of the north are individually strong, but collectively not strong enough. The whole is less than the sum of its parts. So the powerhouse of London dominates more and more. And that's not healthy for our economy. It's not good for our country. We need a Northern Powerhouse.... Not one city, but a collection of northern cities – sufficiently close to each other that combined they can take on the world. (Osborne, 2014)

Three key themes would emerge from Osborne's speech that would underpin this agenda. The first is the UK's productivity gap that was, again, becoming an increasing concern. This not only reflected concerns regarding London's increasing absorption of its surroundings (Hall and Pain, 2006) and drawing in economic migrants (particularly young professionals) from other areas of the UK, but also the effect that this growth was having with regards to planning for the capital – not least the three policy preoccupations discussed in Chapter 1: housing, transport and jobs.

Second was the acknowledgement that individual cities could no longer 'go it alone' in a global economy. Now, and developing the government's own sub-national agenda that had increasingly become focused on broader city regions, the idea was to go one step further and foster economic cooperation between (and within) those regions to attempt to create an urban agglomeration comprising several major city regions. This, the government acknowledged, would require significant investment – not least in transport infrastructure – of which more later.

The third and most important thematic element would be the focus on Northern England. This would make explicit something that had, thus far, only been a sub-narrative of the post-2010 policy agenda. Indeed, the phrase 'Northern Powerhouse' came to encapsulate the entire devolution agenda, even after Osborne left office two years later. In hindsight, Osborne's 2014 speech was a key waypoint in the post-2010 devolution agenda. This chapter now turns to the strategic underpinnings of the proposals

The 'Northern Powerhouse'

If Osborne's ambitions for a 'Northern Powerhouse' can be considered to be the starting gun on a new period in the coalition government's post-2010 reforms, what followed was a period of rapid advancement as the details of what this Northern Powerhouse would entail became clearer. This happened at two scales: strategically, that is, at the level of the North, and also within individual city regions. In line with the thematic issues outlined in this chapter so far, here the discussion of the Northern Powerhouse centres on the former, discussing those strategic issues relating to Northern England. The latter, that is, the specifics of city region-level devolution and subsequent issues, are explicitly considered in Chapter 4.

Although at a top level the strategic aim of the Northern Powerhouse – to foster an urban agglomeration that would provide an economic counterbalance to London – seemed clear, the practicalities of such an undertaking would be complex, and raise fundamental questions relating to both the attainability of such an undertaking and the implications that would arise from it. At the broader scale, the Northern cities would be connected by significant infrastructure spending (Wong and Webb, 2014) including electrification of an ageing Victorian railway infrastructure (HM Treasury, 2017) and, in the longer term, proposals for 'HS3', the third element of the UK's high-speed rail network (NIC, 2015), would also feature. In selecting transport as the strategic issue to connect the Northern cities, the Northern Powerhouse would mirror the Northern Way, albeit with an important difference: the Northern Powerhouse lacked a clear definition of what would constitute Northern England.

Although the 'North–South divide' remains one of the UK's most pervasive issues, and holds a deep-seated place in the British cultural psyche (Wainwright, 2010), the lack of clear definition with regards to the Northern Powerhouse largely reflects the lack of consensus on where the North–South divide actually begins and ends. There are, of course, common jocular expressions of where this might lie, including the area not contained by London's 'M25' ring-motorway, and everything North of the 'Watford Gap' – a geographical feature just north of London through which much major North–South transport infrastructure to the capital passes. Even if tongue in cheek, both emphasise the hegemony of London. At the more serious end of the scale, perhaps the clearest articulation of the composition of Northern England came through the 'Northern Way', which used the three English GORs of North East, North West and Yorkshire and the Humber as its boundaries.

While the 'Northern Powerhouse' branding stuck in the months and years that followed, no such clarity with regards to its boundaries was forthcoming, leaving others scrambling to fill this void with their own definitions. Often going further than the government's own policy position, there was a widespread sense that the Northern Powerhouse should aim to be more than just the sum of several city regions linked by an improved transport infrastructure, while others argued that this Northern Powerhouse should draw in surrounding areas including Wales, with the Under-Secretary of State for Wales arguing in parliament that:

> The Northern Powerhouse, which stretches from north Wales to Newcastle, is reviving the economic and civic strength of our great northern cities. It is central to our vision for rebalancing the economy, and north Wales is already benefiting from large-scale infrastructure investments. (*Hansard*, 2016)

This lack of clarity also created the space for other organisations such as the Royal Town Planning Institute (RTPI) and Institute for Public

Policy Research (IPPR) to explore the strategic opportunities that might be available – something we return to later. Consequently, reflecting both the lack of strategic clarity and the absence of an overarching Northern policy architecture, this space increasingly, generically, and often pejoratively referred to as the 'Northern Powerhouse' was left to develop in a piecemeal fashion in the following years. Of course, the Northern Powerhouse is not the first of its kind, and in Box 3.1 we can observe just a few international examples of where similar approaches have been attempted.

Box 3.1: The Northern Powerhouse's international comparators

The urban agglomeration economy is far from a new idea, having first found favour in the early 1970s in the USA (Bergsman et al, 1972), and the effects of polycentric areas, often comprising multiple towns and cities that interact in a symbiotic fashion, is similarly well explored – not least in the European context (Hall and Pain, 2006).

There are two prominent examples from Europe that give insights as to how the Northern Powerhouse might achieve its broader goals. They are the Rhine-Ruhr in Germany, a region of 11 million people that comprises Dortmund, Essen, Bochum and Duisburg (Blotevogel, 1998), and the Randstad in the Netherlands, which principally comprises Amsterdam, Rotterdam, The Hague and Utrecht (Kloosterman and Lambregts, 2001). In both cases, the agglomeration economy is driven by the competitive advantages that can be gained through good transport links and consistent urban planning. Yet, as we shall see, all that glitters is not always gold, and the Rhine-Ruhr and Randstad face similar challenges to those faced by the putative Northern Powerhouse.

In Germany, while the Rhine-Ruhr is premised on cooperation across its constituent areas (Knapp, 1998), the most clearly transferable lesson to the putative Northern Powerhouse relates to transport, where a unified system runs across the metropolitan area. In achieving this, the Rhine-Ruhr also overcame markedly similar contexts – both in terms of an area forged in long-standing industrial competitiveness (Blotevogel, 1998), but also as one in which that zero-sum entrepreneurial competitiveness still lingers.

In the Netherlands, the UK can draw much from the Randstad's strategic planning (van Oort et al, 2010; Dieleman et al, 1999), which encompasses new urban developments, as well as integrating and connecting the existing urban areas into what is already a compact and well-connected area. As with the Rhine-Ruhr, the parallels to Northern England are marked – especially with regards to the seemingly contradictory nature of the urban realm that sees distinct areas, often existing cheek-by-jowl, blend into conurbations, all the while resisting attempts to integrate into the broader whole (van Oort et al, 2010).

In the absence of a spatial strategy from Northern England, organisations like the RTPI – that has, at points, begun work on a *Great North Plan* (RTPI, 2016) – have much to learn from this context. In particular, it is clear that the idea of broader and more strategic collaboration and buy-in to these agendas is an issue that is not isolated to Northern England. Although not insurmountable, it suggests that while there is value in attempting to overcome those barriers, it cannot be done overnight.

In practice the spatial reality of the Northern Powerhouse would emerge through the signing of 'devolution deals', a package of funding, devolved powers and reforms (discussed at length in Chapter 4) that included control over transport and economic planning, and formed the novel basis through which individual city regions could exert control over their economies. In the longer term, combined authority areas with a 'devo deal' would also be expected to hold elections for a directly elected 'metro mayor' – again, something we discuss at length in Chapter 4.

A prerequisite of signing such a 'devo deal', as they became known, was that it be an agreement between a combined authority and central government. This set an important tone as, given that by 2015 only five city regions (all still located in Northern England, and premised on a core city) had attained combined authority status (Sandford, 2017b), the extent to which power would be devolved to Northern England would be limited. Even the addition of Teesside, becoming the sixth northern combined authority in 2016 as part of an expansion programme, would make little dent in this. This spatial limitation can be seen in Figure 3.2, which shows the Northern combined authorities. If taking the Northern Way's boundaries of Northern England (in the absence of any other clear definition of where Northern England is, as per the previous discussion), it is clear that geographically, there is a comparatively small area covered by the devo deals, with a principal cluster broadly corresponding to the M62 motorway corridor. Consequently, despite the initial rhetoric surrounding the Northern Powerhouse evoking a resurgent Northern England, in practice its functional area (that is, the area with devolved power) was (and presently, remains) tightly bounded, with swathes of the country remaining outside of its reach. As well as larger urban centres such as Preston and Hull that had previously signed City Deals with the coalition government, this tightly delineated space also excluded many areas located in the 'spatial in-between' (Dembski, 2015), that is, those areas not within a city region but located within a wider functional economic area, something supposedly at the heart of government thinking. This includes large towns such as Warrington, located between Liverpool and Manchester, as well as areas such as Burnley and Blackburn, and their exclusion challenges the broader commitment to functional economic area-based thinking. Moreover, from Figure 3.2 (and the comparison with the DEFRA, 2011 urban–rural classification) it is clear that this devolution is an urban agenda with much of rural Northern England, and even large rural towns (for example, Penrith, Carlisle and Harrogate) excluded.

In effect, the tightly bounded reality of the devolved Northern Powerhouse meant that much of Northern England would be reliant on the benefits of a 'trickle-out' effect – either from newly successful urban cores, or proximity to proposed transport links. This would lead to questions connecting the comparative success of the Northern Powerhouse idea to the fates of those places reliant on 'the rising tide lift[ing] all boats' (Nurse, 2015b p 697).

Devolution dilution and difficulties

While Northern England and latterly the *Northern Powerhouse* have undoubtedly taken centre-stage in the post-2010 sub-national reforms, other English areas did experience reform along similar lines, even if receiving less fanfare.

Most notable among those areas was the West Midlands. With Birmingham at its core, and a boundary mirroring that of a namesake metropolitan county abolished in 1986, the West Midlands Combined Authority came into being in June 2016. Just as Greater Manchester would be the pioneer combined authority in the Northern Powerhouse, the West Midlands would take the lead in what Osborne termed the *Midlands Engine*. The rationale behind this Midlands Engine was exactly the same: to encourage economic growth in a post-industrial area as a means to counterbalance London.

In practical terms, the Midlands Engine reaffirmed many of the issues raised earlier, that is, a tightly bounded devolved area, the role of the spatial in-between and the exclusion of other viable urban centres (for example, Wolverhampton). However, with areas including

Figure 3.2: The effective Northern Powerhouse alongside Northern England's urban–rural classification

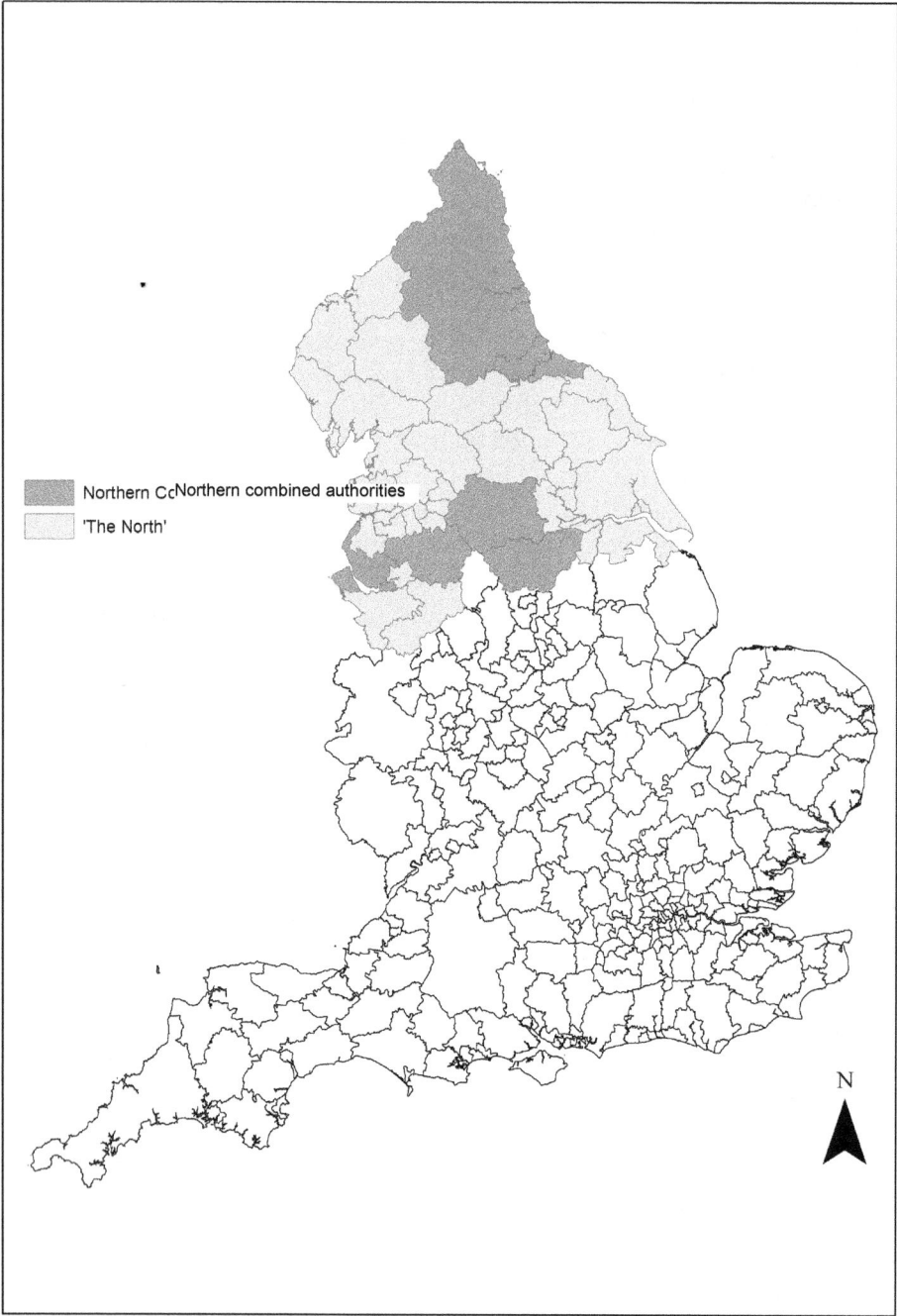

Source for urban and rural classification: DEFRA (2011)

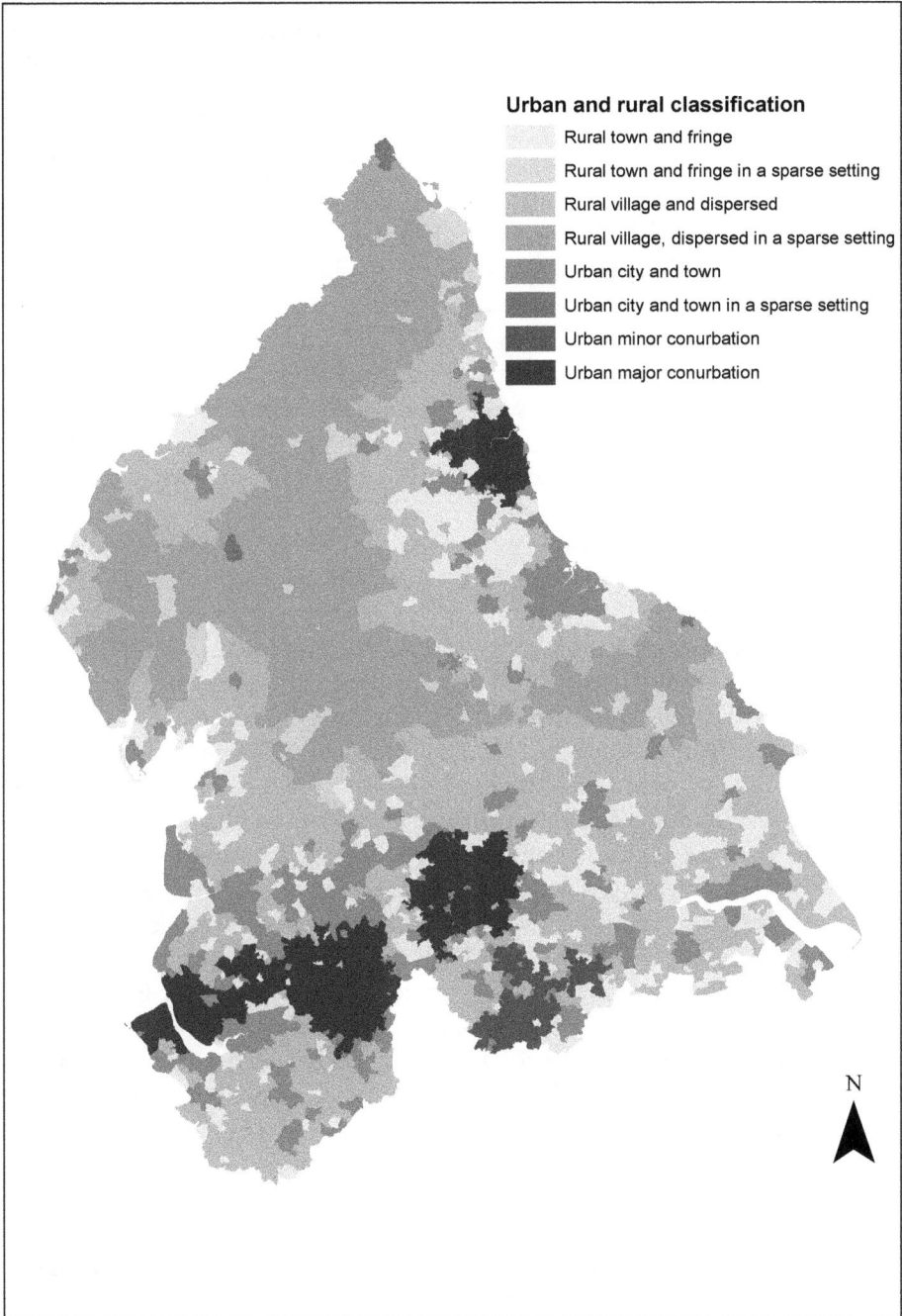

Urban and rural classification

- Rural town and fringe
- Rural town and fringe in a sparse setting
- Rural village and dispersed
- Rural village, dispersed in a sparse setting
- Urban city and town
- Urban city and town in a sparse setting
- Urban minor conurbation
- Urban major conurbation

N

Cornwall, Greater Lincolnshire and East Anglia also working towards their own deals with central government during this period, this also had a diluting and muddying effect on the Northern Powerhouse brand. That said, this expansion (either through being granted, or trying to attain combined authority status and agreeing devo deals) granted greater geographical coverage to the sub-national devolution agenda, and effectively, if slowly, began filling the gaps left by the abolition of regional governance in 2010. Despite this, there remained a piecemeal geographical coverage, and devolution remained largely limited to the major cities outside of London.

In 2016, however, the prospects for this entire agenda were cast into doubt. As we discuss across this book, it is certain that June 2016, and the UK's vote to leave the EU, will be a key marker in the UK's political history. Its changes were seismic and far-reaching, and sub-national devolution was not protected from this. This period of change effectively began following Theresa May's ascent to Prime Minster in July 2016 and the subsequent removal of George Osborne as Chancellor shortly thereafter. With devolution, and the Northern Powerhouse in particular, viewed as Osborne's pet project, any concerns around the longevity of the reforms were deepened when taken alongside May's inaugural comments, which indicated that her administration would support industrial policy that focused on *all* regions of the UK (May, 2016), something interpreted at the time as a direct slight on Osborne's Northern Powerhouse agenda.

However, in the immediate aftermath of May's installation, some argued that with many parties already selecting their candidates for the 2017 metro mayoral elections, and with some funds already allocated to the city regions, 'the genie was out of the lamp' (Cox, 2016). Perhaps reflecting this, the re-appointment of a dedicated Northern Powerhouse minister, alongside comments from George Osborne's replacement as Chancellor, Philip Hammond, suggested that the political commitment to the project would remain. Similarly, in 2018, the government announced a new grouping dubbed 'NP11', comprising the chairs of the 11 Northern LEPs, and tasked with acting as a policy council to advise government on the strategic linkages required to make the Northern Powerhouse work (MHCLG, 2018a). In practice, therefore, the underlying commitment to the post-2010 devolution agenda demonstrably remained.

That said, the government's broader actions did support the spirit of Prime Minister May's inaugural speech. In England, less urbanised areas such as Cambridgeshire and Peterborough attained combined authority status and negotiated a devo deal, and sub-national devolution would also reach the devolved states where Swansea negotiated a devo deal. Yet, while the May government did expand the city-regional devolution agenda, this was not an agenda to be undertaken at all costs. For example, despite a growing sense of identity and unity in Yorkshire (Giovannini, 2016) in which Sheffield City Region Combined Authority members Doncaster and Barnsley withdrew from the devo deal to support a 'One Yorkshire' proposal covering the entire Yorkshire area (Singh, 2018), the government would rebuff those attempts. In doing so, the government indicated that it would only negotiate new deals once existing devo deals had been fulfilled. In broader terms this had the effect of retaining the geographical limits of the Northern Powerhouse – even where there was appetite for its expansion – further demonstrating the limits to the government's commitment to the North as a spatial policy construct. In practice, and as we shall discuss in Chapter 4, this also had further implications for Sheffield City Region's newly elected metro mayor, Dan Jarvis, who would find his capacity to govern severely limited.

There are also other instances of where the May government did not endorse the pre-2016 landscape carte blanche. For example, there were attempts to retreat from elements of the transport agenda including rail electrification and, in late 2016, following a period of protracted infighting, the North East's devo deal was withdrawn by then-incoming Secretary of State for Communities and Local Government, Sajid Javid (Halliday, 2016). As argued earlier, with the functional Northern Powerhouse being premised on those city regions that have access to devolved fiscal and governance arrangements, the removal of the North East's devo deal served to weaken the idea of a 'Northern Powerhouse' that became even more centred on the East–West corridor identified in Figure 3.2. Thus, while devolution was being expanded in some areas, by the end of 2016 in others it was in retreat.

Developments in the post-referendum space: Third parties and statutory limitations

Despite this tumultuous period, the devolution agenda, and the Northern Powerhouse concept in particular, had a clear effect in energising policy-makers, and largely remained resilient to wider political turbulence. This is something also discussed further in Chapter 4, but reflects Cox's (2016) argument that 'the genie was out of the lamp' – in that leaders had done too much to prepare for the devolution that was to come. However, it is clear that it is more than just policy-makers deciding to press their advantage, and there is a broader argument that the Northern Powerhouse (in particular) attained something akin to a critical mass, whereby actors across Northern England recognised the value of the long-term goal, began working towards it anyway, and deployed their own resources in pursuit of those goals. This occurred in a variety of ways.

Indicating his commitment to this agenda, and despite being removed as Chancellor and subsequently standing down as an MP, George Osborne helped to establish the 'Northern Powerhouse Partnership' (NPHP), a business-focused think tank advocating for economic opportunities across Northern England. This group would be chaired by Osborne, and with a board consisting of private sector interests, alongside city-based politicians (for example, the Mayor of Liverpool and the Leaders of Sheffield and Manchester Council), would work to foster those strategic connections between the cities. In doing so, the NPHP would, in effect, be one of few groups acting at a strategic level, either statutory or otherwise.

Elsewhere other groups attempted to address the lack of statutory linkages in a more direct way. Unlike the NPHP, which was able to attract a wealth of institutional and private sector support, many of these activities were carried out through an advocacy model. The leading actor on this front is the think tank IPPR North that produced a number of reports advocating for the opportunities arising from a more strategic outlook (see, for example, IPPR North, 2017a, b). IPPR North has also collaborated with other actors in order to explore these ideas – for example, IPPR's work with the RTPI and others on a 'Great North Plan' (RTPI, 2016). Although the RTPI would recognise that any 'Northern Plan' would lack statutory status, their work (RTPI, 2016) correctly identifies many of the strategic elements that are currently missing or require significant focus if this sub-national project is to succeed. This includes the need to plan for housing, transport and energy, and to give more thought to the ways in which the city regions link, thus enabling them to agglomerate more efficiently. In attempting this, Box 3.2 reflects on an international example where attempts at decentralisation have not worked well in part because of the lack of this strategic thinking.

Box 3.2: It doesn't always work: Decentralisation in South Korea

After the effective end to civil war in the 1950s, the following 50 years saw a period of rapid development in which South Korea has been transformed from one of the world's least-developed countries to one of the most-developed (Amsden, 1992). This development, premised on industrial growth focused on manufacturing, accelerated during the 1980s and 1990s, and led to South Korea being labelled as one of the Asian 'Tiger' economies (Clifford, 2016).

For much of this period, South Korea's government was characterised by authoritarian leadership, leaving a legacy of a highly centralised government based in Seoul (Park, 2008; Sonn, 2010). Although there are other industrial activities (for example, the port of Busan in the South) elsewhere in the country, this centralisation has been consolidated by the substantial focus on development within Seoul and its metropolitan area, where chaebols (major South Korean companies such as Samsung, Hyundai and Korean Air) have their headquarters and foreign transnational companies often prefer to locate (Lee, 2009).

Seoul is neither out of kilter with other global cities (Sassen, 1994; Beaverstock et al, 2000; Smith and Timberlake, 2002), sharing many characteristics with cities such as London, Paris and Tokyo, nor is it unfamiliar with efforts aimed at decentralising this power (Lee, 1996). Indeed, successive South Korean governments largely resisted pressure for decentralisation until 2003, when the government of Roh Moo-Hyun brought forward a devolution agenda that included transferring state-held powers to local governments (Sonn, 2010). Going further, the Roh administration sought to further break up the dominance of Seoul by creating an administrative capital, similar to Brasilia or Canberra, located in Sejong in the centre of the country (Kwon, 2015), and intended to host nearly 50 of South Korea's 400 government agencies (Sonn, 2010).

When the plans were brought forward in 2005 they were hotly contested and, following a successful court challenge that decreed that South Korea's government must remain in Seoul, the Roh administration pressed ahead with plans to make Sejong an administrative centre, as opposed to a capital (Kwon, 2015). In the following years a number of South Korean ministries were moved to the site, including the Ministries of Land, Agriculture, Education, Trade and Health. This is no small undertaking, and the movement of major ministries away from Seoul necessitates not only the appropriate governmental infrastructure, but also accommodation, housing and leisure facilities for the civil servants moving to populate Sejong (KRIHS, 2013).

In practice, however, the major barrier to Sejong's success remains education, a Korean obsession encapsulated by the annual university entrance exam, the *Suneung*, which brings the country to a near halt every November (Sorensen, 1994; Seth, 2002; Park and Abelmann, 2004). Success in the *Suneung* can be a key gateway for class mobility – allowing access to South Korea's best universities and ultimately jobs with chaebols. As such, South Korean families pay significant amounts for private tutoring for their children. Crucially, like many other aspects of Korean life, the best facilities remain concentrated in Seoul. Therefore, Sejong's proponents are presented with a problem in that, while South Korea wants its best civil servants to relocate to their respective ministries, they are often reluctant to do so – and certainly remain reluctant to remove young family members away from schooling. The result has been the emergence of an effective 'bedroom community' (Fishman, 1994) in which those able to afford it retain their primary residence in Seoul while maintaining accommodation for weekday working in Sejong. This highlights the other concerns that usually blight bedroom or dormitory communities, including the sense of community – something that then limits attractiveness to others.

While Sejong is a modern example of a central government wishing to physically move its own institutions in order to break up the strength of its capital city, after being undermined by successful political opposition the early indications suggest that it has failed to break Seoul's stranglehold on Korean life. While it does bear comparison to some of its forbears (for example, Canberra and Brasilia), for now it seems destined to face the same fate as an administrative centre that lives well within the shadows of the illustrious city it was designed to challenge.

Although this chapter finds significant shortcomings in a sub-national agenda that lacks an overarching strategy, but instead relies on trickle-out benefits, transport is the one area where such a strategy is forthcoming. Formalised in April 2018, Transport for the North (TfTN) serves as a statutory body working on transport strategy across Northern England – considering, and attempting to plan for, the strategic role of road and rail transport in particular. In doing so, TfTN has helped to reintroduce a more thorough, broader, regional element, bringing cities and towns back into the fold that might otherwise have been left out. However, TfTN's first year would lay bare many of the issues that a statutory body would face.

Foremost of those issues was the widespread disruption caused after Northern Rail, a private sector company that provides many of the rail services within Northern England, was forced to postpone the implementation of a new timetable in mid-2018, resulting in numerous cancelled journeys and stranded passengers. That Northern was a franchisee, reflecting the UK system in which rail contracts are awarded by central government, left TfTN and the North West's mayors and metro mayors with little recourse but to complain to central government and request that Northern Rail's franchise be reconsidered

(Rotheram and Burnham, 2018). This disruption was exacerbated by delays resulting from over-running engineering works, coordinated through the body responsible for national rail infrastructure, Network Rail. With Network Rail also holding responsibility for the delivery of future upgrades to the rail network, the situation underscored how, while significant chunks of Northern transport infrastructure are ostensibly coordinated by a statutory body in TfTN, they remain reliant on funding and implementation from the central state which, statistics show, favours transport funding in London at a rate of 2.6:1 (Raikes, 2018). Simultaneously, Northern leaders would also criticise a series of leaked email messages, in which London-based civil servants described rail connections between Southport and Manchester as 'not really valued', and maintained as a 'sop' to passengers (Perraudin, 2018b). This furthered perceptions that devolution in its current form still lacked buy-in from central government in London – a view only entrenched further when, in late-2018, the government funded an additional £2.15 billion for London's Crossrail project (Plimmer and Pickard, 2018).

The way in which these transport issues were handled contributed to a widely held sense that the devolution agenda was not taken as seriously as it might be, and left open questions as to the extent and limits to which Northern actors are able to act in their own self-determined interests. Such was the extent of this frustration that, in the wake of the Crossrail bailout, the Mayor of Liverpool, Joe Anderson, resigned from the board of the NPHP, saying that:

> When it is now crystal clear the government isn't committed to delivering the step-change in rail investment in the North that we so desperately need ... the Northern Powerhouse will remain a pipedream. (Anderson, 2018)

As we draw this chapter to a close, the fate of 'The North' remains an open question. For some, enthusiasm is clearly dimming as they lose patience with a lack of concrete action to back up the rhetoric of reform. Elsewhere, however, and more broadly, it does appear that Cox's (2016) suggestion that the 'genie is out of the lamp' holds true. Yet, at the same time, and with Northern Powerhouse Minister, Jake Berry, mirroring Labour's 2010 manifesto pledge (Labour Party, 2010) by calling for a dedicated Minister for the North (Collins, 2019), there are indications that this discussion is coming full circle.

Across this chapter we have seen that many of the ideas behind the government's devolution agenda are not necessarily 'new' – not least the pivot back to metropolitan thinking that fell out of favour in the 1980s. In the call for regional ministers we see another previously sidelined idea gaining a similar airing. The UK sub-national debate has been cyclical in its nature for much of the last century – driven by a mixture of ideology and policy experimentation. Other countries that have experienced comparative success at this have done so in part because of comparative policy stability. Without doubt the centralised nature of the UK state, in which successive governments feel compelled to take a role in local economic development, has been the main driver of this cyclical trajectory. Thus far, the evidence suggests that, as far as English devolution goes, the UK state's grip remains as firm as ever.

Conclusion

At a strategic scale, it is clear that the post-2010 devolution agenda raises a number of issues. As the Northern Powerhouse, in particular, becomes increasingly tightly bounded – and the economic 'rising tide' would be delivered through an agglomeration economy comprising the North's major cities and their immediate surrounds – this is, undoubtedly, an urban-focused agenda. However, it also presents us with some novel conceptions regarding how such agglomerations form and work in practice.

While traditional concepts of agglomeration economies (Saxenian, 1994) suggest that those agglomerations, whatever their size, tend to have naturally settled boundaries that have formed over time, the post-2010 experiences suggest that this is an attempt to artificially create an agglomeration economy through policy architecture. This also runs counter to Saxenian, in that those cities have been historic economic competitors (Nurse, 2015b) that have formed their own economic relationships over time and crucially, never organically formed such a cooperative agglomeration. Thus, through both the *Northern Powerhouse* and the *Midlands Engine*, the post-2010 period offers insights into whether (a) artificially creating such an agglomeration economy is a feasible undertaking and (b) whether it can serve as a platform to meaningfully challenge another naturally formed competitor agglomeration (that is, London). The answer to both questions will be of significant interest across a global audience, not least in those countries with an agglomerated capital city that enjoys economic hegemony in the way that London does in the UK.

Simultaneously, there is a need to consider the implications arising from the heavily prescribed nature of the post-2010 reforms where some, mostly urban, city regions are granted access to the process while others must await 'trickle-out' benefits. Going further, even within those urban areas there are questions regarding not only who can access the process, but also in what order. This has led to a piecemeal and patchwork-like landscape that allows us to question whether top-down selectivity is at play, and the implications that this may create as cities try to function in this uneven environment. The most emblematic indication of this selectivity is that, despite its geographical size, there are currently only six Northern areas with combined authority status, and only five with an active devolution deal. This means that of Northern England's 74 local authorities (based on the old GORs), more than half are, effectively, strategically deselected from this process, and reliant on trickle-out benefits to reach them.

We can observe this top-down privileging in two main ways. The first is a traditional gateway, whereby Whitehall can confer combined authority status and agree the extent of local powers through the devo deal. While this can be seen within the Northern Powerhouse and Midlands Engine (that is, who has combined authority status or a devolution deal and who does not), the concept of the Northern Powerhouse and Midlands Engine are also acts of spatial strategic selectivity (see the discussion in Chapter 1), in which other core cities such as Nottingham and Bristol, as well as other areas that are no less in the shadow of London's growth, have been forced to sit out for varying periods of time. The second comes through powers of withdrawal – for example, the North East's devolution deal being withdrawn following a lack of progress (Halliday, 2016). This has demonstrated that the government is prepared to effectively 'de-privilege' those groups that had previously been granted access – something that has arguably not been seen in British politics since the abolition of the metropolitan counties and Greater London Authority in 1986 (see Chapter 5 for more on this).

Simultaneously, there is evidence to suggest that during this process, bottom-up or horizontal privileging also took place. We argue that this is most evident during the formation of the LEPs, in which all local authorities were 'invited' to form an LEP based on their functional economic area. Here there are numerous examples of local authorities including and excluding partners with their respective LEPs.

Naturally, the selectivity that permeates the post-2010 devolution agenda raises a number of questions for devolution at the macro scale – not least in its ability to realise the overall goal of driving growth that can counterbalance that of London. Ultimately, and per the literature, the spatial selectivity outlined earlier has resulted in a devolution that resembles a patchwork quilt, that is, the spatially uneven development discussed by Jessop (1990) and described by others (see, for example, Beel et al, 2018, in their discussion of city-regional devolution in Wales). In turn, this uneven development necessitates a number of questions – each effectively focusing on the prospects and outcomes for those places that are currently sitting outside of this process. This includes places in the 'spatial in-between' and urban peripheries (Dembski, 2015; Dembski et al, 2017), places that had previously engaged within the devolution agenda (for example, Preston), and the swathes of rural Northern England which, as Pemberton and Shaw (2012) argue, are significant contributors to overall growth and development. The answers to those questions lie at the very heart of post-2010 devolution, and will shape what we can expect to see. Is the outcome the resurgent Northern England that links all-comers to serve as a pan-national agglomeration economy that rivals London? Or is the reality in effect a deepening of what Dorling and Thomas (2004), themselves building on the work of Veltz (1996), dubbed 'an archipelago economy' in which cities act as islands of growth amid seas of decline characterised by their exclusion from the main thrust of economic agendas?

'The North': A spatial imaginary?

Overall, while it is clear that Northern England has had a significant share of the focus, and the *Northern Powerhouse* will be one of the enduring legacies of the post-2010 period, some five years after Osborne set out his intentions for Northern England, the extent to which his vision has been realised remains in doubt. Instead, and with much of the real policy activity taking place at the city-regional level, it is possible to view Northern England as a spatial imaginary, defined by Davoudi et al (2018, p 97) as something that is 'often adopted and enacted as [an] unproblematic representation of places of yesterday, today and tomorrow'.

Although others have cast city regions in a similar light (Beel et al, 2018), it is clear that there are greater problems with the government's conceptualisation of Northern England – foremost of those being that no clear boundaries, demarcations or definitions of the extent of this area exist. It is just 'the North'. This, alone, meets Davoudi et al's definition in its unproblematic nature. But there is more beyond this. In particular, this includes the lack of clarity about how the various city-regional economies will agglomerate in practice – something, as we will see in Chapter 4, that leaders have now begun to address on their own terms. Against this criticism, there is evidence of strategic thinking, most notably through TfTN – but again, we can see a solution that, while unproblematic in its presentation, is beset by problems, many of which are beyond its control.

The extent to which public figures and public-facing organisations (for example, the RTPI and IPPR) have bought into the idea of the Northern Powerhouse demonstrates that the idea has traction. This is clearly demonstrated by the ongoing commitment to the ideas and principles that underpin it, even when, following the sacking of George Osborne, the entire project looked in jeopardy. Yet, despite this commitment, it remains an idea that, in the absence of any unifying 'Northern' strategy, will only be realised by a patchwork quilt of smaller reforms – each contributing to make something that is greater than the sum of its parts (Nurse, 2015b). This is something we turn to now in Chapter 4. Yet, with evidence that suggests that Northern England is growing further apart, not closer, to London (McCann, 2016), people are perfectly entitled to ask: is this good enough?

4

City regions and the cities within them: Connecting two overlapping scales

Introduction

In Chapter 3, we explored how the post-2010 devolution agenda has developed at the strategic level, framed as an agenda that has goals to realign the UK's economy by creating a series of agglomeration economies which could, on fruition, counterbalance the success of London. This discussion centred on a new economic orthodoxy that extols the benefits of agglomeration (for example, critical mass, economies of scale and enhanced connectivity), and suggests that city regionalism is the 'natural' level of governance for contemporary economic thinking (Pike et al, 2016). In doing so, however, Chapter 3 argued that while there is a wealth of rhetoric at this scale, the structures of regional governance that were abolished in 2010 have not been replaced but rather, there now exists a suite of effective 'spatial imaginaries' (Beel et al, 2018; Davoudi et al, 2018) that characterise the sub-national space. Devoid of significant statutory power, and amid limited efforts at strategic linkages, the rhetoric that surrounds devolution at this level far outpaces progress.

In this chapter we build on this discussion, developing our argument that while the sub-national rhetoric (that is, the *Northern Powerhouse* and the *Midlands Engine*) has dominated the headlines and the wider public conscience, the thrust of those reforms is primarily delivered at the city and city-regional level. In doing so, we explore the mechanics of devolution as it has manifested at this city and city-regional scale – moving beyond the broader reforms discussed in Chapter 3, and placing a greater focus on the practicalities of what is different for those tasked with policy delivery. This discussion largely centres on the democratic reforms relating to city and city region mayoralties, which can be argued as being the centrepiece of this agenda.

This agenda became increasingly complex as it developed – with reforms that began with cities, before fully expanding into the city-regional space. Across the chapter, we argue that much of this complexity arose not in individual reforms, but rather that each reform was layered onto existing structures. In doing so, we explore the interactions between those different – often competing – scales to consider how, despite seemingly having the same opportunities made available to them, areas developed devolution in different ways, with distinct characteristics.

Developing the timeline of the reforms since 2010, the chapter begins with a discussion that focuses on the city level. This discusses the City Deals brought forward early in the coalition's term and the instigation of directly elected mayors. Following this, developments in the city-regional space are introduced – examining the city-regional 'metro mayors' and their main activities. In doing so, the chapter consistently highlights the interactions between the city and city-regional level – with a particular focus on the relationship between the core city and its wider surrounds. This serves as a vehicle to discuss the extent to which these scales do, truly, connect, and to examine whether the reintroduction of metropolitan governance – abolished in England in 1986 – can be a success, or otherwise.

Early movements: A focus on the cities

Although the coalition government's sub-national reform began in earnest with the abolition of regional governance and the instigation of LEPs, beginning the broad shift towards the city regions (Bentley et al, 2010; Pugalis, 2010, 2011; Nurse, 2015a), for some time, beyond pre-election policy documents and the 'Coalition Agreement' (NLGN, 2009; HM Government, 2010a), there were few significant indicators of what policy in this area might look like. Rather, early attention focused on initial responses to austerity and cuts in local funding, and reorganisation in response to both the abolition of Local Strategic Partnerships (LSPs) – through which local service delivery was coordinated in the tail end of the 'New' Labour administration (Bailey, 2003; Geddes and Davies, 2007; Nurse and Pemberton, 2010), and the advent of LEPs.

In the case of the LEPs, and as discussed in Chapter 3, in the absence of identifiable good practice and alongside clear variations in local buy-in, this early period revealed varying degrees of function (Pike et al, 2015). By early 2011 the local-scale policy environment was akin to a vacuum in which local actors, facing the starkest challenge to their viability in decades in austerity, were simultaneously getting to grips with new and largely unfamiliar scales of working in which cities weren't the explicit focus.

The first significant change to this came in 2011 when the Deputy Prime Minister, Nick Clegg, announced a series of 'City Deals' (DCLG, 2011c) to be negotiated between cities and central government, granting greater control over local economic and labour market priorities as well as transport (Marlow, 2013; Deas, 2014; Harrison and Heley, 2015). As such, the City Deals represented the first significant element of coalition policy to focus on the cities, even if not explicitly discussed in the 'Coalition Agreement' (HM Government, 2010a). This first 'wave' of City Deals would focus exclusively on the core cities, with Greater Birmingham, Bristol, Leeds, Liverpool, Greater Manchester, Newcastle, Nottingham and Sheffield all agreeing a deal with government by 2012 (DCLG, 2012d). The focus on these cities is no coincidence, and reflects the collective work of their leaders under the guise of the Core Cities Group since its formation in the mid-1990s, their positioning of their cities as being central to the UK economy, and their advocacy for the decentralisation of power. However, the lack of clear delineation of the relationship between the new broader LEPs and the core cities would give the first indication of a major issue within the coalition's reform agenda: namely, a scalar conflict between organisations trying to operate in and for the same space. This is something we discuss throughout this chapter.

With each City Deal agreed on a case-by-case basis, the City Deals would also mark the first occurrence of one of the hallmarks of the coalition's devolution programme: bespoke deal-making. This was encapsulated by O'Brien and Pike (2015, R14), arguing that:

> Regional and urban public policy is being recast as a process of deal-making founded upon territorial competition and negotiation between central national and local actors unequally endowed with information and resources, leading to highly imbalanced and inequitable outcomes across the UK.

In promoting a devolution agenda, therefore, the coalition made clear that while they were content to cede control under certain circumstances, the level to which this occurred would rely on the extent to which cities could negotiate this control away from government ministers in London. In line with O'Brien and Pike (2015) highlighting the unequal spread of information and resources, this could be affected by a number of factors, including the skills of negotiators and the extent of local ambition to have control devolved – perhaps reflecting the skills held locally, or perceived value to be drawn from that local control. In the same way, negotiations of this kind are also contingent on politics – normally in one of two ways. The first is an area's political history – for example, if an area has a history of mismanagement or intransigence, then they may find it more difficult to negotiate additional powers and responsibilities away from central government. The second is its existing political landscape where a positive relationship between local leaders and leading national political figures can be key in leveraging extra concessions (Nurse, 2012), while history shows that differing political ideologies can close doors rather than open them (Frost and North, 2013).

Regardless, and as discussed in Chapter 3, in this new world of negotiations and deals the English cities found themselves exposed to precisely the sort of conditions set out by Jessop and others (Jessop, 1990; Jones, 1997) – namely, that a strategic selectivity could be liable to dictate what conditions they would operate under, and therefore the potential benefits that could be attained. As such, from the outset critics highlighted one of the fundamental ironies of the coalition's agenda – that in order for their localism attempts to succeed, local areas would be reliant on a willing central state to release or agree the requested powers.

Experiments in sub-national democracy: Part I – Devolution through deal making

The concept of devolution via 'deals' was not the only hallmark of the coalition's agenda, and the first raft of City Deals also sought to introduce a second underpinning principle: additional levels of local democracy. To achieve this the government insisted that, in return for the controls released through the City Deal, each city would hold a referendum on whether to replace existing 'leader and cabinet' systems – the predominant form of organising local government – with a directly elected mayor. The promotion of directly elected mayors certainly came at a time when mayors were re-entering the urban vogue (Barber, 2013), and it is clear that the government was influenced by experiences from London, which had a mayoralty in place since 2000 (Gash and Sims, 2012), and which had benefited from the national profile afforded to it by its first two mayors, Ken Livingstone and Boris Johnson (Worthy et al, 2018). However, at the same time there was also a sense that the reforms sought to respond directly to a blind spot in the post-2010 reforms thus far: that is, that some of the early coalition reforms (for example, LEPs) had a democratic deficiency comparable to those of the recently abolished GORs (Bache and Flinders, 2004).

In the run-up to the mayoral referenda, held in May 2012, the benefits of the mayoral model were widely extolled (Gash and Sims, 2012), not least the experiences of London. However, this would overlook one obvious thing: that the UK cities are not London, face differing prospects and opportunities, and operate within a markedly different environment. For example, while London enjoyed high-profile politicians battling to even attain nomination for the position of mayor, and who could act as policy entrepreneurs (Kingdon, 1984) to front high-profile projects (for example, bids for the Olympic Games) within a global city (Sassen, 1991; Tonne et al, 2008; Worthy et al, 2018), it was unclear whether any other English city could attract candidates of a similar calibre, or whether these new city mayors could achieve similar outcomes. Along similar lines, another significant difference with the London model was that the directly elected mayors brought forward through the City Deals were to operate at the local authority rather than the city region scale – in contrast, the mayor of London is, more specifically, the mayor of Greater London, which comprises all 32 London boroughs – an area of 8.5 million people. Elsewhere, others pointed to the shortcomings of the mayoral model, not least that divorcing local leaders from traditional checks and balances can leave local leaders open to corruption (Elcock and Fenwick, 2007), while leaders who operate within mayoral systems can often struggle to adapt to differing and limited powers than they might have perceived (Copus, 2009). Often, these perceptions can be influenced by well-known examples of mayoralties such as the Mayor of New York (see Box 4.1) despite operating in very different contexts.

Box 4.1: In comparison, mayors from around the world

Although mayors are currently in vogue in terms of English policy-making, they are a comparatively new import. Indeed, the most well-known office of the English mayors – the Mayor of London – has been in place for less than two decades. The English fascination with mayors is, however, undoubtedly inspired by leading international cases where this model has worked well.

Arguably the most well-known mayoralty is that of New York City, an office created in 1665, and selected via direct elections since 1834, to preside over the city's five boroughs (Brooklyn, The Bronx, Manhattan, Queens and Staten Island).

For many years, and particularly during the 1970s and 1980s, New York was a city characterised by high crime rates and inner-city blight (Kelling and Bratton, 1997; Greene, 1999). It is the work of one mayor – Rudolph Giuliani (in office 1994–2001) – who is credited with reversing this trend, while simultaneously benefiting from broader trends of gentrification that reached many of the city's neighbourhoods during his tenure. Giuliani and the New York City mayoralty would, however, gain its greatest public exposure in the aftermath of the 9/11 terrorist attacks, turning international attention to the role of the mayor in responding to a major disaster.

Giuliani would be succeeded in office later that year by billionaire Michael Bloomberg. Although Giuliani probably enjoys greater recognition, it would be Bloomberg who has really demonstrated what the mayoralty can do – and showcasing Kingdon's (1984) policy entrepreneurship on several different fronts. The most prominent work in this regard is *PlaNYC* (Rosan, 2012), the city's 20-year strategy to avoid global warming while simultaneously accommodating projected population growth. Major policies brought forward under PlaNYC included the 'million trees initiative' (Foderaro, 2011) and more famously, the city's High Line, which repurposed an elevated railway as a ribbon park (David and Hammond, 2011). Across this period, although Bloomberg did enjoy many significant policy successes, not everything he proposed did pass. This included a high-profile and controversial campaign to introduce bans on high-sugar drinks. This activity, while still in the spirit of a policy entrepreneur, demonstrates that there are limits to this type of action.

Ultimately, the mayor of New York highlights examples of strategic leadership in a complex world city. However, with its population of just over 8 million people, there are limits to the utility of this example in the UK's city mayor debate. New York City readily compares to London and, perhaps, some of the larger combined authority areas beginning their metro mayoral model. Therefore, while there are valuable lessons from across the Atlantic, it is important that they are taken in their context, and reflect the same issues the UK's second cities must heed when drawing down policy lessons from London.

Ahead of the referenda the councillors of one city, Liverpool, decided that the mayoral model presented an opportunity rather than a risk, and passed legislation to ensure that Liverpool would replace its leader and cabinet model with a mayor (Bartlett, 2012a). Therefore, on the day that other cities would host their referenda, the residents of Liverpool would actually vote for their mayor. Flying in the face of a broader view that suggested the reforms were unpopular, even in spite of practical successes (PSA, 2012), this represented a significant early challenge and inherent contradiction to the underlying principles of the reform – that is, local leaders would bypass democratic mechanisms in order to install democratic reforms.

This approach was further called into question when all but one authority voted to reject the mayoral reforms in their referenda. This was, perhaps, unsurprising given that in many cities leaders across the political spectrum campaigned against the issue, but the scale of the rejection – the third rejection of democratic reforms in 10 years, following regional governance (2004) and the 'Alternative Vote' (2011) (Shaw and Robinson, 2007; Curtice, 2013) – left the coalition open to accusations that it was attempting to fix a model that, in the general public's view, wasn't fundamentally broken. Such accusations did not subside when, following the referendum, all City Deals were allowed to proceed regardless of their referendum choice, and the second wave of City Deals were not subject to a referendum at all (Sandford, 2015).

For their part, the only English city to vote in favour of a directly elected mayor was Bristol, albeit with the lowest turnout of any of the participating areas (Bristol City Council, 2012). Consequently elections for Bristol's mayor were scheduled for later that year and, in November 2012, the independent candidate George Ferguson would join the Labour Party's Joe Anderson – elected as mayor of Liverpool – as England's two newest directly elected mayors. The activities of the two mayors are discussed in Chapter 5, but here we reflect on the success of this model in 'democratic' terms.

Democratic reform: City mayors (and city regions)

On their advent there was scepticism about what difference city mayors could make away from London, where political celebrity could, to some extent, overcome the limitations of the office (Worthy et al, 2018). Here, and while Worthy, Bennister and Stafford (2018) deploy Sweeting and Hambleton (2015, p 16) to suggest that the new mayors could be an 'antidote' to 'the managerialisation of urban politics', they also note the complex, and increasingly mixed role that the mayors must play in which they 'have had to move between being a "civic, political and corporate leader" [Copus, 2009, cited in Worthy et al, 2018] and use their influence to persuade due to limited powers and constitutional weakness' (Worthy et al, 2018, p 25). In their analysis of the first term of Liverpool's mayor, Headlam and Hepburn (2017) argued that the new mayoralty was less about 'city management' and more about representation – that is, through the entrepreneurial activities outlined in Chapter 5 – suggesting that while the mayors may have played an important role, perhaps other 'traditional' management functions went overlooked.

Although the mayors of both Bristol and Liverpool each had relatively clear programmes of work – discussed in Chapter 5 – from the outset it was not entirely clear how they would sit within their wider city regions. While the LEPs preceded the creation of the mayoralties (as discussed in Chapter 3), from an early stage there were tensions between the two institutions. In Liverpool, these tensions became apparent early on in Anderson's term through several incidents. The first came with the mayor making clear that Liverpool City Council alone would retain control over planning decisions relating to Liverpool Waters, a major redevelopment of disused dockland, and the city's UNESCO World Heritage Site (WHS) status (Nurse, 2015a), despite both Liverpool Waters and WHS informing Liverpool City Region's LEP strategy (Dembski, 2015). The second would come through the 2012 allocation of the Regional Growth Fund, for which Liverpool City Council and Liverpool City Region's LEP (representing Liverpool City Region's five other local authorities) would submit separate bids. Although this initially raised questions about the functional relationships (both economic and governance) between a core city and its periphery, this was further complicated when the Liverpool City Region LEP bid was successful, while Liverpool City Council's was not (Bartlett, 2012b). The rejection of Liverpool's bid – framed as a snub in local media – served as one of the first indications that the Liverpool City Region was not functioning as coherently as it might.

Thus, from the early stages there were already indications that the post-2010 devolution reforms would be affected by a lack of coherence between operations at these two scales – that is, the city, and its wider city region. Without clear and defined links between the two, places that historically enjoyed greater policy experience (that is, cities) would find themselves at a natural advantage compared to those that were new, or had grown unaccustomed to this style of working (that is, city-regional LEPs). Although the mayors would feed into their respective LEPs, the clear lack of democratic accountability structures left a situation in which the LEPs could either be integral to a city's strategic outlook, or easily sidelined, depending on the will of those involved.

For their part, the broader public opinion of England's city mayors remains mixed. While it is clear (and understandable) that neither Anderson nor Ferguson enjoyed anything like the national profile held by any mayor of London – both failed to break into the national conscience – more tellingly they also received mixed opinions within their own cities. This is most striking with Ferguson who, in 2016, was roundly beaten in his attempt at re-election by Labour's Marvin Rees. Although this might be partly down to the difficulties facing independent candidates on re-election (Copus, 2004), in that they are often initially elected on anti-establishment sentiments only to find their re-election challenged by both sides of a 'hostile political environment' (Copus, 2009, pp 44–5), for Ferguson it perhaps goes further than this, with his entrepreneurial activity (see Chapter 5) failing to catch the popular imagination. For his part, Anderson was re-elected in 2016, albeit with a reduced majority. While his victory is perhaps little surprise in a city recently dominated by Labour, his reduced majority could be seen as being indicative of a city that was tiring of austerity measures and the handling of other debates including the management of the city's built heritage.

Further democratic developments ahead of the Northern Powerhouse

In the immediate aftermath of the broader rejection of the mayoral referenda, and the subsequent removal of mayoral reforms from the later rounds of the City Deal programme, many thought that the coalition had 'put to bed' (Marsh, 2012) their desire to create more democratically elected positions in local areas. They would be mistaken.

Under reforms set out in late-2012, and only six months after many communities rejected mayors for their cities, as part of their LEP area citizens would have the opportunity to elect a 'police and crime commissioner' (PCC) to provide democratic and civilian oversight of policing priorities (Joyce, 2011; Jones et al, 2012; Lister, 2013; Lister and Rowe, 2015). If the mayors enjoyed a lukewarm response, the reception given to the PCCs was positively anaemic – with many elected on turnouts that struggled to break into double figures (Rallings and Thrasher, 2016). Although this may be put down to the PCC elections being held in November away from traditional voting periods in early summer, the poor turnouts suggested a public that was, at its most charitable, less enthusiastic about the reforms than the coalition had anticipated. This limited democratic mandate also had the effect of undermining the PCCs from the outset, and barring occasional interventions, they struggled to make significant headway.

Following the PCC elections there was a comparatively long pause in the rate of local government reform – lasting until the reinvigoration of combined authorities in 2014. Although the combined authorities were largely intended to respond to the lack of democratic accountability of the LEPs, this time the coalition would take a different tact and, rather than creating new posts, would attempt to deploy existing leaders (that is, mayors and local authority leaders) who would lend their own democratic legitimacy to the process. For their part (and as discussed in Chapter 3), the early experiences of the combined authorities in large part mirrored experiences from the LEPs, in that the levels of local effectiveness were largely reflective of existing working relationships between the authorities. For example, in Greater Manchester long-standing working relationships and its 2011 designation as a combined authority meant they could absorb the new powers over economic and transport planning with little fuss. Elsewhere other combined authorities would again struggle – both in regards to the core–periphery relationship, the roles of member authorities and policy priorities (Nurse, 2015a).

In practice, and as we saw in Chapter 3, the stable governance window of the combined authorities (that is, before they were altered by further reforms) was comparatively short. However, within a year they would be cast as one of the early central actors in what many argued was the culmination of the coalition's devolution agenda: George Osborne's vision for a Northern Powerhouse. In hindsight, and having possession of the post-hoc narrative, it is clear how the combined authorities served as a springboard to the further developments of the Northern Powerhouse, but at the time they played an important role for which they were unheralded – bringing democratic accountability to bear on the devolution process and, in doing so, stabilising what was becoming an embarrassing set of electoral returns for the coalition's agenda. If it was not for their work in bringing their respective 'heft' to the process it is entirely possible that the city region project may have withered on the vine of electoral indifference. Instead, however, combined authorities helped lay the groundwork for the most significant shift in city-regional governance in a generation: devolution deals and the metro mayors.

Devolution deals and towards metro mayors

In June 2014, when George Osborne gave his speech announcing his intent to create a Northern Powerhouse that could unite the northern cities so that they could 'take on the world' (Osborne, 2014), it was made clear that this goal would be achieved by building on the themes of the previous five years of reform. City regions would remain the focus, the extent of devolution would remain premised on bespoke 'deal'-making, and the process would be selective, not elective. In the combined authorities, and to a lesser extent the LEPs, the coalition had the beginnings of a city-regional architecture to which they could begin to devolve power and they would be granted an important role – agreeing the devolution deals which, in time, would underpin the Northern Powerhouse.

Each 'devo deal' had one underpinning principle: it could only be agreed between a combined authority and central government. As discussed in Chapter 3, the geographical coverage of the combined authorities was extremely limited, with only five Northern-based combined authorities in place by 2014, and even within this, the rate at which the devo deals were signed reflected a mixture of the long-standing working relationships discussed previously. As well as this, and reflecting the strategic selective nature of the post-2010 reforms (among others, see Jessop, 1990), the relationship with central government would also play a role. Thus, it was to the surprise of few that Greater Manchester would be the first to agree its devolution deal as the centrepiece of Osborne's vision, and would extract significantly improved concessions.

When agreeing their respective devo deals, each city would be offered a basic package of reforms, on which they could make further 'asks'. In some ways, there would be little novelty in this package, with the greater control over transport and economic planning largely seen as modest extensions of existing powers already held locally, either through the City Deal or combined authority. Similarly, the headline figure of £900 million of extra funding would, in fact, be spread over 30 years. This would mean an annual injection of £30 million of extra funds. A welcome addition to cash-strapped authorities, perhaps, but others would argue that this was a cynical offer to cities that had seen debilitating budget cuts in the preceding years (HM Treasury, 2010; Lowndes and Pratchett, 2012; Lowndes and McCaughie, 2013; Lowndes and Gardner, 2016).

In planning terms, the basic devolution package would grant the ability to designate a Statutory Spatial Strategy (SSS) for the city region, providing a strategic vision for transport planning and housing allocations. This would mark the end of a six-year hiatus of planning that went beyond the local authority level following the scrapping of RSSs in 2010. The planning reforms also suggested that the city-regional policy architecture would be as much carved out of local authority powers as it would by devolution of powers from central government (Lupton et al, 2018), and would set the scene for tensions between authorities – something we will return to later in this chapter.

In developing these devo deals, the coalition did not stray far from their established modus operandi: namely, that the 'deal' came with a quid pro quo, and like the first round of City Deals, the trade-off was democratic reform. In agreeing a devo deal, each city region would be expected to hold elections for a directly elected executive mayor (DEEM), commonly known as a 'metro mayor'. This would supersede the existing political leadership of combined authority, with local authority leaders instead serving as a cabinet to the metro mayor. Importantly, this time there would be no referenda, and DEEMs were central to the deal. While this clearly indicated that the coalition's fervour for democratic reform was undiminished, there was a clear and naked irony in that, given almost all of the English core cities had rejected a directly elected mayor for their city, they would now have one imposed on them for their city region. Localism, whether you like it or not.

For their part and under the auspices of the 'basic package' devo deal, on election the new DEEMs would also consolidate a number of locally held powers including assuming the responsibilities of the PCC – implicitly acknowledging the anaemic support PCCs received at the ballot box, and reflecting another feature of the 2010–onwards policy environment – short-lived experiments in governance.

Beyond this, any further concessions within each devo deal would be extracted through the 'deal'-making process. As discussed earlier, this would reflect a mixture of political ambition, local negotiating prowess and relationships with central government. As the first combined authority to agree its devo deal, and held up by Osborne as the potential shape of things to come, Greater Manchester was notable in gaining several significant concessions. Foremost of those would be the transfer of health priorities and budgeting – something hitherto unseen since the formation of the NHS nearly 70 years earlier. While the devolution of control over NHS priorities attracted significant attention, others pointed towards the potential risks (Nurse, 2015b; Hambleton, 2017). With the NHS frequently ranking among voters' top priorities (Ipsos MORI, 2017), and with health services increasingly pressed by austerity, there were clear concerns that the move might simply be a ploy to divorce central government from a hot-button political issue while simultaneously flipping it to political rivals locally (Nurse, 2015b). In negotiating their devolution deals, therefore, there was a balance to be struck between pushing as far as they could, and pushing as far as they dare – particularly in light of the constraints already placed on local areas by austerity (Shaw and Tewdwr-Jones, 2017). So far, in practice, Greater Manchester is the only combined authority to agree such a deal on the NHS – suggesting that either combined authorities are perhaps wary of a 'poisoned chalice' or perhaps that central government is not setting up the combined authorities to fail by devolving this control to them at all cost.

Experiments in sub-national democracy: Part II – Metro mayors

By late 2015, and with several combined authorities signing their devo deal, attention turned to who would become metro mayor – with the first elections to be held in May 2017. With many of the UK core cities characterised by relatively predictable voting patterns, in practice the process through which the political parties would decide their candidates would carry more importance. Ahead of time, and with several candidates expressing their interest in becoming metro mayor, it was initially unclear how parties – not least Labour, that dominated Greater Manchester and Liverpool City Region, and whose candidate would be almost certainly guaranteed victory – would select their candidate. As the fields began to emerge, most parties decided that, if required, US-style primaries would be held in the summer of 2016.

Several high-profile MPs declared their interest, including then-Shadow Home Secretary Andy Burnham and former Minister Ivan Lewis (Greater Manchester), as well as then-Shadow Minister for Mental Health, Luciana Berger and Steve Rotheram (Liverpool City Region). In the West Midlands and in the absence of other primary challengers, the former Chief Executive of John Lewis, Andy Street, was selected to represent the Conservatives. There were, perhaps, numerous motivations for the substantial number of MPs and other high-profile candidates seeking election. For some, particularly in the major cities, the powers on offer would represent a meaningful policy platform while simultaneously affording a national profile. For others, particularly within the Labour Party, there was also an element of political expediency, as success would also mean a convenient exit from an increasingly turbulent political environment at the national level. Either way, their presence granted an exposure that lent legitimacy to processes of local governance which had, thus far, failed to capture the public imagination. Importantly, the pre-election period was not the exclusive domain of those high-profile candidacies, and a number of candidates with experience of local government – for example,

Tony Lloyd, interim metro mayor for Greater Manchester, and Joe Anderson, mayor of Liverpool – also sought election, while elsewhere the fields were comprised almost entirely of councillors and council leaders.

The primary period was generally good natured. In many areas debate focused on broad themes of high-profile star power versus local knowledge. Here MPs would argue that their relationships with Whitehall would leave them well placed to get the best value for their city regions while, conversely, more locally rooted candidates argued that their rivals lacked the necessary experience of local government (Rustin, 2016). However, in the places where MPs went up against local candidates they invariably won the day, and Andy Burnham, Steve Rotheram and Siôn Simon were selected as Labour candidates in Greater Manchester, Liverpool City Region and the West Midlands, respectively.

By early 2017 the scene was set for the mayoral elections. In some areas, particularly in the Labour-dominated North of England, the elections were seen as a foregone conclusion – with the key issue being turnout. In other areas, however, particularly those in which Labour's control of the core cities did not extend to the surrounding areas of a combined authority, the result was much harder to predict. Reflecting this, and amidst a torrid 2017 local election period for Labour overall, there were several surprises. While Burnham and Rotheram won elections as metro mayor for Greater Manchester and the Liverpool City Region, in the four other combined authority areas the Conservatives were successful. Although Andy Street's narrow victory in Birmingham was the most significant win, Ben Houchen's surprise win in Tees Valley, an area with a long-standing Labour voter base, was the real shock.

In bringing forward metro mayors, it was clear that the government was undiminished by the anaemic responses their earlier reforms had received – either through outright rejection or low turnout. Any hopes that the metro mayor reforms would break this cycle would be ill-founded. Although the turnout for the metro mayor elections was higher than those of the PCCs, even the area of greatest turnout, Greater Manchester, could only muster 29% of its 1.9 million voters (GMElects, 2017), while Tees Valley saw a turnout of only 21%. While some of this may be accounted for by traditionally lower turnouts for local elections (see Chapter 5), in this case there were other mitigating factors. Most notably is that in mid-April, and less than one month before the mayoral elections, Theresa May made a surprise announcement that there would be a general election, to be held on

8 June 2017. This had the immediate effect of drawing attention away from the mayoral races just at the period in which they would expect to attract more prolonged coverage. Ultimately, mayoral campaigns were simply dwarfed by broader election debates.

The general election, held just over one month after the mayoral elections, meant that there was almost no time for the dust to settle on the mayoralties before attention shifted elsewhere. This meant that there was little immediate detailed analysis of the new mayoral dynamics: a patchwork quilt that reflected differing political configurations and differing institutional arrangements (see Table 4.1).

Of the six metro mayors elected in 2017, three (Cambridgeshire and Peterborough, Tees Valley, and West Midlands), would have a comparatively straightforward arrangement where the incoming metro mayor would be able to work with their own political party in central government. To a lesser extent, in Greater Manchester, the new mayor would only have to contend with one differing political relationship. However, in the cities that had installed directly elected mayors which, crucially, remained in post, there would be greater complexity. In those places, namely, Liverpool City Region and the West of England, the metro mayor would have to manage the responsibilities of their new role while also managing the relationship with the existing city mayor, who would not only control many of the core city's priorities and thus be central to broader ambitions, but also had control or significant influence over a number of overlapping policy areas. As discussed earlier, this was a real-and-present issue in this debate, and is something we will return to later in this chapter.

After the EU referendum and ahead of the metro mayoral elections, much of the talk was around the longevity of the city-regional agenda without Osborne to drive it. Here the resounding Conservative victories may have gone some way to giving this agenda a new lease

Table 4.1: Mayoral configurations in England 2017/18

Area	City mayor	Metro mayor	National government
Cambridgeshire and Peterborough	N/A	Conservative	Conservative
Greater Manchester	N/A	Labour	
Liverpool City Region	Labour	Labour	
Tees Valley	N/A	Conservative	
West of England (Bristol)	Labour	Conservative	
West Midlands (Birmingham)	N/A	Conservative	
Sheffield	N/A	Labour*	

Note: *Elections held in 2018.

of life. However, the nature of those victories caught several candidates flat-footed and, compared to candidates like Burnham and Rotheram, who had time to plan their policy agendas, they would have to think on their feet when it came to governing.

Governing the city regions

Taking office on 5 May 2017, the incoming metro mayors had to navigate their new powers, the city-regional apparatus and the interrelationship between the individual authorities within their regions, and over the following year mayoral agendas developed at slightly different paces, each reflecting a mixture of mayoral assuredness, preparedness and institutional support. Some metro mayors found their voice quickly; others took longer to grow into their new role.

As might be expected, the metro mayor for Greater Manchester, Andy Burnham, settled into his new position with the greatest ease. This reflected his experience as a national-level politician, his position as overwhelming favourite, which granted him time to craft his agenda, and inheriting control of a city region that had several years to shape its devolution activity prior to his election.

On taking office, Burnham quickly turned his attention to the transport brief – in particular, Manchester's issues with congestion. Given Burnham's manifesto focus on 'active travel' as a solution to those issues (Burnham for Mayor, 2016), shortly after entering office, former Olympic champion Chris Boardman was appointed as Commissioner for Walking and Cycling. Guided by Boardman, Burnham embarked on an ambitious programme that fundamentally revisited planning attitudes to cycling across the city region. Buoyed by the success of individual initiatives, in June 2018 Burnham announced a centrepiece initiative dubbed 'Beelines' (TFGM, 2018), a £160 million, 1,000-mile active travel network spanning Greater Manchester, including 75 miles of segregated cycleway, and funded out of Manchester's £250 million share of the Transforming Cities Fund (DfT, 2018; TFGM, 2018).

Although air quality was not an explicit focus of Burnham's manifesto, the issue would arise in late 2018 following the release of data that suggested Manchester was among many UK cities whose air quality exceeded legal limits. Although he had spoken out earlier against congestion charging – even as something instigated to modest success by the first mayor of London (Tonne et al, 2008) – the urgency of Manchester's air quality issue resulted in a partial *volte face* in which congestion charging across Greater Manchester was discussed

(Williams, 2018a). That Burnham would return to a publically unpopular decision displays some of the characteristics of a policy entrepreneur (Kingdon, 1984). However, compared to the Beelines which conforms more naturally to the idea of a policy entrepreneur, in this case Burnham's hand was forced by political necessity and thus, while he is not averse to taking politically unpopular decisions, suggests he is reluctant to spend his political capital in doing so.

In other aspects, even Burnham did not always enjoy smooth sailing, and the early period of his tenure suggested he was navigating the political realities of governing as opposed to campaigning. For example, Burnham would find controversy in his attempts to engage with his new-found strategic planning powers. This would stem from the fact that, on taking office, he would inherit an outline SSS begun under his predecessor, the interim metro mayor, Tony Lloyd. Under Lloyd's leadership, planners drawn from Greater Manchester's authorities had prepared a draft SSS named the Greater Manchester Spatial Framework (GMSF) (GMCA, 2016), which specifically attempted to engage with strategic housing allocation for the city region. In doing so, the draft plan would propose a sizeable number of developments on green belt land across Greater Manchester to meet expected demand. Reflecting similar experiences in London (Thornley et al, 2003; Morphet, 2011), the GMSF would directly engage with two of the most contentious issues in English planning – housing supply (Millward, 2005) and its location (Sturzaker and Mell, 2016). Amidst substantial public outcry, Burnham followed through on pre-election comments (Fitzgerald, 2017), if not the word of his election manifesto, and announced that he would not support the GMSF in its current form. Instead, he announced that planners must 'go back to the drawing board' and find 80% reductions in green belt land release while still meeting overall housing targets (Middleton-Pugh, 2018). This would exacerbate tensions within Greater Manchester's 10 local authorities and particularly their councillors who, perhaps understandably, harboured concerns over the political implications of the scale of green belt land release and recalibrated housing allocations for their areas.

Ultimately, experiences from the first 18 months of the GMSF suggest that the devolution of strategic planning powers to the city regions has done little to remedy pre-existing concerns – not least relating to tensions between the executive and districts, as powers previously held by local authorities are transferred upwards (Lupton et al, 2018). With the consent of all 10 of Greater Manchester's authorities required in order for the GMSF to pass, the planning process would set competing political realities against one another.

In doing so, the focus on housing which, at the time of writing, has prompted four re-writes of the GMSF, also served to push other spatial planning issues – not least designating land for employment and economic growth – down the agenda.

Away from Greater Manchester, the other newly elected metro mayors appeared more inclined to become accustomed to their roles on a gradual basis, and as such their mayoral agendas unfurled more slowly. Here, they would rationalise that while Manchester would enjoy first mover advantage, there was value in being second mover, and thus learning from policy mistakes (Kopel and Löffler, 2008). This second mover advantage was most keenly observed in the spatial planning process in which, while Greater Manchester's interim metro mayor pressed ahead with the GMSF ahead of full elections, other combined authorities such as the Liverpool City Region preferred to hold back, using the lull before the 2017 elections to prepare the ground for their own spatial frameworks (Liverpool City Region, 2016), and ultimately wait for the incoming mayor to set the tone. Although the fruits of this endeavour may not be seen for some time, given that these areas are no less susceptible to the same debates regarding housing allocation, it can be seen as a case of more haste: less speed.

In holding back on their spatial planning processes, other city regions made conscious efforts to address the tensions between the core and peripheries, and their spatial in-between (Dembski, 2015), something long seen as a key factor to success in the devolution project, and something aggravated in Greater Manchester through the GMSF. In particular, the metro mayors of both Cambridgeshire and Peterborough and the Liverpool City Region developed initiatives focusing on the towns within their area with each, rightly, recognising that they are under-prioritised within the current system of reforms. In Cambridgeshire and Peterborough, one of the few combined authorities not to be centred on a Core City, the metro mayor, James Palmer, would place an emphasis on market towns. Specifically, the combined authority announced a fund of £500,000 to bolster the planning process in 10 market towns (Cambridgeshire and Peterborough Combined Authority, 2018), with each market town expected to produce a masterplan setting out a strategy for its growth. The nature of this 'growth' is broadly cast, with the first 'Masterplan for Growth' (St Neots, 2018) taking an expansive view that covers transport, housing and regeneration, indicating that, while it may defined by its market, there is substantially more to the strategy. This focus on market towns demonstrates the fundamental differences between combined authorities that include a Core City and those that don't. First, the Market Towns strategy recognises that, without a Core City to underpin economic growth, it is even more important that all areas able to make an economic contribution are working to their full effect. While other combined authorities undoubtedly do share the same issues, for those without a Core City there is less space to hide, and thus there is greater impetus to act. Second, this also reflects the political reality in that, without a heavily populated Core City that may skew election outcomes, the metro mayor of any non-Core combined authority will likely find an even greater proportion of their electorate to be located in those places.

In the Liverpool City Region, the metro mayor announced £5 million of funding, to be allocated through a new Town Centre Commission (Houghton, 2018). Rather than the broader planning focus of Cambridgeshire and Peterborough, the focus would be on raising the retail prospects of ailing town centres across the city region. In doing so, the Liverpool City region is driven by the same core–periphery focus, albeit while reflecting a slightly different political reality. Here, with an often tempestuous relationship with the Core City that robustly defends its existing planning rights from city-regional interference (Nurse, 2015a), and having stood on a platform that emphasised the role of the broader city region (Rotheram, 2016), Rotheram's focus could be seen as a realistic exercise of his powers while simultaneously speaking to his perceived electoral base.

In theoretical terms, the focus on towns by those metro mayors offers useful insights into the strategic selectivity raised by Jessop (1990) and others. At the broader level, these efforts go against the perceived flow of an agenda largely seen as favouring city-regional thinking while emphasising the cities within them. The efforts to specifically connect towns to this agenda can be seen as an attempt to redirect some of the flow of this activity to areas widely seen as missing out (McCann, 2016; Dembski et al, 2017). In doing so, however, we can see a more localised privileging emerge. For example, in the Liverpool City Region, any funds for the towns are allocated through a Commission. Here, the local locus of power becomes a de facto 'centre' that, per the original literature on strategic selectivity, can privilege allies or perceived special cases at the expense of others. While efforts in Cambridgeshire – for example, to allocate all successful towns £50,000 – attempt to even out any approaches, the focus on towns raises fresh challenges: while many talk of the rising tide lifting all boats, first the metro mayors must work to ensure the tide reaches them at all.

Are metro mayors delivering the broader post-2010 devolution vision?

As argued earlier in this book, the mechanics of post-2010 devolution meant that while there is a significant degree of focus on the fruits of agglomeration, the reality is the bulk of meaningful policy change – and policy outcomes – would, in practice, be delivered through the city regions themselves. In doing so, this raised questions as to whether (a) devolution to the city regions would support this agglomeration effect and (b) if it did, whether the installed mayors would buy into it – effectively seeing the value of collaborating with long-standing rivals.

In practice, the early evidence on this front is mixed. While there are indications that many of the city regions did experience tensions between core and peripheries, as outlined earlier, on a strategic level it is clear that many of the metro mayors did see the value in agglomeration-focused thinking. Foremost of those were Steve Rotheram and Andy Burnham who, following victory in their respective primaries and set against the background of the politically uncertain summer of 2016 following the UK's vote to leave the EU, spoke of their willingness to work together and how, regardless of the future of the Northern Powerhouse, they would use their offices to create a 'North West Powerhouse' along the same principles (Walker, 2016). In doing so, Burnham and Rotheram were among the first to engage with the idea of smaller agglomerations within the Northern Powerhouse, something that others (see, for example, Headlam, 2014) had previously identified as a market gap that was, perhaps, unexploited owing to a lack of strategic leadership.

However, there are other indications that the metro mayors have failed this test and, per Peck and Tickell (1994), remain fierce entrepreneurial competitors. One key demonstrator of this is the relocation of Channel 4's television studios away from London and for which, in early 2018, cities were invited to declare their interest. Seeing the potential of such an undertaking, and influenced by the positive effects of BBC's partial relocation to Media City in Salford, over 30 areas expressed their interest. Of the seven shortlisted applicants, three (Manchester, Liverpool and Leeds) were in the putative Northern Powerhouse, and of those, Leeds and Manchester made the final shortlist of three. With each drawing significant support from their respective leaders, including the metro mayors, the Channel 4 relocation demonstrated that while there may be overtures regarding the benefits that agglomeration may bring, nonetheless, leaders remain rooted in entrepreneurial completion for the benefit of their cities.

This is natural, and represents what mayors would argue as seeking the best outcomes for their citizens (and voters). However, while this may be so, it also indicates that, in the absence of clear incentives, ahead of any true agglomeration the devolved city leaders will make sure that they will reap any benefits first.

The Channel 4 bidding process, ultimately won by Leeds (Waterson, 2018), also unveiled entrepreneurial tensions *within* the city regions – with reports suggesting that both Manchester and Salford (as part of Greater Manchester) vied for the project (Williams, 2018b). This has echoes of the tensions between Liverpool and its city region relating to the allocation of Regional Development Funding (Bartlett, 2012b) and again, suggests that despite governance architecture that aims to foster cooperation, entrepreneurial tendencies based on individual success remain. Although this is, perhaps, an inevitable side-product of the nature of the city-regional working, the reported unwillingness of the metro mayor to intervene (Williams, 2018b) gives further credence to the idea that the metro mayors may struggle to arbitrate between the competing needs of their districts. This is an issue we will return to in the following section.

One of the rarely discussed hallmarks of the post-2010 devolution agenda is that while the rate of change has been comparatively rapid, there has been little, if any, 'tidying up' of earlier reforms. The most notable example of this is the directly elected city mayors which, in two cities, now also sit within a governance environment in which they have strategic overlap with the metro mayors (see Table 4.1). In failing to 'tidy up', the conflicts that have flared since 2010, not least between the Core Cities and their regions, have not gone away. In reality, this has meant that in cities with a directly elected city mayor, the metro mayors have been forced into strategic compromise in order to engage with the fundamental economic drivers of their city regions, and ultimately advance their own policy agendas. Similarly, elsewhere, metro mayors have found themselves treading on the toes of their districts. Although the Town Centre initiatives do provide examples of addressing centre–periphery gaps (Dembski et al, 2017), this lack of political clarity remains the undoing of the city regional agenda.

Those concerns have not gone unnoticed, and there have been efforts to conduct this 'tidying up' locally – such as an unsuccessful internal campaign to remove the 'spare [city] mayor' in Liverpool (Thorp, 2018). However, given almost all of the post-2010 structures remain in place, the reality is an often confusing landscape in which power overlaps, lines of authority are not clear and ultimately, political reality casts potential collaborators as competitors. Therefore, against the backdrop of some interesting work, this abundant lack of clarity remains one of the biggest challenge facing this city-regional agenda.

Metro mayors: Populists, or policy entrepreneurs?

In bringing forward metro mayors, the overarching intention was to add a level of democratic accountability to the government's reforms. In doing so, and in deliberately setting out with the intention to counterbalance London's growth, there was also a hope that the new mayors would capture some of the 'stardust' seen in other mayoralties – not least London itself. In short, it was hoped the new metro mayors would act as policy entrepreneurs (Kingdon, 1984), who would lend their newfound political capital in order to get things done.

In reality, just over halfway into the metro mayors' first terms of office, the evidence for this is mixed. Certainly, there are examples of policy entrepreneurial behaviour in which incoming mayors have sacrificed political capital on novel projects. Arguably the best example of this comes through the first mayor of the Sheffield City Region, Dan Jarvis. Elected in 2018, a year after the initial raft of metro mayors, following delays owing to political in-fighting regarding the composition of the combined authority (see the discussion in Chapter 3), Jarvis took office despite his role being unpaid (Perraudin, 2018a). In taking on the role on an unpaid basis, and with the scope of his powers un-agreed at the time of his election, the scale of Jarvis' sacrifice is significant, and clearly represents the spirit of a policy entrepreneur. In policy terms, Burnham's efforts on active travel and the 'Beelines' have clear mirrors with London's cycle superhighways and the efforts of Livingstone and Johnson (Worthy et al, 2018). However, elsewhere thus far the broader evidence that metro mayors have made any such breakthrough remains scant.

Conversely, rather than staking political capital, in some cases there are clear examples of metro mayors positioning themselves so as to preserve it – effectively embracing populist positions. In particular this includes Burnham's position on housing within the GMSF, which clearly sought to deflect the negative political ramifications of building on the green belt, despite broader local agreement over the original proposals. Elsewhere, and while there is a clear indication that the incoming metro mayors have taken their democratic accountability seriously, with some actively engaging with their broader city region area, there is also reason to suggest that policy initiatives such as the Town Centre Commission and Market Towns initiatives are, to some extent, strategic moves that will appeal to voters in the round.

Conclusion

As we have seen across the period since 2010, and as discussed in Chapter 3, while the policies that have captured broader attention during this period have been the pan-regional projects such as the Northern Powerhouse and the Midlands Engine, in practice there is little policy architecture to support this work. Consequently, in reality, while there has been much talk of agglomerations, the significant thrust of policy reform has been located in the pivot back towards city-regional/metropolitan thinking. Here, there has been a wealth of policy reform, and it is the leaders – some new, some old – at this scale who have been at the coalface of implementing much of the post-2010 sub-national agenda. This work has been characterised by several key themes – each of which contribute, for good or ill, to the nature of UK governance as we find it today.

While one of the major themes of this period is the government's persistent attempts at electoral reform, the post-2010 period is as much characterised by the public's equally-as-persistent rejection of those reforms. In the period since 2010, city mayoral and electoral reform referenda were roundly rejected, while other top-down initiatives (for example, PCCs) received a lukewarm reception at the ballot box. Yet despite those rejections, further reforms were brought forward as part of an advancing agenda. The reasons behind this are contested. Some would argue that the coalition viewed local electoral accountability as the lynchpin of its localist agenda; others would view those reforms as either a mask for further centralisation (Hambleton, 2017) or a mechanism to shunt politically unpopular decisions on to local leaders (Nurse, 2015b). Nevertheless, a significant raft of those reforms did stick – either through local political manoeuvring or top-down reforms – in itself hinting at another major theme of the period: local reform *in spite* of a lack of public enthusiasm for that reform.

Regardless of debates around their genesis, the city and city region mayoralties that form the main thrust of discussion in this chapter are arguably the most significant element of sub-national reform in the post-2010 period. Until that point, with London and a few small examples excepted, directly elected executive leadership has never been a key feature of local policy landscapes in England and as such, the city mayors were a venture into the unknown. Thus far their records appear mixed.

At the city level, the mayors of Bristol and Liverpool never attained the level of national acclaim enjoyed by the mayor of London, even if this is an unfair yardstick. For their part, the city mayors, alongside the majority of local authorities across the country, would argue that their agendas for office were hamstrung by the government's programme of austerity. There is no doubt that these arguments carry weight, and there is clear evidence of the urban austerity outlined by Peck (2012), meaning that cities were struggling just to stay still. However, there were clear signs of tensions between the cities and the emerging city-regional space raised through increasing complications regarding compatibility and overlapping agendas and consequently, the city mayoralties increasingly struggled for political oxygen in an environment that had moved on.

While the city-regional agenda has taken longer to coalesce, it is without doubt the centrepiece of the post-2010 reforms. Importantly, while sold on the premise of 'devolution' in carving out a space for these new metropolitan areas, powers have been absorbed upwards from local authorities as much as they have been released downwards from central government (Lupton et al, 2018). For proponents of this agenda it is comparatively easy to point to Greater Manchester as an example of what devolution can achieve, and there are undoubted successes here. However, at the same time, in the GMSF which is (at the time of writing) on its fourth iteration, we can observe the challenges of planning for a multi-authority city-regional space – even in what is commonly regarded as a well-run area. While Greater Manchester is the leading light, other city regions have opted for a more sedate pace – instead, learning from mistakes made in Greater Manchester's haste. Whether by coincidence or not, it is those places that also seem to have made greater efforts in bringing the entirety of their metropolitan area with them – with both Cambridgeshire and Peterborough and the Liverpool City Region both bringing forward concrete proposals to channel funding into smaller and traditionally more peripheral areas. Across this activity there is, for certain, clear evidence of policy entrepreneurship. However, by the same stroke, we can also see evidence that hints at more populist behaviour – particularly through the allocation of housing through the spatial planning process.

Ultimately, and in contrast to the city mayors, perhaps as a result of direct democratic accountability to a broader metropolitan area, there are clear indications that the metro mayors do not necessarily prioritise the Core City at the heart of the city region, and rather are attempting to balance the broader needs and expectations of their area. In doing so, we should be aware of the potential for a spatial selectivity in that, just as central government can privilege others through its policy action, the inclusion or exclusion of areas from metro mayoral activities can be seen as a strategic choice. This is, understandably, something that is underexplored in this nascent agenda but, as the balance of the core–periphery relationship appears to remain front and centre, it is something we should not lose sight of.

An era of deal-making

If there is one unifying theme of the government's post 2010 agenda, it is deal-making. The nature of any deal, however, involves two parties in negotiation – and this is no less true here. The government was prepared to release powers, but in each instance there was a quid pro quo. In the majority of cases this came in the shape of electoral reform that became a fervent pursuit. Similarly, the very nature of 'dealing' suggests that better negotiating skills can lead to better or more preferable outcomes, and this can be observed across the entire deal-making process – both in City Deals and the devolution deals at the city region scale. This, inevitably, has led to spatial variations in policy, as combined authorities were able to extract greater or lesser extents of powers. In doing so, this also reveals a clear strategic selectivity at play in that, while negotiation skills and capacity would play a part, they would require the government to sign them off. Thus what we saw is the government agreeing bespoke deals that led to an uneven foundation on which areas would work – effectively giving some an explicit advantage in an environment where collaboration was, ostensibly, the goal. Similarly, the government would not be hesitant in punishing those who did not play by the rules, and would withdraw deal-making opportunities from those who would not play along.

Across this period, deals were made of all shapes and sizes, and it is important not to lose sight of this. While the Northern Powerhouse may garner much of the attention, many of those earlier deals and their after-effects (for example, City Deals) remain in place. The result is a complex patchwork agenda, with each reform layered on the one that preceded it. It is therefore difficult to understand one reform without considering the totality. The government did not clear as they went, and thus we can observe a web of reform, often overlapping, often conflicting, and ultimately not as efficient as it might be.

Local authorities:
Powerhouses or scapegoats?

Introduction

It has been argued that the reforms to governance in England since 2010, and the intensified focus on both city regions and neighbourhoods that have resulted (see Chapters 4 and 6 respectively) have, in turn, led to a loss of focus on the tier of governance in between these two − that of local authorities (Lowndes and Gardner, 2016). At the same time, the massive cuts in public spending consequential on 'austerity' are both exacerbating the problems local authorities have to deal with, such as social and welfare issues, and also limiting their scope to deal with them as their budgets have been severely reduced (Lowndes and Pratchett, 2012). So a great deal of power and responsibility remains at local authority level. Before exploring the parameters of this power and responsibility, it is necessary to consider some definitional issues.

First is the question of scale. In this chapter we are dealing with what are referred to as *municipalities* in other countries. As discussed in Chapter 1, there are theoretical arguments against 'territorial' thinking, and the imposition of boundaries on places that are rendered false by 'the multiplicity of connections formed across them' (Cox, 2013, p 49). However, while lived experiences may be increasingly relational rather than territorial (Harvey, 1989; MacLeod and Jones, 2011), local authorities remain a fixture in urban governance, as they have for more than 100 years (John, 2014), and it is to 'the council' that most residents of UK cities instinctively first turn to deal with problems faced in day-to-day life.

A related scalar issue is that of the significant variability in size of urban areas represented by local authorities: the population size of local authorities on the English mainland, for example, ranges from 7,500 to 1.1 million, and population density from 24 to 13,700 people per square kilometre (ONS, 2018). In this book we have primarily focused on the 'more urban' parts of the country, that is, the largest (in terms of population) and most dense towns and cities. We maintain that focus in this chapter, being principally interested in the 74 urban areas in England with more than 100,000 people (Pike et al, 2016). We also, however, concur with Jennings et al (2017) that it is important not to ignore what is happening in smaller towns that are also urban in character.

The chapter first considers the scope and parameters of autonomy at the local authority level, how this has changed over the last 100 years in the UK and the impacts of austerity. It then reflects on the 'entrepreneurial turn' in local governance, with local authorities increasingly exploring different ways to generate income. Finally it considers prospects for the future, reflecting on examples of alternative models for city governance at this local scale, including informal, radical or otherwise non-state-sponsored activity such as the Transition Towns initiative and local currencies.

Localism and local government autonomy

Theoretical and practical arguments

An essential requirement for the existence of local government is that there is *some* degree of autonomy from central control – an entity cannot justifiably be called a government without controlling some activity within its jurisdiction (King, 2007). In some contexts, perhaps most famously the USA, the extent of national government power is specified in the constitution and thus carries significant legal weight. In the absence of a written constitution, the approach taken in the UK is one that depends to a great extent on the attitude of central government; everything that local authorities are able (or obliged) to do is specified in statute and hence subject to the authority of the UK parliament (Stanton, 2018).

Since around the Second World War, and particularly since the 1980s, UK governments have tended to take the position that local government should be an 'agent' of the central state and help to deliver its aims. There are a number of tensions inherent in this assumption, not least that local authorities have a mandate from, and responsibility to, their electorate. The low turnout at local elections has, however, been identified as one reason for a reluctance to give more autonomy to local authorities (Stanton, 2018). Since 1973 turnout at local elections in England is typically between 30% and 40%, compared to turnout at general elections of 60% to 70% (Dempsey, 2017). This might, however, be a circular argument – local authorities have little autonomy, so people are reluctant to turn out in large numbers to vote in local elections, which means central government is, in turn, reluctant to devolve power to local authorities (Hambleton, 2015; Stanton, 2018).

The nature of any power devolved is also important. For devolution of power to be effective, it must be both *substantive* and *procedural*. The former relates to the specific provisions that delegate power; the latter the broader processes of governance – delegating power is pointless if 'the lack of an appropriate procedural framework prevents councils freely exercising that power' (Stanton, 2018, p 433). Similarly, if central government devolves responsibilities that it does not want 'because they are troublesome or politically contentious' (John, 2014, p 697), local authorities can find themselves in an invidious position.

A more recent factor is the increased devolution to city regions discussed in the previous chapter. Sometimes power or funding is genuinely 'new', but it can equally be the case that devolving power from central government to a new tier of city-regional government involves centralising power *from* local authorities (Lowndes and Gardner, 2016). For example, the city region may now take responsibility for some strategic planning decisions that were the responsibility of the local authority. Whether or not powers are new, participating in city-regional government demands attention on the part of local authorities. Lowndes and Gardner (2016, p 370) were concerned that 'local elites … are turning like moths towards the bright light of devolution' and away from the challenges faced at the local level, compounded by the austerity we return to shortly.

The changes to governance arrangements introduced since 2010 may have been particularly radical, but they are also merely the latest example of the constant change in local government structures in the UK since the Second World War. This change has had significant costs – both financial, which is often underestimated, and cultural, in terms of the loss of expertise and knowledge that builds up around established ways of doing things (Jones and Stewart, 2012). In the next section we review some of the significant changes that have taken place.

Some key areas of change in modern local government in England

A number of textbooks have been written on the history of local government in England (see, for example, Chandler, 2007), and this review is by no means intended to distil this literature – instead, we use it to flag up some of the critical areas of change that remain most relevant today.

The first was the emergence of local government as an active participant in civic life, in contrast to '19th-century principles of *laissez-faire* and minimal government' (Gehrke, 2016, p 24). The classic example of what became known as 'municipal socialism' was perhaps that of Birmingham, and Joseph Chamberlain, the city's mayor from 1873 to 1876. In this brief period, Chamberlain instituted major interventions in local utility, housing and transport provision (Gehrke, 2016). While Chamberlain was unusually active, the first half of the 20th century saw a steady growth in local authority powers, for example, in planning through legislation including the Housing, Town Planning, etc Act 1909, the Housing and Town Planning Act 1919, the Town Planning Act 1925 and the Town and Country Planning Act 1932. At the same time there was a growth in the number and size of urban local authorities and a rivalry ensued between these and the older rural county councils, along with attempts by national Conservative governments to limit the powers of urban local authorities due to 'fears that urban government might be captured by socialists' (Chandler, 2007, p 141).

The election of the Labour government in 1945, immediately after the Second World War, is rightly heralded as bringing about the creation of the National Health Service (NHS) along with nationalisations of various other industries and the creation of the town and country planning system (Cullingworth et al, 2015). However, Hanna, Guinan and Bilsborough (2018) argue that it also heralded the end of municipal socialism, as alongside nationalisation came a tendency towards centralism. It is certainly possible to see initiatives such as the New Towns programme, introduced in 1946, as somewhat centralist – the classic example being the residents of Stevenage protesting about plans to turn their small town into a New Town. The Minister of Town and Country Planning, Lewis Silkin, addressed a hostile public meeting with the distinctly anti-localist '"it's no good you jeering; it's going to be done"' (Boughton, 2018, p 79). Development Corporations, the bodies created to deliver New Towns, were relatively independent from government, but also from the local authorities whose jurisdictions they were imposed over (Alexander, 2009).

The New Towns are just one example of the more interventionist and centralist state that characterised the post-war years, with Labour and Conservative-led governments alike inclined to reduce local government autonomy in both fiscal and policy terms (Chandler, 2007), at the same time as using local authorities as the delivery vehicle for much of the welfare state. Central government grants for the provision of council housing are one example, through which local authorities briefly became the biggest providers of housing

(Short, 1982). From the 1950s to the late 1970s, local authorities' expenditure and size (in terms of employees) grew, as their scope for independent action shrank (John, 2014). The 1980s, 1990s and 2000s saw several rounds of reform of local government, but the 'system of local government political management carried on as before and was even strengthened by the reforms' (John, 2014, p 696).

Another important aspect of local government which has been the subject of regular change is that of organisational structure(s). The Municipal Corporations Act 1835 'created the legal person of the local authority' (John, 2014, p 689), and at various points these subsequently took the form of *county councils, rural* and *urban sanitary districts, county boroughs, municipal boroughs, urban* and *rural district councils.* This complex picture was comprehensively simplified by the Local Government Acts of 1963 and 1972 that reformed, respectively, London and the rest of England and Wales. The 1972 Act was introduced under a Conservative government consequent to the Redcliffe-Maud Commission set up by the previous Labour government to explore possibilities for reform. The change of government was seen by many to have favoured rural areas at the expense of urban (Sturzaker and Mell, 2016), including the drawing of very tight metropolitan boundaries around cities. The 1972 Act created a comprehensive two-tier system of counties and boroughs (in urban areas) or districts (in rural areas). It dramatically consolidated the arrangements for local government, reducing the number of directly elected local authorities from 1,300 to 401 (Dearlove, 1979).

Since these reorganisations, there have been almost constant reviews of local government boundaries (Jones and Stewart, 2012), a particularly significant example being that of the Local Government Act 1985, which abolished metropolitan counties and the Greater London Council. The latter was something of a thorn in the side of the Conservative national government, led as it was by a radical left-wing Labour administration. The Greater London Council was experimenting with a resurgence of municipal socialism, appalling the then Prime Minister Margaret Thatcher. Hence the 1985 Act 'legislated out of existence' (Hanna et al, 2018) these 'radical policy experiments' (John, 2014, p 695), and other legislation during that period placed strict limits on local authorities building new homes and borrowing against their assets. The advent of the Labour government in 1997 was initially seen as 'a return to a more consensual mode of relations' (Midwinter, 2001, p 311). However, the programme of 'modernisation' which was brought about, as we discuss later, arguably introduced more stringent controls, albeit indirectly, than under previous administrations. In terms of reorganisation, this was not an initial priority (Jones and Stewart, 2012), but by the early 2000s there was the failed attempt to introduce elected regional authorities (see Chapter 3), and the introduction of unitary authorities in some county areas, alongside changes such as a move from the traditional system of 'inefficient and opaque' local government committees (DETR, 1998) to a 'cabinet and leader model', following the model of national government or cities with prominent mayors, for example, New York.

In the face of these initiatives, 'local government adapted to the changes and made them its own' (John, 2014, p 696). John argued that local government is 'The Great Survivor' and that, whatever is thrown at it by central government, it adapts and, at its core, persists. Some, however, have highlighted fundamental shifts in the relationship between central and local government, which may mean the challenges faced by local government at the time of writing are as significant as they have ever been (Lowndes and Pratchett, 2012; Sandford, 2016). By no means the least of these challenges is the programme of fiscal 'austerity' that began under the 2007–10 Gordon Brown-led Labour government as a consequence of the 2008 onwards global financial crash, but was radically ramped up after the 2010 General Election. This is discussed in more detail in Chapter 2, but here it is worth highlighting the consequences for local government.

Austerity

As we will go on to discuss, thanks to the extremely centralised nature of the fiscal system in the UK, a significant proportion of local authority income has historically come from central government grants. At the time of writing in 2019 these grants have been cut by 50% since 2010, and estimates as to the extent of cuts by 2020 vary between 56% and 77% (Bounds, 2017; Hanna et al, 2018). These cuts have not been evenly spread, with more deprived local authorities seeing sharper reductions in their grants (Hastings et al, 2015; Lowndes and Gardner, 2016).

A number of commentators have argued that the scale of these cuts means that, contrary to claims made by successive governments, local authorities have *not* been empowered through localism (see, for example, Stanton, 2018; Williams et al, 2014). Indeed, some have argued that the localism reforms are an attempt to 'shift the blame for implementing austerity' (Hanna et al, 2018). The counter-position put forward by the then-Prime Minister David Cameron was that the apparent paradox between austerity and devolution could be addressed through local government reforms and efficiencies in order to 'spend less but deliver more' (Cameron, 2015). Perhaps reflecting the adaptability noted by John (2014), local authorities were initially able, through making the kinds of efficiencies urged by Cameron (that is, through reducing the number of staff they employed) to protect the delivery of their core services (Lowndes and Gardner, 2016). However, there is growing evidence that there are no more efficiencies to be made (Ryan, 2017). There is, for example, a huge backlog in roads maintenance (Dempsey et al, 2016), and as we return to in the conclusion of this chapter, more than one local authority appears on the verge of bankruptcy. The challenge is not just that local authorities' budgets have been cut, but also that at the same time demands on their services are growing. The 'graph of doom' (also known as the 'jaws of doom' or 'scissors of doom') is used by some to illustrate an 'existential crisis' for local government as the gap between income and perceived need for spending grows (Butler, 2012).

Cuts from central government are a particular problem for local authorities in England (and indeed, the wider UK) due to their inability to raise money themselves through taxation.

Fiscal autonomy

In the UK, a tiny proportion of GDP (1.6% in 2016) is raised through local taxation, in contrast to what is spent on local services (13%). There is usually a difference between these two figures – for example, local government in Australia is reliant on federal grants (Burton, 2017) and in Japan, one-third of tax revenue is collected locally while two-thirds of expenditure is at the local level (Jacobs, 2003). The UK is, however, a particularly centralised economy in comparison to others in Western Europe (Ferry et al, 2015; Hambleton, 2015).

The extent of this centralisation is a relatively recent situation – until 1990, local authorities set their own taxes (known as rates) on domestic and business properties. From 1991, business rates were centralised at a flat rate, and the revenue centralised and redistributed on the basis of need. From 2013–14 onwards the government moved away from a purely needs-based approach and introduced the *Business Rates Retention Scheme* (BRRS), whereby local authorities are permitted to retain a proportion of the growth in their business rate revenue, thus resulting in a small increase in fiscal autonomy at the local scale. However, this clearly disproportionately benefits those local authorities with growing economies, adding to the regressive approach to cuts in central grants noted earlier (Sandford, 2016).

At the same time as business rates were centralised in 1991, domestic rates were likewise replaced by the ill-fated *Poll Tax*, a flat-rate tax on domestic properties. This was a spectacularly unpopular political move, eventually leading to the ousting of Margaret Thatcher as Prime Minister. It was swiftly dropped, replaced in 1991 by the *Council Tax*. This was, and remains, the only fully local tax available to local authorities, making up around 20% of their income (Sandford, 2016). The combined effect of the business rate and Poll Tax/Council Tax reforms were to reduce local income significantly. This was largely replaced by an increase in central grants, making local authorities yet more dependent on those grants (Ferry et al, 2015).

So, while the reduction in grants from central to local government can be painted as an incentive for local authorities to become more self-reliant, there is central government control on local authorities' ability to increase Council Tax or business rates. Only councils led by directly elected mayors, the government's preferred model (see Chapter 4), can increase business rates (Stanton, 2018). Likewise, if local authorities wish to increase Council Tax by more than a figure set by central government (currently 3%), they must hold a local referendum – clearly an attempt to limit local authority autonomy, given that 'populist referendums' tend to 'promote short-term self-interest over broader community concerns' (Lowndes and Pratchett, 2012, p 28).

There are various other means by which the centre seeks to control local government. In the following sections we discuss three of these – direct control, monitoring, and liberalising nationally set legislation. In all three of these areas, land-use planning is used as an illustrative example – and in all three, the ongoing policy preoccupation with increasing the delivery of new housing is often behind the intervention.

Direct control

As mentioned in Chapter 2, the planning systems in the UK are based around the 'discretionary' system in which local authorities make decisions on development proposals, guided by their own local policy. That local policy is in turn *informed* by national policy guidance but should reflect local circumstances (MHCLG, 2018e). In addition, the UK government minister responsible for planning, currently the Secretary of State for Housing, Communities and Local Government, has various powers that can be used to exercise direct control over planning decisions, including by taking decisions on development proposals that would otherwise be made by local authorities or, if those decisions are appealed, by the independent Planning Inspectorate. At times this approach has been used to enforce national policy on local areas, for example, the forcing through of approvals for fracking near Blackpool in the North West of England (Vaughan, 2016). A previous Secretary of State was accused of taking decisions in line with local political manoeuvring, with 93% of decisions made by him on development proposals between 2016 and 2018 being in Conservative constituencies in comparison to the 56% of constituencies in England held by the Conservatives at that time (Johnston, 2017). The Secretary of State also has the ability to place a 'holding direction' on local authorities to prevent them from adopting a new local plan, used to guide development in their area. Similarly, the next incumbent, James Brokenshire, twice issued such a direction at the behest of the Conservative MP for Stevenage (Dewar, 2018b) in relation to proposals for housing development on the green belt – this intervention on behalf of Stevenage's residents in ironic contrast to Silkin's adventures in 1946.

Indirect control through monitoring

The 'New' Labour government that came to power in 1997 was intent on 'modernising' local government. They did this partly through internal reorganisation – see the previous discussion above – and partly through bringing in a system of 'compulsory top-down benchmarking with severe sanctions' (Kuhlmann and Bogumil, 2018, p 544), a practice that Coulson (2009) termed 'targets by terror'. The purpose of this was to indirectly control what local authorities did by evaluating their activities and requiring them to comply with various performance indicators. If they met the required standards, then they could 'earn' additional autonomy; if they failed to do so, then they would lose some autonomy (Lowndes and Pratchett, 2012). A similar approach operates in Japan, where failure to comply with national guidance results in loss of funds from central government (Jacobs, 2003). A comparison of this system with the more voluntary model operated in Germany and Sweden concluded that a punitive approach was far from ideal if the aim was to identify best practice, learn from others and adapt what local authorities did (Kuhlmann and Bogumil, 2018, p 555).

The targets system, and the organisation that undertook it (the *Audit Commission*), was abolished as part of the 'bonfire of the quangos' (Curtis, 2010) carried out by the 2010–onwards government. While this was done on the basis of saving money and empowering communities, as with much of the localism reforms (DCLG, 2010b), it can also be seen as a way to avoid the benchmarking or comparison of local authorities and the consequent publicising of 'high-profile failures' (Lowndes and Pratchett, 2012, p 36). Land-use planning was one of the areas of activity to be monitored and controlled by central government, and initially at least this control was loosened under the 2010–onwards governments. However, in recent years the approach has moved back towards monitoring and punitive control. In 2013 a 'special measures' regime was introduced to penalise local authorities that were deemed to be underperforming in relation to processing planning applications (Geoghegan, 2018b); and in 2018, if local authorities had not produced their local plan in what was considered a timely manner, they faced 'intervention' in the form of a plan being produced on their behalf (Donnelly, 2017; MHCLG, 2018c).

Since the announcement of intended reforms to the planning system in the run-up to the 2010 General Election (The Conservative Party, 2010b), the various Conservative-led governments have been wrestling with an ongoing tension between giving local people more say over planning and increasing housing supply. Their reforms to the planning system, including the abolition of regional planning and the introduction of Neighbourhood Planning (see Chapters 3 and 6), were predicated on the notion that 'Regional Strategies built nothing but resentment – we want to build houses. So instead we will introduce powerful new incentives for local people so they support the construction of new homes in the right places and receive direct rewards from the proceeds of growth to improve their local area' (DCLG, 2010a). However, it quite swiftly became clear that this approach was not working. The pattern evinced by the previous system – consistent undersupply of homes where demand was highest (Sturzaker, 2010) – continued. So the government resorted to what were effectively the 'Soviet tractor style top-down planning targets' (DCLG, 2010a) used under that previous system. Central government's planning policy for England (DCLG, 2012b; MHCLG, 2018e) introduced a requirement for local authorities to be able to demonstrate they have a five-year supply of land that is 'deliverable' for housing. If they cannot, housing developers are effectively given *carte blanche* to build housing in that area – often in direct opposition to the views of local people.

Loosening national controls over development

Since very early in the evolution of the modern English planning system (introduced by the Town and Country Planning Act 1947), certain forms of development have been categorised as 'permitted development' and thus exempted from the requirement to obtain formal planning permission. This includes small-scale domestic alterations for householders, and some changes of use of land and buildings. Since 2013, the latter category has been significantly expanded to allow the conversion of commercial and agricultural buildings to residential use, with the aim of increasing housing supply. When these changes were introduced, the UK government predicted that the changes would be at least cost-neutral and would lead to a very small number of applications in areas that were generally in line with where local authorities wished to see housing developed (DCLG, 2013).

Two studies of the impact of these changes between their introduction and 2017 have found that these predictions were inaccurate. One study looked at just five local authorities and found there had been 487 schemes for office–residential conversion in the first four years across the five, in contrast with the prediction of 140 per year nationally (Clifford et al, 2018). The lack of quality control meant that permitted development 'residential quality was significantly worse than schemes which required planning permission' (Clifford et al, 2018, p 10). Another study looking at the conversion of rural buildings to agricultural uses found there had been around 17,000 additional homes created between 2014 and 2017 (Clifford and Henneberry, 2018). Beyond the loss of control on the part of local authorities 'to take proactive spatially- and community-informed decisions' (Clifford and Henneberry, 2018, p 385), the loosening of permitted development regulations has been a 'fiscal giveaway from the state to private real estate interests' of in excess of £50 million[1] (Clifford et al, 2018, p 11).

In the preceding sections we have discussed a range of issues related to the autonomy of local authorities, identifying how in many cases this is circumscribed, limiting the scope for local authorities to act and to raise money. But there is some room for manoeuvre, and in the next section we move on to discuss how local authorities can be more proactive.

Sisters are doing it for themselves: Local authority entrepreneurialism

Grants to local authorities from central government continue to be cut, and 'local government is also being "written out" of services that were previously its core business' (Lowndes and Gardner, 2016, p 367) as, for example, schools are moved to academy status rather than being managed by local authorities. As we have discussed at several points, this is not the first 'crisis' that has occurred in the existence of local authorities. In the 1980s and before, local authorities responded to such crises by being more proactive in the realm of economic development. This 'entrepreneurialism' has received much attention from scholars, David Harvey principle among them (Harvey, 1989). We discussed the key theoretical contributions of Harvey in Chapter 1, and in what follows we illustrate these with examples from contemporary practice.

Liverpool: A case study in entrepreneurialism

Liverpool, a city we are particularly familiar with, is an excellent case study to illustrate the entrepreneurial options Harvey identified, as it has perhaps become the archetypal entrepreneurial city in recent decades. As discussed in Chapter 4, it is also one of very few UK local authorities with a directly elected mayor, who, since 2012, has been Joe Anderson, previously (since 2010) the appointed leader of the local authority.

The first of Harvey's options is the 'creation of exploitation of particular advantages for the production of goods and services' (Harvey, 1989, p 8). These might be naturally occurring (for example, oil fields in Texas), but territories can also invest in physical and social infrastructures to make their place more attractive. There are various examples of this in Liverpool, but particularly key is the creation of an environment conducive to investment in the waterfront area, once the heart of Liverpool's economic strength as a dock city, but now typical of many such areas in post-industrial cities as needing new uses to be found for it. The Royal Albert Dock and the area around it has been the focus of much entrepreneurial activity since the 1980s (Parkinson and Lord, 2017), but an area of more recent focus is the north docks area, further from the city centre. The centrepiece of this activity is the Liverpool Waters scheme, a multibillion pound mixed-use development incorporating offices, leisure and residential space (Peel, 2016). Figure 5.1 shows the Liverpool Waters site, the redevelopment of which is hoped to create 25,000 new jobs. Jones (2015) has cogently explored how models of the site have been used during the process of obtaining planning permission to make bold claims about it, which are open to question, but the role played by the local authority, Liverpool City Council, in enabling the development is also key.

One aspect of this is the creation of a joint 'Mersey Waters' enterprise zone (something we expand on later in this chapter) between the Liverpool and Wirral local authorities to cover the Liverpool Waters and Wirral Waters redevelopment sites. On the Liverpool side of the Mersey river, the Liverpool Waters site is also part of the North Liverpool Mayoral Development Zone (MDZ), itself part of a 'Mayoral Development Corporation' (a body that the Cities and Local Government Devolution Act 2016 allowed for the creation of) established by Joe Anderson and supported with funds worth £120 million.[2] The mayor is very keen to ensure that the Liverpool Waters development succeeds, placing the city into direct conflict with the United Nations Educational, Scientific and Cultural Organization (UNESCO). Liverpool waterfront is a WHS as designated by UNESCO, and in 2012, that organisation put the site on its 'in danger' list because it was concerned at the impact of the Liverpool Waters scheme (*Liverpool Echo*, 2014). UNESCO subsequently requested that the development be put on hold for two years, a request which Anderson 'flatly rejected'. He said, 'Part of the problem that we face is if we go out and say to people "please come and invest in our city" but then say "you can't put in a planning application for two years" then our growth is going to suffer' (quoted in Weston, 2016), an archetypally entrepreneurial comment. A further

Figure 5.1: Part of the Liverpool Waters site

Source: Authors' own

illustration of this entrepreneurialism is in relation to one of the largest parts of the Liverpool Waters development, a new stadium for Everton Football Club. Liverpool City Council have offered to loan the football club (owned by a billionaire) £280 million, in order to take advantage of the preferential loan rates available to local authorities (P. Wilson, 2018). Although controversial with the general public, the initiative had been tested on Everton's Finch Farm training ground, with Liverpool City Council making a profit through the repayments on a similar loan.

The second option identified by Harvey is in relation to the consumption side of the economy – 'the city has to appear as an innovative, exciting, creative, and safe place to live or to visit, to play and consume in' (Harvey, 1989, p 9). Liverpool, both at the city and city region scale, has devoted considerable resources to this aspect of its development in recent years (Liverpool City Region LEP, 2014; Parkinson et al, 2017). The proliferation of high-profile events in the city is emblematic of this: 'There's always something going on' (Liverpool City Region LEP, 2018). The city was selected as the European Capital of Culture in 2008, and the City Council's commissioned analysis of this estimated that the programme of events associated with it 'had a total income of £130 million over six years, the highest of any European Capital of Culture to date' (Garcia et al, 2010). That analysis does not specify the cost of the programme, but analysis of similar mega-events such as the Olympic Games concludes that they tend to make a loss in economic terms (Groothuis and Rotthoff, 2016). That has not stopped Liverpool City Council unsuccessfully bidding for the 2022 Commonwealth Games (Halliday, 2017), and putting on various other large-scale events. However, as Harvey notes, there can be benefits beyond the economics in improving a city's image – this can 'help create a 'sense of social solidarity, civic pride and loyalty to place' (Harvey, 1989, p 14). This is certainly evident in the scale of the crowds seen in images of 'The Giants' walking around Liverpool (see Figure 5.2). These huge puppets, operated by a French theatre company, have now made three visits to the city, at a cost of around £2 million per visit (Bradbury, 2014), bringing an estimated 1.3 million visitors into the city centre on their third visit in 2018 (*Liverpool Echo*, 2018).

Harvey's third option is 'the acquisition of key control and command functions in high finance, government, or information gathering and processing (including the media) …' (Harvey, 1989, p 10). Liverpool has also tried to pursue this approach, historically and since Anderson became leader in 2010. Anderson inherited a city that had overcome

Figure 5.2: The 'Giants' perambulating around Liverpool

Source: Thanks to Andrew Davies

significant decline to post growth figures that would be outperformed only by London (TMP, 2009), and he has attempted to continue that trend. In this spirit, Liverpool hosted an International Festival for Business in 2014, and again in 2016, serving as a platform to bring key business leaders and investors into the city. The city joined the bidding to be the new location of the headquarters of the state-owned Channel 4 television station, losing out to Leeds (Place North

West, 2018), but were successful in attracting an office of the UK government's tax department (Houghton, 2017).

We can view the entrepreneurial turn in local authority activity as a pragmatic response to a lack of resources (John, 2014) – and it is one that has been adopted across the world (De Boeck et al, 2017; Lauermann, 2014). It can also be problematic, whether on ideological grounds or practical. As Harvey concludes, while urban entrepreneurialism need not necessarily be zero-sum, that is, one place 'winning' while another 'loses', it often is. The advantage a city gains in attracting capital by, for example, making itself an attractive place for business to locate through cutting taxes, can quickly be diminished as other cities do the same. In terms of infrastructure, there is a limit to the number of successful convention centres, sporting stadia, and so on that can be built. Nevertheless, most local authorities in England continue to take the entrepreneurial approach, as we will show through various other examples.

Investing in housing, infrastructure, and so on

It has been estimated that 65% of local authorities are now engaged in directly delivering housing, as are a number of county councils (Edgar, 2018). Some local authorities are doing so in order to meet a local need for housing and to address homelessness, while others seek to use rental income from housing development to fund their 'essential services' (Morphet and Clifford, 2017, p 4). The latter, while pragmatic, is an example of urban entrepreneurialism while the former is perhaps nearer to municipal socialism.

Another example of entrepreneurialism is the Dutch model of housing delivery, which has long been commended as a way for local authorities to stimulate the housing market (Lord et al, 2015), while also acting as a 'very welcome source of income' to Dutch municipalities (Woestenburg et al, 2018, p 803). In this model, Dutch municipalities buy land, provide it with infrastructure and then sell it on to private developers to build homes upon it. This allows the municipalities to ensure that the plans they make are implemented, in contrast to the systems in the UK that are criticised for not being implementation-focused (Geoghegan, 2018a). The Dutch system gives local authorities a great deal of autonomy, but has been problematic in recent years as land values have fallen and local authorities have had to take increasingly large risks in order to make profits from their land dealings – some sustaining losses as a consequence (Woestenburg et al, 2018).

Contracting out

A different type of entrepreneurial activity involves local authorities, rather than undertaking activity, opting to not undertake it by contracting out services that used to be core to its purpose. This was enabled initially by legislation in the 1980s that required local authorities to put work such as construction, maintenance and street cleaning out to competitive tender on the basis that the private sector would be able to do this work more cheaply (Dempsey et al, 2016). More recently the range of activities that can be contracted out has grown, with Barnet Council in London earning itself the moniker 'easyCouncil' as it proposed contracting out £1 billion of activities and moving to a model whereby residents would need to pay to access anything beyond a basic level of services (Golding, 2010; Blunden, 2012). Some have suggested that a wish to exercise more control over services is leading to an end to contracting-out. For example, in 2005, Salford Council formed a public–private partnership to contract out much of its planning regulatory services, but in 2018, it announced that when the contract expired in 2020, this would be brought back in-house in order to '"maximise social value for the city"' (Johnston, 2018, p 8).

Enterprise zones and similar approaches

Enterprise zones in their current form are, in fact, allocated at the LEP level (see Chapter 4), but we discuss them here because they are a local place-based policy initiative that typifies the entrepreneurial approach to local governance (Squires and Hall, 2013; Monaghan et al, 2016). They are a global phenomenon, with an estimated 3,500 around the world (Monaghan et al, 2016), and prior to being reborn under the 2010–15 government, were a major policy initiative in the UK in the 1980s. Between 1981 and 1995, 38 enterprise zones were established through powers contained in the Local Finance and Local Government, Planning and Land Acts 1980 (Squires and Hall, 2013). The main focus of these early zones was derelict industrial sites, and a range of incentives were introduced to encourage economic development, including significant tax breaks, a relaxing of planning controls and intervention from local authorities to assist with acquisition, assembly and decontamination of land. So, while enterprise zones were introduced as a deregulatory initiative, they required significant public subsidy – estimated at £1.5 billion in tax breaks and local investment (Squires and Hall, 2013). It is further claimed that although the zones employed many people, a high proportion of these were not 'additional', that is, they were already in existence in other locations, and is it estimated that 60% of the benefits of designation went to private interests rather than local areas (Monaghan et al, 2016). Similar results have been found in enterprise zones in other European countries (De Boeck et al, 2017), and a comparative study of the UK and USA experiences concluded that a critical success factor of US zones was found in mobilising a range of local actors to work collaboratively (Squires and Hall, 2013).

Given these findings it is perhaps surprising that the new wave of enterprise zones introduced in 2011 mirrors the approach adopted in the 1980s – they are, again, premised on deregulation and private property rights, with no strong link to wider benefits or leadership in local areas (Squires and Hall, 2013). New enterprise zones were announced in 2011, 2015 and 2016, bringing the number of new wave zones in England to around 50 (Ward, 2016). The focus of the new wave is on 'green growth', and there is some evidence that they may be more effective in encouraging more sustainable development (Monaghan et al, 2016). Some of these were allocated after a competitive bidding process, illustrating again the role of local authorities (through LEPs) in local entrepreneurial activity and showing, in both the 1980s and current waves, a 'pragmatic local desire on the part of most, if not all, councils to exploit central government subsidy during a period of crisis' (Squires and Hall, 2013, p 83). That pragmatism may also explain the more radical approaches to local governance we discuss in the next section, as might a genuinely more progressive intent.

Radical alternatives

'Green' and local approaches

Local currencies involve the creation of a complementary currency that is intended to operate alongside the national currency. The idea of these currencies, which operate in cities in the UK including Manchester and Bath, are that they 'keep wealth flowing locally' (North, 2016, p 1444) as local people spend their local currency in their local shops, which, in turn, procure stock locally and employ local people. However, while they may succeed in that limited remit, they do not generate additionality, that is, they do not stimulate production on top of that which would otherwise have existed (North, 2016).

Transition currencies are a particular example of local currencies, associated with the Transition Towns movement (Hopkins, 2008). Transition Towns are 'designed to get ordinary citizens involved in participatory initiatives that contribute to the sustainability of their local communities' (Fischer, 2017, p 214), such as local low-carbon energy provision, food gardens and banks and a wide range of other projects. Transition Town projects are predicated around local people investing their time and cash locally. There are a growing number of Transition Towns around the world, but they have been criticised for being insufficiently radical, as participants are not encouraged to formally engage in politics (Fischer, 2017).

More clearly led by local authorities are programmes such as that to make Vancouver more resilient by making decisions that incorporate climate change mitigation with other issues (Fischer, 2017) and the Low Carbon Liverpool initiative, which sought to balance economic development with the pressing need to limit climate change (North et al, 2017). The latter highlights the political precarity of such activity, as during the project's lifespan central government changed from Labour to Conservative-led, and policy correspondingly changed from one that included climate targets to one prioritising economic growth above all else. This change in policy changed the local authority's focus, leading to politicians who had previously supported the project to attack it (North et al, 2017).

The city of Bristol has in recent years cast itself as something of an exemplar of alternative approaches to urban governance. As discussed in Chapter 4, Bristol was the only city in England that voted through a referendum to adopt a directly elected mayor in May 2012, and in the subsequent election chose an independent candidate, George Ferguson. The election of a political outsider perhaps opened up some opportunities for lateral thinking. While appointing a 'rainbow' cabinet drawing from all major political parties as a reflection of his position as an independent who would nonetheless still need to achieve policy ambitions, Ferguson would still pursue policies perhaps seen as outside the political mainstream. This included advocating for sustainable transport solutions, with a standout example being the closure of some roads in the city centre on Sundays (BBC News, 2013). Similarly, the mayor agreed to take part of his salary in Bristol's local currency. In 2015, following several attempts, Bristol was designated European Green Capital, a year-long award from the European Commission intended to celebrate and promote environmental efforts within cities (North et al, 2017).

While pursuing the award of the Green Capital can be seen as reflective of Ferguson's general approach, strengthening Bristol's environmental credentials, it clearly also had entrepreneurial benefits for the city – not least as a branding exercise in which Bristol was the first UK city to win the award, mirroring the efforts of Liverpool after it won the European Capital of Culture (Garcia, 2017). Ferguson also attempted to make use of all the instruments available to the city to promote Bristol, including using the City Deal apparatus and £12 million to support the development of a new concert arena in the city centre which was abandoned after Ferguson lost his re-election bid (Ashcroft, 2018).

The Preston model: Municipal socialism and the foundational economy

In recent years, the city of Preston in the North West of England has begun to be known for something other than its football team, the inaugural winners of the English football league in 1889, and its famous bus station (Moore, 2018). The 'Preston model', a form of 'community wealth building' (Sheffield, 2017), has been likened to 'municipal socialism' (Hanna et al, 2018). Since 2012, Preston City Council has led an initiative whereby large local institutions, including the council itself, spend more of their money locally, focused where possible on cooperatives and other community-led institutions. Inspired by the examples of Cleveland in the USA and the Mondragon Corporation in Spain, this approach appears to have had an immediate impact, as Preston saw a rapid improvement in its deprivation statistics (Sheffield, 2017). There was likewise some evidence of a political impact, with the Labour Party increasing its majority on the local council in 2018 and ascribing this in part to the new approach (Hanna et al, 2018). There are limitations on what it might be able to achieve given the context of the UK in contrast to the examples of Cleveland or Spain – cooperatives may be harder to set up in the UK, with its 'weaker city governments, less availability of philanthropic capital and the looming shadow of austerity' (Sheffield, 2017). It is also legitimate to wonder whether Preston would have gone down this route had the £700 million shopping centre 'the council had bet everything on' (Chakrabortty, 2018) not been abandoned after the 2008 financial crisis.

Regardless of Preston's motives, the idea of community wealth building at the heart of the Preston model can be seen as an example of placing more emphasis on the *foundational economy*. The foundational economy comprises the goods and services that are the essential daily needs of all the population – education, health, food and infrastructure, including transport, pipes and cables (Engelen et al, 2017). The argument for placing more emphasis on these foundational activities is that they have been neglected by the focus on competitiveness inherent in the entrepreneurial turn – but that they 'act as an important buffer and stabiliser of the city economy' precisely because of their enduring and ongoing nature (Engelen et al, 2017, p 416). They can be difficult to fund by cities that are not flourishing – regardless of whether the tax base has declined due to unemployment, they still have to be provided, which has historically explained the redistributive nature of central government grants on the principle of 'funding following duties' (Sandford, 2016, p 638). Those advocating for a greater emphasis on the foundational economy argue that rather than focusing on competing with each other, cities should measure the deficiencies in local provision of foundational services and prioritise addressing those deficiencies on the basis of equality for everyone within their jurisdiction. They advocate for taxes to provide services, capturing land values and 'defending national settlements around declining cities' (Engelen et al, 2017, p 420) – noting, of course, that this requires change beyond the scale of the local authority, particularly in heavily centralised states such as the UK, bringing us full circle to the problems of (a lack of) local autonomy.

Conclusion

It would be fair to call local authorities the 'piggy-in-the-middle' of devolution. In the period since 2010, new tiers of governance at the city region and community level have received new powers and some funding while local authorities have seen their grants from central government cut by more than 50%. The re-focusing on the levels above and below local authorities appears in many ways to be ideologically motivated – the old Conservative distrust of Labour-dominated local councils allied to a belief in a smaller state. Other countries (see Box 5.1 for an example) see the opportunities available in working together.

Box 5.1: An alternative to 'zero-sum'

An example from Portugal highlights the importance of ideology. The UK government currently appears to believe in a 'zero sum concept of the relationship between civil society and the state, whereby more "society" involvement equates to less "state" activity' (Lowndes and Pratchett, 2012, p 32). In fact, the actions of local authorities can enable and encourage community activity. The City Council in Lisbon, for example, developed a 'co governance model' (Departamento De Desenvolvimento Local, 2017, p 2), bringing together communities and the municipality to help address deprivation. While there are some examples of such co-governance in the UK, they are not particularly common.

It is unsurprising in this context that the Localism Act 2011 in fact arguably reduced local authorities' powers – Jones and Stewart (2012, p 356) suggest 'it could well have been called the Centralism Act'. Central government continues to intervene in local government, whether through adapted forms of the monitoring regime that became central to the New Labour administration or through other forms of direct and indirect control.

The result is a situation where 'local government lacks the freedom and the resources to govern local areas effectively, provide local services and serve local people' (Stanton, 2015, p 985), and what some see as a fundamental re-casting of the relationship between central and local government (Sandford, 2016). The period of reductions in local authority grants has gone on for approaching a decade, and while the UK Prime Minister promised 'an end to austerity' (Kentish, 2018), this has not prefaced an immediate change in approach. It has been claimed that local authorities are now at 'breaking point' (Ryan, 2017) and will soon be unable to deliver their statutory services – leading to, as previously noted, claims of an 'existential crisis' for local authorities (Butler, 2012). Some have gone bankrupt, apparently partly as a result of refusing to raise Council Tax over a sustained period (Lowndes and Gardner, 2016; Butler, 2018).

However, local government has a long history of resilience in the face of claims of terminal decline (John, 2014). This is, in part, due to its flexibility and adaptability, illustrated by the evolving role of local authorities over the last century. In recent years they have become increasingly entrepreneurial, branching into areas of activity at times some distance from their traditional managerial purpose (Harvey, 1989). This adaptability, while arguably ideologically questionable and certainly practically risky, means that there are some grounds for optimism as we look forward (Lowndes and Gardner, 2016). It is impossible to say with any certainty what the future will bring for local authorities, but the example of the Preston model has been seized upon by some as providing a model for more progressive city governance, and evidence of the need to reject 'the twin temptations of fatalism – that *nothing can be done* – and deferral – that *nothing can be done until Labour is in power in Westminster*' (Hanna et al, 2018; original emphasis).

Notes
[1] Calculated by adding together the loss of planning fees and planning gain (which would normally be extracted from residential development) and subtracting the savings to local authorities of not having to process planning applications.
[2] http://regeneratingliverpool.com/mayoral-enterprise-and-development-zones/

6

Community-led governance: Opportunities and constraints

Introduction

The notion of devolving power to local people, whether as communities or individuals, has a long history but became a focus of academic attention from the late 1960s onwards, with the oft-quoted landmark work of Arnstein (1969). It has now become a cliché for politicians, whether on the left, right or centre of the political spectrum, to boast of their commitment to (re-)empower citizens. Devolving or decentralising power to communities is a hard proposal to argue against – who is in favour of *not* giving people more say over their futures (Rodriguez-Pose and Sandall, 2008; Lord et al, 2017)? The popularity of the idea, however, hides a great deal of complexity and contention (Sturzaker and Gordon, 2017).

This chapter first presents a brief historical overview of community-led urban governance and selected international examples. It then looks in depth at experiences in England, an exemplary case study in complexity and contention since the introduction of policies such as Neighbourhood Planning through the Localism Act 2011 claimed to empower communities and citizens. There has been a great deal of entirely justifiable scepticism about this, with concerns including the likelihood of these powers being taken up mainly by the wealthy. Conversely, there may be scope for Neighbourhood Plans to play a progressive and emancipatory role in cities through allowing communities to challenge decisions made by city governments and/or create their own plans. This chapter includes some new empirical material on experiences of Neighbourhood Plan production in the North West of England, which casts an interesting new light on the role played by higher tier actors in framing and controlling community activity.

Community involvement in urban governance: A brief historical review

Damer and Hague (1971), in their early review of the evolution of public participation in planning, note that some discussions on the topic were taking place in the 1950s. Opposition to urban renewal in the USA and elsewhere in the 1960s is often credited with provoking larger-scale interest (Shipley and Utz, 2012), with keystone authors such as Jacobs (1961) and Arnstein (1969) bringing both polemical and theoretical arguments in favour of community involvement in planning. Arnstein's ladder of citizen participation, adapted in various ways in the years since (for example, the spectrum of participation developed by the International Association of Public Participation, 2014), remains hugely influential, making important distinctions between *manipulating* the public, *informing* them, *consulting* them, *partnering* with them and giving them *control*. However, despite these distinctions, such terms continue to be used interchangeably by policy-makers, one of the definitional issues that bedevils a review of this sort.

The second of these is the distinction between the *neighbourhood* and *community*. Again, there can be a tendency to assume these are synonymous. They are, however, different – 'neighbourhood is about place while community is about people' (Barton et al, 2010, p 30). This distinction has always been important, for example, in the shape of faith-based communities. In recent decades the idea of a non-spatial community has become even more significant as migration is now the norm, so diaspora communities are part of many people's identities, and virtual communities can be as important as any other. Adding the word 'planning' to either *community* or *neighbourhood* can, in turn, complicate the picture further, with some using the term *community planning* to refer to 'a wider, more inclusive' (ACRE, 2014) form of activity than *neighbourhood planning*.

Related to the neighbourhood vs community confusion is a tendency on the part of some, particularly state actors, to use either term to refer to policies targeted at deprivation. That tendency has itself been ascribed to the approach, from the 1960s onwards, of attempting to 'tackle huge social and economic problems [urban poverty and deprivation] with tiny financial resources' (Green and Chapman, 1992, p 242). This approach was (and is) justified according to the ethic of 'social pathology', whereby the problems found in areas of deprivation are seen to be due to individual or collective failures on behalf of the people living there, rather than a consequence of larger-scale economic trends or deliberate government policy. So, rather than addressing these trends or revising that policy, the approach is to focus resources on a small number of problematised places ('neighbourhoods' or 'communities') in an attempt to remedy the failures of those places and the people living within them. A different, but equally top–down, way of viewing neighbourhoods is illustrated in Box 6.1.

Box 6.1: 'Neighbourhood' planning in the USA

Due to its federal nature, the USA is comprised of many different governance systems, with similarly many ways in which communities are involved, although there are some common themes. Bennett (2017) observed that neighbourhoods were used as a key scale of planning in the USA in many cities from the 1920s onwards, but this tended to be a top-down and technocratic approach, initially using neighbourhood 'modules' as building blocks to plan the city, and using them in the same way to regenerate post-war cities. In the 1970s 'neighbourhood advisory systems' were used, but again, these tended to be used for information or consultation purposes rather than being citizen-led. Bennett highlights cities such as New York and Portland as having some form of apparently genuine Neighbourhood Planning involving the collaborative production of community-oriented plans, although not always sufficiently supported financially by the cities – an issue we return to later.

The national Community Development Project (CDP), running from 1970–78, was an early example of this approach, but unusually had a strong element of genuine community participation. This participation led to a series of reports from the projects that challenged the social pathology ethic and instead viewed poverty as a consequence of structural inequalities (Green and Chapman, 1992). The danger of communities not following 'the party line' in this way perhaps explains the reluctance of planners and others to embrace this experimental way of working – despite the advantages of this approach identified by Green and Chapman, it was not widely adopted. There have, instead, been a series of 'sporadic' and 'short-lived' (John, 2014, p 693) legislative and policy-based attempts to encourage more active community participation at intervals since the time of the CDP.

The 1980s is usually characterised as being a fallow period for community involvement in governance, particularly in urban areas, due to the emphasis by the Conservative governments in this period on property-led regeneration. Box 6.4 later illustrates that this was not always the case, with the Conservative national government happy to support community-led development in Liverpool given the hard-left 'militant' Labour local authority as the alternative. In general, however, there is something of an inherent conflict between schemes such as Urban Development Corporations, designed to expedite development and opening up decision-making to communities (Church, 1988). It has been suggested that Margaret Thatcher's 1987 repudiation of society – and emphasis on individuals and families – led to the development of 'a particularly Conservative notion of community' (Hickson, 2013, p 409) in the early 1990s. This view of community, drawing on Edmund Burke and others (Tait and Inch, 2016), emphasised the organic development of communities with minimal state involvement, and then only to enforce basic societal rules rather than pursue wider social objectives.

The election of the 'New' Labour government in 1997 introduced a new emphasis on community engagement that in many ways drew on these Burke-ian ideas, as evidenced by quotations from two publications from the Office of the Deputy Prime Minister in the early years of the administration: 'councils need to listen to, lead and build up their local communities' and 'everywhere there should be forms of local governance which listen to the voice of local people and give strong leadership for communities …' (ODPM, 1998, p 2, 1999, p 2). This was initially operationalised as the *Community Empowerment Fund* and *Community Chest Scheme*, two programme of funding designed to support engagement in community governance (Cullingworth and Nadin, 2006). Subsequently, the *New Deal for Communities*, an example of the use of 'communities' to refer to deprivation-related investment, had a requirement for community involvement as a condition of receiving funding (Jones and Evans, 2008). There were questions about how influential this community involvement was – and these approaches were resisted by local authorities, particularly elected councillors, as they feared diminution of their control (Lowndes and Pratchett, 2012). As we will see, there is some evidence of a similar resistance to Neighbourhood Planning today.

The questionable influence of the community is one of the perennial issues that recurs in relation to these types of initiatives – evidence from early experiences through to the Labour years is that citizen participation tended towards, at best, tokenism (Green and Chapman, 1992; Jones and Evans, 2008). There were a number of reasons for this: a lack of capacity at the community level; the complexity of bidding processes meaning that genuine engagement is difficult; and differences in opinion between neighbourhoods, local authorities and national government, with the final decision (and hence the power) remaining with the latter (Cullingworth and Nadin, 2006) – problems not unique to the UK, as Box 6.2 shows.

Box 6.2: Power and devolution in Australia

Like the USA, Australia operates a federal system with states and territories holding a great deal of power but tending not to delegate this to local authorities (Burton, 2017) that are generally quite small – Sydney, for example, is controlled by 30 local authorities with no metropolitan authority. Brisbane City Council is an exception to this (Brown and Chin, 2013). A further innovation in Brisbane is the statutory Neighbourhood Plans in place over much of the city. These include formal public participation that Brown and Chin (2013) critiqued for being poor in both process and outcome terms, exacerbating the 'disconnect' felt by citizens from the planning process. They concluded that private sector developers were unduly privileged in the Neighbourhood Planning process, and that professional planners continued to wield considerable power – we see echoes of this in the current English system that we return to later.

It is ostensibly to address imbalances of power that the 'localist' reforms of the 2010–onwards Conservative-led governments were introduced, inspired by, among other things, David Cameron's ideas about 'the Big Society' (Sparrow, 2009). As discussed in Chapter 1, and which we return to shortly, these reforms were accompanied by rhetoric that suggested they would lead to, for the first time, a genuinely participatory form of (urban) governance. There are examples of such governance elsewhere, with Porto Alegre in Brazil often cited (see Box 6.3).

Box 6.3: Radical distribution of power in Brazil

The Porto Alegre case involves a city run by the Workers' Party aiming 'to open up the state machinery in the municipalities and involve all citizens – the poor especially – in deciding how it should work' (Wainwright, 2009, p 120). Between 1989 and 2004 the Workers' Party was in power in Porto Alegre, and instituted participatory budgeting in the city. This involved the opening up of decisions on the city's investment budget. Delegates were elected at the community level to decide on the budget. Cuts in the city's budget by the national government began to hamper the efficacy of this arrangement, but the principle has subsequently been adopted in other cities in Brazil and elsewhere.

As local government struggles to deliver its core services, we are in some places seeing, perhaps out of necessity, a strand of activity that appears to be genuinely driven by community members themselves. Commonly identified reasons for such activity to develop are to seek better *outcomes* for communities from decision-making (Brown and Chin, 2013); to improve the *process* of decision-making for communities (TCPA, 1999); and as a reaction against perceived unfavourable decisions made by others (Moore, 2014). The relationship of this activity with the formal state is complex and variable – sometimes the activity comes about through opposition to actions of the state (Wainwright, 2009), sometimes it is supported by the state (Healey, 2006), and sometimes it is co-opted by the state (de Magalhaes et al, 2003).

These various reasons for activity and the relationships with the state can be encapsulated in one example of such activity, which is growing more prominent in the UK – the use of development trusts and community land trusts (CLTs). Both types of organisations are predicated on the acquisition, development and management of assets for community rather than private gain, with CLTs usually focused on (affordable) housing while development trusts may have a broader remit, including economic, social and environmental activity (Moore and McKee, 2012; Healey, 2015). CLTs in particular emerged in the USA in the 1960s, but have rapidly grown in number since around 2000; likewise, community ownership of land in the UK has a long history in Scotland at least, with it being used as an alternative to feudalism since the early 20th century, and growing in popularity since 2000 (Satsangi, 2007). In England CLTs have been promoted and encouraged since around 2008 (Moore and McKee, 2012), generally small in scale and in rural areas – although there are now some successful examples in cities such as Liverpool (Moore, 2014; Thompson, 2015), which is an exemplar for this type of activity (see Box 6.4).

Box 6.4: Liverpool as a community governance innovation hub

As noted by Thompson (2015, p 1029), Liverpool has been 'at the forefront of urban policy innovations to tackle its persistent housing crisis.' Examples of these innovations include:

Pioneering resident-led housing cooperatives, such as the Weller Streets Housing Cooperative in 1982. These 61 houses in Toxteth, and very close to the rioting the year before, were designed by their residents, working with local architects, but funded by the state (Wates and Knevitt, 1987).

In North Liverpool, the Eldonian Community Based Housing Association has been in operation since the late 1970s – a reaction against Liverpool City Council plans to demolish 'slum' housing and redistribute the population, this cooperative was supported by the national government, in conflict with the 'militant' Labour local government of the time (McBane, 2008). It is now the largest scheme of its type in operation in the UK (Thompson, 2015).

Some of the first urban CLTs were in Granby, Toxteth (Thompson, 2015) and Anfield (Moore, 2014). These CLTs developed in opposition to activity by Liverpool City Council (a recurring theme), and in the Anfield case, Liverpool Football Club (Southern, 2014), illustrating the diverse motivations for community activity.

Neighbourhood Planning in England

A brief introduction to Neighbourhood Planning

As noted earlier, the New Labour governments of 1997–2010 invested at a significant scale in urban poverty reduction programmes, and emphasised the need to empower communities. They were, however, also criticised for accompanying this rhetoric and funding with an increasing range of targets and other monitoring measures (see Chapter 5) – what has been called 'managerial localism' (Evans et al, 2013). There may have been moves towards a more genuinely community-driven localism, with the publication in July 2009 of a consultation document entitled *Strengthening Local Democracy*, which proposed 'a radical dispersal of power both to the citizen *and* to their local elected representatives' (DCLG, 2009, p 6; emphasis added).

This approach never got beyond the consultation stage, as in May 2010 the Labour Party lost the general election and a Conservative–Liberal Democrat coalition government was formed. The swiftly written *Programme for Government* of this coalition promised, in a strikingly similar form of words, 'a radical redistribution of power ... to councils, communities and homes across the nation' (HM Government, 2010a, p 7). The Localism Act 2011 was a key piece of legislation in relation to this supposed empowerment, introducing as it did a series of 'community rights' to do things. Neighbourhood Planning is arguably the most effective of these 'rights'. More than 2,400 communities have begun the process of preparing a Neighbourhood Plan (MHCLG, 2018d). Other 'rights' introduced including the 'community right to bid', involving communities bidding for assets such as libraries or pubs, have thus far been rarely used (Sandford, 2017a).

In brief, the process for producing Neighbourhood Plans begins with communities voluntarily coming together to define the area they wish to produce a plan for, and defining the membership of the body that will produce the Plan. In rural areas this is by default the parish or town council, bodies that have existed since 1894 in their current form, but with a longer history in many places (see Sturzaker and Shaw, 2015, for a discussion of Neighbourhood Planning in rural areas). In urban areas, which we emphasise here given the focus of this book, parish and town councils tend not to exist, so a new body – the Neighbourhood Forum – must be formed. The draft Plan boundary and Neighbourhood Forum must be submitted to the local authority for approval. Once approved, the Neighbourhood Forum can begin production of the Plan. There are various statutory stages of consultation, after which the Plan is submitted to the local authority, which then appoints an independent examiner who tests whether the Plan meets a set of 'basic conditions' (MHCLG, 2018f), including whether it is in general conformity with the strategic planning policies of the local authority. Assuming the Plan passes this examination, a referendum is held of all those who live and work in the neighbourhood, a feature of Neighbourhood Planning that makes it distinctive in terms of the English planning system, and indeed, most other systems around the world. In addition to the *representative democracy* which, as we will discuss further, remains the overriding source of power and legitimacy within planning decision-making, Neighbourhood Planning incorporates *participatory democracy* in the Plan production process and *direct democracy* in the referendum. How these forms of democracy intertwine and work together (or not) is analysed in detail in Sturzaker and Gordon (2017). If a Plan passes the referendum (and all but two have passed at the time of writing), then the local authority is obliged to 'make' it, meaning it becomes part of the *Statutory Development Plan* and hence has equivalent status to the local authority's own Local Plan when decisions on planning applications (development proposals) are made. One local authority has gone further, devolving the power to determine planning applications to a town council (Dewar, 2018a).

The Localism Act became law in late 2011, with secondary legislation introducing Neighbourhood Planning powers in mid-2012. Since the introduction of the draft legislation in December 2010, concerns have been raised about various aspects of it, particularly Neighbourhood Planning. These concerns are not in general about the principle of localism in planning, although some are (Orme, 2010); most have taken the view, as argued in Chapter 1, that concepts such as localism are broadly ideologically neutral. What matters is how localism is operationalised, that is, the 'devil is in the detail' regarding the extent to which power is genuinely shifted and any changes in power structures benefit elites or otherwise (Bradley and Brownill, 2017). It is concern about the limits of UK localism and the potentially regressive nature of Neighbourhood Planning that has prompted much criticism – yet some have observed that there is scope for optimism. In the following section we summarise two of the main criticisms that are raised and their counterpoints – the opportunity spaces 'among the neoliberal canvas' of UK localism referred to by Williams, Goodwin and Cloke (2014).

Pre-implementation concerns and spaces for hope

Despite the bold claims put forward for it as a radical shift in power (DCLG, 2012a), Neighbourhood Planning was criticised from its inception for offering communities the power to plan under only 'limited terms' (Parker et al, 2015). These limits include that Neighbourhood Plans must accord with 'strategic' policies in Local Plans and cannot be used to reduce the level of development proposed in neighbourhoods by those Local Plans. This restriction was introduced during the passage of the legislation through parliament, in response to concerns that without it, Neighbourhood Plans would be a 'NIMBY's charter' (O'Connor, 2010) as they would allow local communities to prevent housing and other forms of necessary development being built. This, of course, immediately highlights a substantial crack in the façade of UK localism – communities could make their own choices only if these aligned substantively with that of Local Planning Authorities, and indeed, the national government that continues to express in strong terms the view that the planning system is to blame for the 'housing crisis' (MHCLG et al, 2018).

However, limiting though this bias is, the law requires only that Neighbourhood Plans accord with 'strategic' policies – not everything planned by Local Planning Authorities. There is scope, then, for Neighbourhood Plans to facilitate 'spaces of resistance' (Haughton et al, 2013, p 230). There is some evidence that this is happening in some places, with Neighbourhood Plans tending to promote smaller housing sites, often on previously developed, as opposed to greenfield, land – in contrast to the standard model of housebuilding in the UK (Bradley and Sparling, 2016). Further, in places where this standard model is not working, and development is not currently happening due to a lack of interest from the private sector developers who drive most building activity in England, Neighbourhood Plans may be able to be used to promote development that might not otherwise take place (Bradley, 2015; Southern, 2014; Brownill, 2017).

The second significant area of criticism of Neighbourhood Planning was that it would act to entrench existing inequalities of access to the planning system. The argument here is that middle-class people and communities are better able to engage with the planning system, for various reasons (Matthews and Hastings, 2012), and that Neighbourhood Planning, and localism more broadly, would further empower these already privileged individuals and groups (Matthews et al, 2015). A key aspect of this fear was the variable ability of individuals to be able to volunteer to produce Neighbourhood Plans (that is, to do unpaid planning work). Peter Hall argued that those more likely to do so were 'well-meaning, well educated people living in nice places – mostly rural – with time on their hands' (Hall, 2011, p 60). Hall was drawing on work by Sutcliffe and Holt (2011), which showed significantly higher levels of voluntarism among wealthier rural communities than more deprived urban equivalents. This breaks down into two socio-spatial issues: first, that rural communities (on average, more wealthy than their urban counterparts in England) were more likely to take up Neighbourhood Planning powers; and second, that within those communities that did produce Neighbourhood Plans, wealthy and/or retired people (Hall's 'well-meaning, well educated people with time on their hands') were more likely to get involved (Stanton, 2015). The latter reflects existing experience, such groups representing the so-called 'usual suspects' who tend to be over-represented in voluntarism (Goulding, 2013) and existing participation processes in planning (Dandekar and Main, 2014). The concern was that the combined effect of these two issues was that Neighbourhood Plans would be spatially concentrated in less deprived areas, and that where they were produced, they were more likely to benefit less deprived people, that is, those who had produced them (Sturzaker, 2010; Hastings and Matthews, 2015).

The converse position from this pessimism is first that, after an initial period of 'bedding in', urban areas may be no less likely than rural areas to prepare Neighbourhood Plans. Beyond the broad-brush demographic differences between urban and rural areas of England, rural England features a pre-existing governance architecture of town or parish councils, which gives them an automatic head start in terms of both formal governance structures and the accompanying capital to prepare Neighbourhood Plans (see Gallent, 2013; Sturzaker and Gordon, 2017, for a fuller discussion). After an initial lag it may be that some (but not all) of these advantages become less influential. Moving to the second issue, that of intra-community variations in involvement, the government's claim was that Neighbourhood Planning might broaden or deepen democracy in terms of the proportion of people who engage in the planning process (Parker et al, 2015). This could happen because moving governance arenas 'closer' to people's lived realities makes it easier and more appealing to get involved (Lowndes and Sullivan, 2008), or because Neighbourhood Planning, unlike most planning activity, 'addresses people's emotional commitment to place' (Bradley, 2017b, p 163). The hope would be, then, that Neighbourhood Planning can 'challenge rather than entrench inequalities between and within places' (Featherstone et al, 2012, p 180). Evidence from less deprived parts of the country suggest that this may be happening within some places (Healey, 2015; Sturzaker and Shaw, 2015), although profound tensions remain (Sturzaker and Gordon, 2017). There is as yet little published work analysing how Neighbourhood Planning is happening at the 'micro' scale, that is, beyond broad national-level studies (cf Parker and Salter, 2016). This is particularly the case in relation to more deprived or urban places, in part because of the lag in activity in such places noted previously. Given that this book is interested in changes to urban governance, and whether they can be said to have had progressive impacts, we feel it is essential to try and remedy this gap in research. In the following section, therefore, we present some empirical data on this topic, at first quantitative, and then qualitative.

Six years in: Quantitative findings in England and the North West

Parker and Salter (2016) found that around 90% of the first Neighbourhood Planning areas to be designated, and those subsequently passing referendums were in parished (that is, rural) parts of England. Looking now at the *Index of Multiple Deprivation* (IMD), the measure used to quantify relative deprivation at various scales across England, half of the 1,625 areas were in local authorities within the upper two IMD quintiles (that is, the least deprived 40% of England), while only a quarter were in local authorities within the lower two IMD quintiles (that is, the most deprived 40% of England). So overall there is a very strong bias towards rural areas, and a less strong but still clear bias towards wealthier areas, among the 'early adopters' of Neighbourhood Planning – although it is important to note that this data is at the local authority level, which does not reflect any variability in deprivation within those local authorities.

In early 2017 we were commissioned by RTPI and Planning Aid North West to undertake a desk-based review of all Neighbourhood Planning activity in the region. This was to comprise first, an analysis of the information and support offered on the website of each of the 40 Local Planning Authorities in the region, and second, the compilation of a database of Neighbourhood Planning activity within each Local Planning Authority (we focus on the latter here). We used the Local Planning Authorities' own information on Neighbourhood Planning activity within their area, and collected information as to where in the Neighbourhood Planning process (see above) each Neighbourhood Plan had got to. We further mapped the level of deprivation in each Neighbourhood Planning area using the UK government's mapping tool for the IMD.[1] This map shows the IMD ranking of each of the 32,844 Lower Super Output Areas (LSOAs) in England (the most deprived being ranked 1).

At Local Planning Authority level, a similar pattern is found in the North West of England as Parker and Salter (2016) found in England. Of the 157 Neighbourhood Planning areas designated in the region by June 2017, 130 were within areas covered by parish or town councils – a figure of 83%, slightly lower than the 91% identified by at the national scale, but still a significant proportion. The bias towards less deprived local authorities is more marked than found by Parker and Salter – we found that in the North West, 39% of the areas designated are within the least deprived upper two IMD quintiles (compared to 51.6% in England) and 28% of areas are in the lower two (compared to 23.2% in England). The difference from the national figures in large part is due to the fact that the North West is a comparatively deprived region – only one North West local authority (Ribble Valley, with three Neighbourhood Planning areas) is in the top quintile, that is, the least deprived 20% of local authorities nationally. The North West also contains 4 of the 10 most deprived local authorities in the country by this measure.

If we instead identify how the local authorities rank within the North West, that is, looking at deprivation relative to other local authorities in the region, we see a very stark pattern of concentration of Neighbourhood Planning activity within the less deprived parts of the region. Ranking the 39 local authorities within the North West by deprivation, 77% of the 157 Neighbourhood Planning areas are in the upper two IMD quintiles in the North West, and only 11% of areas are in the lower two IMD quintiles in the North West.

Table 6.1 illustrates the pattern of deprivation and number of Neighbourhood Planning areas at local authority level.

As Table 6.1 illustrates, the figures are significantly skewed by several outlier local authorities – three local authorities have between them 87 of the 157 Neighbourhood Planning areas (55%). These are the local authorities of Cheshire East (42 Neighbourhood Planning areas), Cheshire West & Cheshire (29 areas) and Eden (16 areas). These three are respectively the 37th, 33rd and 31st most deprived of the 39 local authorities in the North West (although only Cheshire East is within the least deprived 40% of local authorities in the country), and given that the mean number of Neighbourhood Planning areas per local authority in the North West is four, they are clearly outliers. Figure 6.1 illustrates this graphically, and shows an overall relationship at local authority level between degree of deprivation and number of Neighbourhood Planning areas within the local authority.

However, as noted previously, analysis at local authority level tells us only so much. Even the most deprived local authority contains wealthier areas, and vice versa. If we move to the level of the

Table 6.1: Local authorities in the North West and their national and regional IMD ranking

Local authority (LA)	IMD rank LA	IMD quintile LA	No of Neighbourhood Planning areas in LA	IMD rank LA (within North West)	IMD quintile LA (within North West)	Population of LA
Ribble Valley BC	290	1	3	39	1	58,826
South Lakeland BC	251	2	6	38	1	103,274
Cheshire East BC	241	2	42	37	1	376,695
South Ribble BC	234	2	2	36	1	110,118
Trafford MBC	222	2	2	35	1	234,673
Fylde BC	218	2	6	34	1	77,990
Cheshire West and Chester UA	192	3	29	33	1	335,680
Chorley BC	186	3	0	32	2	114,351
Eden DC	182	3	16	31	2	52,639
Stockport MBC	178	3	2	30	2	290,557
Warrington BC	176	3	2	29	2	208,809
Wyre BC	167	3	2	28	2	110,261

(continued)

Table 6.1: Local authorities in the North West and their national and regional IMD ranking (continued)

Local authority (LA)	IMD rank LA	IMD quintile LA	No of Neighbourhood Planning areas in LA	IMD rank LA (within North West)	IMD quintile LA (within North West)	Population of LA
West Lancashire DC	164	3	1	27	2	113,401
Bury MBC	132	3	0	26	2	188,669
Lancaster CC	125	4	8	25	2	143,517
Allerdale BC	114	4	1	24	3	96,956
Carlisle CC	112	4	1	23	3	108,409
Wigan MBC	107	4	2	22	3	323,060
Wirral MBC	106	4	5	21	3	321,238
Sefton BC	102	4	4	20	3	274,261
Rossendale BC	98	4	0	19	3	69,886
Preston CC	72	4	4	18	3	141,801
Bolton MBC	64	5	1	17	3	283,115
Copeland BC	63	5	3	16	4	69,307
St Helen's MBC	52	5	0	15	4	178,455
Oldham MBC	51	5	1	14	4	232,724
Barrow BC	44	5	0	13	4	67,321
Pendle BC	42	5	3	12	4	90,588
Halton BC	36	5	0	11	4	126,903
Tameside MBC	34	5	1	10	4	223,189
Hyndburn BC	28	5	1	9	4	80,537
Salford CC	27	5	0	8	5	248,726
Rochdale MBC	25	5	1	7	5	216,165
Blackburn with Darwen BC	24	5	0	6	5	147,049
Burnley BC	17	5	1	5	5	87,522
Liverpool CC	7	5	5	4	5	484,578
Knowsley MBC	5	5	0	3	5	147,915
Blackpool	4	5	0	2	5	139,195
Manchester CC	1	5	2	1	5	541,263

Notes: BC = borough council; MBC = metropolitan borough council; UA = unitary authority; DC = district council; CC = county council.

Figure 6.1: Relationship between IMD rank of local authority and number of Neighbourhood Planning areas within the local authority, with a 'best fit' line added

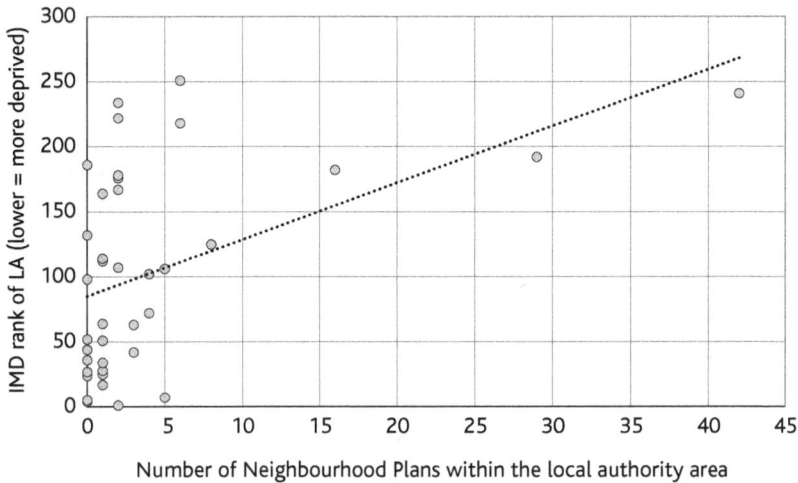

Number of Neighbourhood Plans within the local authority area

neighbourhood we can apply a finer grain of analysis. As discussed earlier, we have used the DCLG map of IMD data from 2015 at LSOA level. Each Neighbourhood Planning area was categorised by the most deprived LSOA within the area, as required by the commission for the research.

Looking at the neighbourhood level, of the 157 Neighbourhood Planning areas in the North West, 38% are in the upper two IMD quintiles for neighbourhoods, and 28% are in the lower two quintiles. These figures are almost exactly the same as at local authority level, suggesting that variations *within* local authorities are less significant than variations *between* local authorities. Considering how activity has increased over time, Figure 6.2 illustrates the relationship between deprivation at Neighbourhood Planning level, time and stage of the process reached. This again illustrates that most activity is in less deprived areas – those towards the top of the vertical axis. It also shows that the level of activity has increased over time, with more activity as the system 'beds in'. Incidentally, it is worth noting the number of areas that have been designated (marked with a cross) but have not got any further with preparing their plan – some from as long ago as 2012 and 2013. This may suggest that estimates of Neighbourhood Planning activity based on how many areas have been designated are not particularly helpful in accurately gauging interest in the programme.

Figure 6.2: Deprivation at neighbourhood level, activity type and activity over time

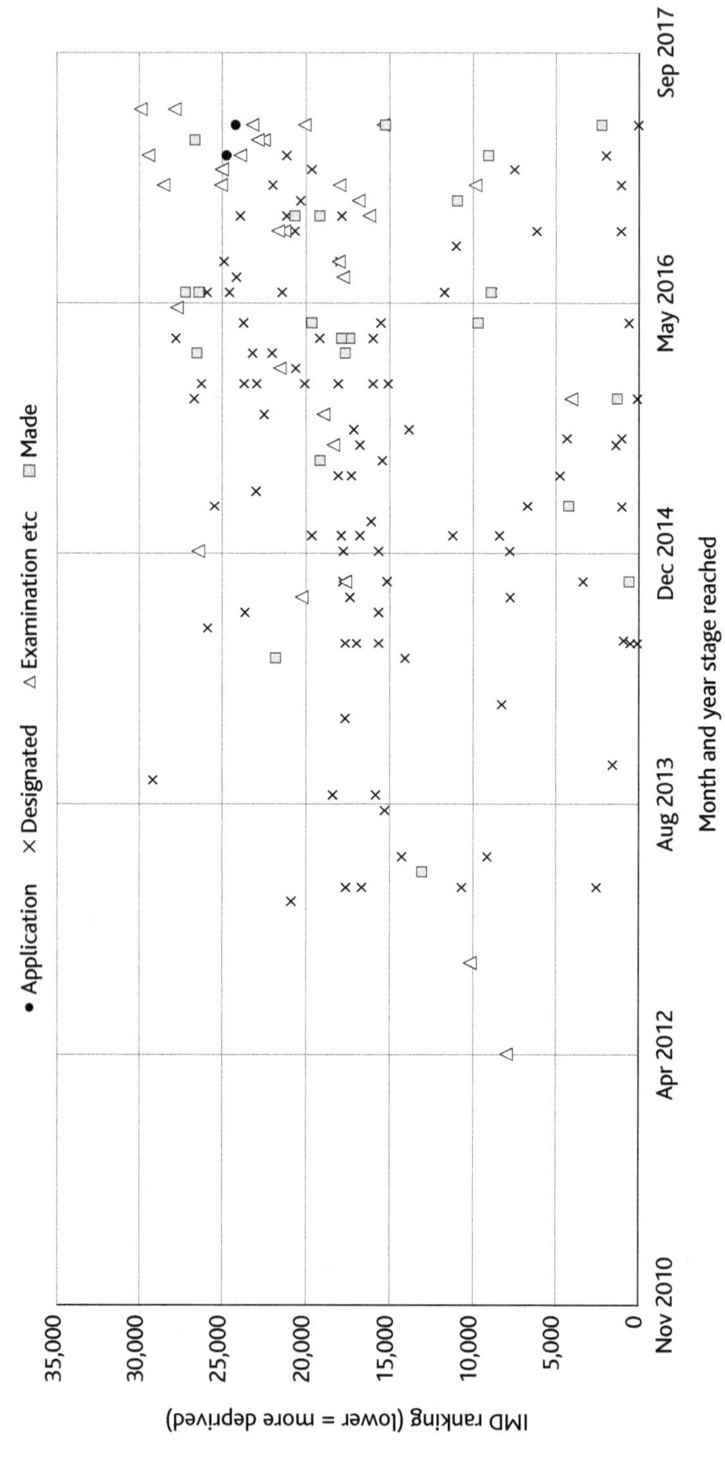

● Application × Designated △ Examination etc □ Made

Figure 6.3 provides more detail regarding how the level of activity has increased, with the Neighbourhood Planning areas divided into IMD quintiles. This shows that activity in quintiles 4 and 5, the top two 'slices' in each column (neighbourhoods within the most deprived 40% of areas in the country), has increased in absolute terms as time progresses but has not increased relative to less deprived areas. This suggests, therefore, that the proposition that as the system beds in, poorer and/or non-parished areas will begin to take up Neighbourhood Planning powers is being borne out, but that the proportion of such areas in comparison to wealthier and/or parished areas may not increase.

So, based on our data, less deprived rural areas are more likely to undertake Neighbourhood Planning than more deprived urban areas, as predicted by Hall (2011) and others, and while an increasing number of more deprived urban areas are beginning the process, the proportion of such is not increasing. As noted earlier, it was to be expected that rural areas would have a head start given their pre-existing institutional architecture, but there was some expectation that urban areas would begin to catch up. To understand more about why this is not the case, we felt we needed to talk to some of those who are working with communities in such urban areas.

Figure 6.3: Activity increasing over time

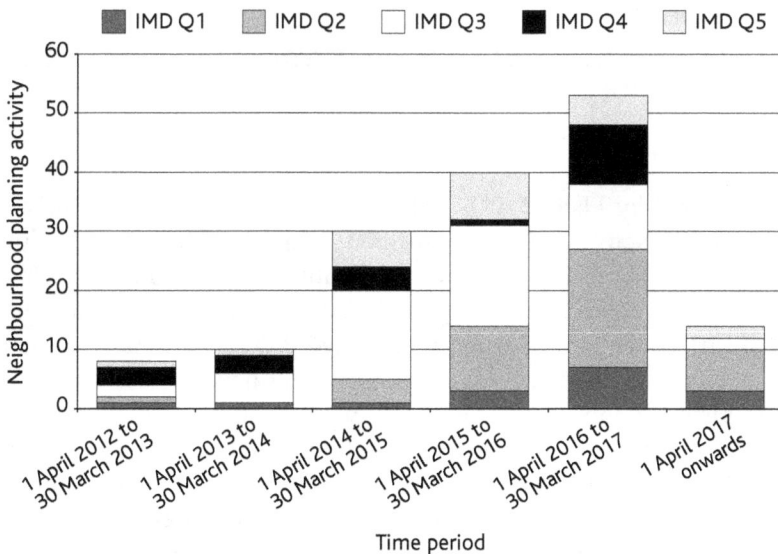

Notes: IMD Q1 = least deprived; IMD Q5 = most deprived.

Qualitative evidence in the North West

We interviewed eight people involved in Neighbourhood Planning in urban parts of the North West. Seven of these were in the most deprived areas of the region, with one in a comparatively less deprived place. Table 6.2 illustrates this, along with the role of the interviewee – either the chair of the Neighbourhood Planning group or a Neighbourhood Plan support worker who had worked, paid by the group through grants from central government, to support the Neighbourhood Planning group in question.

These interviews highlighted several issues that affected the ability of these groups to produce Neighbourhood Plans. Here we discuss three of these issues.

Table 6.2: The interviewees

Neighbourhood Planning area	Role of interviewee	Date of interview
3rd most deprived (Neighbourhood Planning area in the North West)	Chair of Neighbourhood Planning (NP) group	7 June 2018
4th most deprived	NP support worker	7 June 2018
8th most deprived	NP support worker	5 June 2018
9th most deprived	NP support worker	29 May 2018
13th most deprived	NP support worker	17 July 2018
14th most deprived	Chair of NP group	22 June 2018
21st most deprived	Chair of NP group	7 June 2018
112th most deprived	Chair of NP group	18 June 2018

Institutional capacity

As predicted by Hall (2011), a clear issue in deprived urban areas is a lack of capacity for Neighbourhood Planning. This is partly due to the lower levels of volunteering identified by Sutcliffe and Holt (2011). The government suggested that Neighbourhood Planning would motivate more people to get involved in planning for their areas, as they would feel empowered by the new powers they had been given. It appears from our interviews that this is true to some extent – there was evidence that Neighbourhood Planning acted as an invigorating factor to promote interest in place and, consequently, in planning, but sustaining interest is hard – most of those interviewed highlighted the phenomenon of a larger swell of interest (in some cases over 100 people) in the first stages of the Neighbourhood Planning process initially subsiding to a much smaller rump of committed individuals. In the least deprived case study, this rump amounted to a "group of about 20 people, and they are still meeting regularly to discuss different aspects and different issues have arisen in meetings". This level of active membership was exceptional, however, with one Neighbourhood Planning support worker summarising the typical situation as "The reality would be two people are doing most of the work, that's almost always the way".

Despite the rhetoric around a 'light-touch' approach from the government (DCLG, 2012c, p 4), it turns out that producing a Neighbourhood Plan is a long and difficult process. One volunteer expressed her tiredness: "If you've not done it before I can understand how some groups get to a certain point and think you know what? I can't do this…. It's a lot more intense than I thought it was going to be". It is clear from our interviews that getting to the stage this group has, of a draft plan about to go through the public consultation process, takes a great deal of work and support.

Planning knowledge and support

All our interviewees stressed that without the involvement of professional planners, groups would find it all but impossible to proceed. One of the Neighbourhood Planning group chairs was a retired planner, bearing out the findings of others that such individuals are often involved in Neighbourhood Planning groups (Sturzaker and Shaw, 2015; Vigar et al, 2017). This is a factor that appears to vary between wealthier rural areas and more deprived urban areas – a Neighbourhood Planning support worker stated this explicitly:

> 'If you go to a deprived area, there's probably not likely to be a town planner living in the area. But in other areas I've been to … we were sitting around the table with a couple of architects, some engineers, estate agents, there was a planner….'

The knowledge brought by those with experience in or related to planning was both technical in nature – "This is where knowing a bit about how our local government works helps a bit, actually…", and in terms of the tacit 'rules of the planning game' (Lord, 2012). One of our interviewees, a practising planner, tried to sum this up: "There's always an element of that – rules which are embedded culturally, they're not explicit". If there were no planners participating in the process as volunteers, a support worker told us that "the notion that people without professional knowledge of at least something in the field can write a Neighbourhood Plan … is – I kind of think it's laughable". Whether (Neighbourhood) Planning should be a professional activity has been the source of some debate, and Box 6.5 illustrates contrasting views on this from the UK and France.

Box 6.5: Different perspectives on professionalisation and community involvement in planning

A junior minister in the DCLG said, in 2011, 'Planning isn't brain surgery' (quoted in Carpenter, 2011) to illustrate how easy it should be for communities to get involved in Neighbourhood Planning, leading some to express concern about the deprofessionalisation of planning (Lord et al, 2017). The French example can be seen as a stark contrast. The constitution in France 'does not recognise the idea of "community", considered to potentially associate an ethnic or religious minority to a geographical space' (Gardesse and Zetlaoui-Leger, 2017, p 201). Hence, representative democracy remains the dominant model of legitimacy in governance – both in general and as related to planning. Gardesse and Zetlaoui-Leger further note that participation is now mandatory for city council departments in France, but that the notion of the 'planner as expert' is still an important one.

It is because communities have found it essential to involve professionals that the financial package on offer has proved so important, and latterly so controversial. Since the inception of Neighbourhood Planning through the 2011 Act there have been three programmes of grants available to Neighbourhood Planning groups, running from 2013–15, 2015–18 and 2018–22 respectively. The 2015–18 programme offered basic grants of £9,000, which all Neighbourhood Planning groups could apply for. These could be topped up with additional support of up to £15,000, plus additional technical support, if groups were in urban or more deprived areas. The latter top-ups have been removed in the 2018–22 package, to be replaced by additional support for Neighbourhood Planning groups that are proposing more housing. This is in line with the ongoing rhetorical emphasis of the UK government on addressing the 'housing crisis' (Watts, 2017) as discussed in Chapter 1, but was bemoaned by one of our interviewees as being reflective of the government's "one-dimensional approach to planning … it's all about London, London's housing crisis".

The removal of this support was uniformly agreed by our interviewees to lead to problems for deprived urban Neighbourhood Planning groups – most of them argued that more support, not less, was needed, and they suggested that it was likely that fewer deprived areas would now progress Neighbourhood Plans, exacerbating the imbalance discussed previously. One of the Neighbourhood Forums featuring in the research has now withdrawn from the process as without the additional funding it will not be possible to produce a Neighbourhood Plan. The volunteer who was interviewed from that Forum also highlighted intense political opposition to the Neighbourhood Plan from the Labour Party, the party in control of that local authority. This opposition from politicians, specifically from the Labour Party, was highlighted by a number of other interviewees.

Democratic issues and tensions

In seven of the eight interviews we undertook with Neighbourhood Planning volunteers and workers, opposition and resistance to Neighbourhood Planning from elected politicians was highlighted as an issue. In all but the least deprived outlier case study this opposition was from Labour politicians, in some cases holding senior positions in the cabinets of the local authorities. The opposition manifested itself in various ways, including encouraging party members to resign from the Neighbourhood Forum, opposing the designation of Neighbourhood Forums both officially (formally objecting during the consultation phase) and unofficially (encouraging Local Planning Authority officers to reject designations), and publicly denigrating Neighbourhood Planning as "an unnecessary level of democracy".

Our interviewees identified a number of reasons for this opposition – some explicit, others implicit. One Neighbourhood Planning group chair observed that a councillor had expressed the view that "sometimes my worry about Neighbourhood Forums is it becomes a clique, and they're deciding what the community want". There are concerns about the democratic legitimacy of Neighbourhood Forums (Davoudi and Cowie, 2013), in terms of how they are constituted and whether they can be seen to be representative, but it is important to remember that Neighbourhood Planning is not emerging into a vacuum. There is a long-standing critique over lack of participation in the extant English planning system (Davies, 2001), which Neighbourhood Planning was in part intended to address (DCLG, 2010c), and as one of our interviewees put it, "how you could argue a Neighbourhood Planning is less democratic than a Local Plan is actually beyond comprehension to me". One interviewee pointed out the checks and balances in the Neighbourhood Planning system, and concluded that opposition to Neighbourhood Planning on the grounds of legitimacy was "a load of nonsense".

Indeed, several of our interviewees took the opportunity to contrast what they saw as "well organised, very democratic, very well run" Neighbourhood Planning processes with an older, more established set of governance processes that they felt elected politicians were more comfortable with – essentially, being elected every four years and thus having a mandate to represent their constituents. These elected members appeared to view Neighbourhood Planning as "a threat to their power". One Neighbourhood Planning group chair summed up the position well: "I think some people are a bit power crazy". As noted earlier, these interviews were mostly carried out in areas dominated by the Labour Party, but opposition to Neighbourhood Planning on these grounds was not an exclusively party political issue – in the least deprived area, our interviewee noted that "some of the [Conservative] councillors didn't like the idea that somebody else was going to make the decisions".

If this resistance to losing control is common in different areas, an unanswered question from this research is why politicians in more deprived urban areas have successfully limited the take-up of Neighbourhood Planning, whereas in less deprived rural areas they have not. The answer may lie in a return to the theoretical arguments about power and domination in planning, and the ability of certain groups to use planning systems to their advantage more effectively than others (Sturzaker, 2010).

Conclusion

This chapter has focused on experiences of community-led urban governance in England, first, through a historical review of various initiatives and schemes – some led by the state (often referred to as 'top-down') and some led by communities themselves ('bottom-up'). This was accompanied by a brief discussion of some examples of similar experiences in other countries. Together those reviews identify a number of common theoretical and practical issues with community-led governance.

The first is one of community capacity – these approaches rely on volunteers, who have, or can be trained to, some level of expertise in skills such as bureaucracy, communication and – crucially – planning. This is a challenge in many places (Moore and McKee, 2012; Moore,

2014), and particularly so in more deprived and/or urban areas. This is problematic both for the practical success of community-led urban governance and in terms of equity between and within places – if there is insufficient capacity, then both the processes and outcomes of governance practices may be biased against the poor. Some have argued that capacity need not be intrinsic and can be built by introducing better participation processes (Docherty et al, 2001); indeed, the localism reforms in England were partly justified on this basis.

The second issue is related to the first, and it is one of power, along at least two axes – in what we could call 'intra-local' terms, that localism and decentralisation merely further empower the already powerful (Brown and Chin, 2013; Jacobs and Manzi, 2013; Bennett, 2017), and in 'inter-local' terms, that the notion of empowerment is just that – a notion, a form of tokenism which, in fact, does not involve any real devolution of power (Catney et al, 2014; Ludwig and Ludwig, 2014).

A third, again related, issue is that of the role played by other actors in the process – elected politicians and professional planners, for example. The extent to which such actors seek to 'frame' and control the activities of communities as opposed to facilitating and enabling them appears to vary from place to place. In some examples, planners remain clearly in charge (Brown and Chin, 2013; Gardesse and Zetlaoui-Leger, 2017); in others, elected politicians seek to suppress community activities if they are not in line with 'strategic' priorities (Mooney and Fyfe, 2006; Sturzaker and Shaw, 2015)

The Neighbourhood Planning experience in England appears to be exemplifying these issues. Our evidence from the urban North West supports the picture found at national level and in other localities. Neighbourhood Planning is primarily being taken up by wealthier people in more rural areas (Parker and Salter, 2016); professional planners are key to its success or otherwise (Parker et al, 2015); and the processes of Neighbourhood Planning can be dominated by the powerful (Vigar et al, 2017).

A final, overarching issue we wish to briefly touch on is one we touched on in Chapter 1 – the neoliberal critique. Because initiatives such as CLTs, development trusts, Neighbourhood Planning, and so on 'are in part filling the gaps in service provision left by state shrinkage' (Healey, 2015, p 11), they can be criticised on the grounds that they are both produced by and enabling, or at least not challenging, the neoliberal cutting back of the state (Hickson, 2013). Conversely, they can be seen as more radical and experimental changes to governance approaches, 'deepening' democracy and challenging the sort of 'city boss' mentality we heard evidence of in our interviews in the North West of England (Crisp, 2015). Our view is that these positions are not mutually exclusive – that it is possible to criticise and challenge 'austerity' and the swingeing reductions in state spending it presages while still recognising that activity emerging from and with communities may be progressive in nature and worth exploring and encouraging if it is. We agree that local activity can 'challenge rather than entrench inequalities between and within places and regions' (Featherstone et al, 2012, p 180), and that it is worthwhile continuing to look for 'new ethical and political spaces in amongst the neoliberal canvas' (Williams et al, 2014, p 2798) at community level, and indeed, elsewhere.

Note

[1] See http://dclgapps.communities.gov.uk/imd/idmap.html

7

Conclusion:
Rescaling urban governance

The overall aim of this book has been to analyse the cumulative effects of recent reforms (2010–onwards) to city governance in the United Kingdom, explicitly considering whether they can be said to be progressive in nature. We had three objectives: first, to present in one easily accessible volume comprehensive yet concise analysis of results of the changes to city governance that have been seen in the UK since 2010, at a range of scales. Second, to consolidate and disseminate research in this field and new thinking about the overall implications of this research, to facilitate informed discussion and debate about changes to governance practices and the outcomes of those changes. Finally, to challenge policy and practice in the field of city governance in the UK and internationally, strengthening the evidence base for policy-makers to take decisions regarding reforms to governance practices.

This chapter summarises the preceding chapters, bringing together a discussion around a number of key themes, including reflections on the power relationships inherent within governance approaches (that is, 'who wins?'); the success or otherwise of attempts to deal with contemporary issues such as housing, transport and jobs provision; the possible implications of Brexit and other 'external' changes; and alternative forms and modes of localism. It also synthesises international reflections, both in terms of how the UK might learn from elsewhere in how it moves forward, and what other places might learn from the UK.

Planning, localism and institutional change

Planning reform and state spatial rescaling

The opening chapter of this book used a number of key topics to set the context for the subsequent discussion. The first of these was the 'grand challenges' facing cities around the world, including in the UK. Perhaps the most significant of these is globalisation, which has had profound consequences for much of the world. Many of these consequences can be conceived positively, but there is little doubt that the structural changes to economies in 'Western' countries such as the UK and USA had, and continue to have, major negative ramifications for many cities. The 2008 global financial crisis highlighted many of these problems.

The second key topic in the Introduction was a series of conceptual questions that have framed our analyses. Here we considered 'who governs?' (Dahl, 1961), but emphasising that today this question requires broadening to include a scalar issue, looking across levels of government (MacLeod and Jones, 2011). We acknowledged the position that relational rather than territorial understandings of governance are important (Cox, 2013), but argued that, given the continuing importance of the spatial, both as an imaginary (Salet et al, 2015) and in practical terms as the mechanism by which the UK is organised and governed, we would take a territorial approach to the organisation of the book.

Third, we discussed three 'policy preoccupations' that dominate the approach taken by successive UK governments – jobs, housing and transport – and the tendency for the approach taken in all three instances to be one of numbers, that is, increasing the number of jobs and houses and providing more roads, train lines, etc. The failure to satisfactorily do this has been one of the arguments behind the rise in calls for more decentralisation, devolution or localism in the UK, and we placed this rise in the context of a similar pattern elsewhere (Rodriguez-Pose and Gill, 2003). We briefly analysed the particular 'brand' of localism adopted by the UK government to set the context for the discussion in subsequent chapters.

Finally we introduced the theoretical perspectives we have adopted throughout the book to help us analyse the 2010–onwards reforms to urban governance in the UK. These perspectives include how and why power is used; the concept of *strategic-relational approaches*; and the entrepreneurial turn in urban governance.

Devolution: A patchwork quilt of planning reform

Chapter 2 looked at the national scale, considering the peculiarities of the UK's constitutional arrangements – there is no written constitution in the UK, which means that any devolution, whether to national, sub-national, regional, sub-regional, local or community levels, is contingent on the approval of the UK parliament. Any devolved powers are merely 'lent' from the UK to other levels, which means the UK parliament and government retain a great deal of power. Another peculiarity is the lack of an English parliament or other governance structures to match those in the 'devolved nations' of Scotland, Wales and Northern Ireland. In the absence of such structures, the UK parliament is that which issues legislation to deal with English matters – we discussed the proposed alternatives for this, and the reasons they have not taken root in the same way as the devolved nations. The impacts of 'austerity' (the significant cuts in state expenditure instituted in the UK since 2010) were then identified.

Following this, Chapter 2 reflected on the approaches to urban governance in the devolved nations: Scotland, Wales and Northern Ireland. This covered their historical relationship with the UK parliament and the particular policy areas that were devolved to their respective parliaments and assembly. While it is difficult at present to make the case that devolution has led to significantly different outcomes in any of the three devolved nations, we suggest that the tentative steps towards divergence in Income Tax made by the Scottish government (Sim, 2018) may, in the future, lead to a divergence in inequality.

Chapter 2 concluded with a reflection on the 'butterfly effect' and the argument that in pulling out the stops to avoid Scottish independence in 2014, the then-Prime Minister David Cameron set in chain a series of events that led to the UK voting to leave the EU. That argument suggests that the greater powers, including over taxation, promised to Scottish voters before the 2014 Scottish independence referendum led to calls for similar powers for English regions and a wider discussion of *sovereignty*. The increasing influence of UKIP led to Cameron committing to a referendum on membership of the EU if the Conservative Party won the 2015 General Election, which it did. The consequences of that decision have been discussed in depth elsewhere, but one possible outcome of relevance here could be a renewal of calls for Scottish independence – both because 62% of Scottish voters wanted to remain, and because 'freedom' from the EU opens up the possibility of greater policy divergence between England and the devolved nations in some areas, which may be resisted by the UK government (Brouillet and Mullen, 2018).

Replacing the regions: The evolution of English sub-national reform

In Chapter 3 we explored the history of subnational planning and governance reforms in England, including the enduring 'North–South divide' in the economy that has informed successive waves of reform. While the 1997–2010 'New' Labour governments' preferred approach to subnational governance was to use the scale of the eight

GORs regions, the 2010–onwards Conservative-led governments have preferred the scales 'above' and 'below' this – the supra-regional and city regional.

The Northern Powerhouse is the best known example of the former, and as with other government policy initiatives, it reflects the policy preoccupations noted previously – particularly transport and the economy. The Northern Powerhouse, while deliberately undefined (a prime example of a 'fuzzy boundary'; cf Haughton et al, 2010), centres on the urban areas of the North, particularly the 'Core Cities'. Other places are expected to benefit from the 'trickle-out' of any economic growth that might occur as a result of these cities agglomerating. The Northern Powerhouse is in part predicated on the Core Cities cooperating with each other instead of competing – but there is little evidence of such cooperation so far, in part due to the informality of the governance of the Northern Powerhouse. There is, for example, no statutory plan that might focus investment in specific industrial sectors in specific locations.

One trend that is noticeable in recent years, no doubt a consequence of the government's antipathy towards the imposition of formal 'top-down' governance modes, is that of non-state actors taking a lead role in sub-national activity. Notable examples include the RTPI and IPPR and their *Great North Plan* initiative, and the *Northern Powerhouse Partnership* chaired by ex-Chancellor George Osborne.

Local Enterprise Partnerships are a peculiar mix of top-down and bottom-up, in that the government mandated that they should be business-led and that every local authority must belong to one, but there was considerable local discretion in their size and configuration. This led to both a considerable variety in terms of size, and a perhaps unsurprising replication of pre-existing arrangements. A further predictable consequence was that areas that had a history of working at this scale were more successful in doing so, leading to an issue that recurs throughout this book – spatially uneven development. Another recurring theme is a sense of rapid policy experimentation on the part of the UK government, as LEPs, while still in existence, were superseded as the preferred drivers of sub-national devolution by combined authorities.

City regions and the cities within them: Connecting two overlapping scales

Chapter 4 focused on the series of experiments that have played out since 2010 as regards city-regional (and city) governance. These have included directly elected mayors at city level (adopted in only two cities), combined authorities, police and crime commissioners (PCCs), and directly elected mayors at city region level, incorporating the powers of PCCs in those areas.

A number of themes are reflected across these various experiments. One is the tension between different tiers of governance that each claim some form of democratic legitimacy – a tension replicated at community level (Sturzaker and Gordon, 2017). At the city region level this tension is illustrated through the 'spare mayor' in Liverpool, which now has one of the only examples of a city-level elected mayor operating in tandem with a city region mayor. Even without this duplication, arguments have taken place between city-regional and local authorities over matters such as housing policy. A second recurring theme is that city-regional devolution heavily features 'deal-making founded upon territorial competition and negotiation' (O'Brien and Pike, 2015, p R14), with each devolution deal being individually negotiated between central and local governments. This, perhaps inevitably, has led to a great deal of variability between these deals. Linked to this is a third theme: devolved powers being contingent on local areas accepting the imposition of new forms of governance, for example, a directly elected mayor. A final theme is that the citizens who are the subjects of these various experiments are markedly unenthusiastic about them. For example, in referendums to decide whether to have an elected mayor at city level, only residents of Bristol voted 'yes', on the lowest turnout of any of the referendums.

The turnouts in the elections for city region mayors were slightly better, although still below that of most local elections. Once in place, there has been some attempt on the part of several city region mayors to go beyond the focus on the Core Cities that has characterised much of the rhetoric around sub-national governance for the last 20 years or more, with some of the limited funding at their disposal going towards smaller towns. This attempt to include non-metropolitan areas and recognise the patterns of spatial inequality that characterise England is something we return to in Chapter 5.

Local authorities: Powerhouses or scapegoats?

Chapter 5 examined the roles and powers of local authorities since 2010 that, across this period, have often been cast as the 'piggy in the middle' as the government has emphasised policy activity at the levels immediately above and below. Even so, the local authority retains an important role, and a number of key themes emerged.

Set against a background of austerity, in which some local authorities have seen their operating budgets cut by half, the chapter explored how, in what John (2014) describes as resilience in the face of claims of terminal decline, local authorities are finding ways of adapting to the limits austerity has placed on them. In particular, the chapter identifies an increasing reliance on the entrepreneurial thesis, for example, using 'enterprise zones' (last seen in the 1980s) to prioritise economic development, and often focusing on 'green growth'. In doing so, as in the 1980s, there remains a pragmatic reliance on central government subsidy to see authorities through more straitened times, which poses the question: is it worth cutting local authority funding if they will simply require support by other policy activity? The chapter also considers other more radical approaches to urban austerity including what has become known as the 'Preston model', a return to the municipal socialism seen in the 19th century. This identifies a key theme: encouraging the use of local services and contractors as a means to generate positive economic feedback cycles.

The chapter concluded with suggestions that the period since 2010 has left local authorities at financial breaking point, illustrated by Northamptonshire County Council declaring that it is effectively insolvent. Thus, while we argued that there are examples of local authority resilience, we questioned the longevity of such.

Community-led governance: Opportunities and constraints

Chapter 6 examined some of the ways in which, post-2010, communities have been given powers to plan for their own futures, with a particular focus on Neighbourhood Planning as one of the main 'community rights' brought forward as part of the Localism Act 2011. This new form of planning was designed to allow local residents the opportunity to designate their own Plan for their area which, if passed by referendum, would form part of their local authority's Statutory Development Plan – that is, it would have a bearing on planning decisions. However, the chapter highlighted that by having to broadly conform to 'strategic' planning principles, there are limits to what local residents can do with their Neighbourhood Plan.

Through new data presented in this book, we note a clear link between deprivation and the extent to which Neighbourhood Planning is undertaken, with less deprived areas more likely to engage with the Neighbourhood Plan-making process. This work fits with Hall's (2011, p 60) argument that those more likely to engage with Neighbourhood Planning were 'well-meaning, well educated people living in nice places – mostly rural – with time on their hands' – something that can be further seen in terms of those who engage with the Plan-making process in practical terms. Further reflecting Hall's predictions, we found that while there was often a rump of people within a community interested in Neighbourhood Planning, typically work was concentrated in a few hands that were, more often than not, those with professional experience. This again favoured wealthier areas, as the grant funding available to fund professional planning support is conditional and thus, without inherent expertise or conforming to government priorities (that is, housebuilding), areas already predisposed to not engaging with Neighbourhood Planning may find themselves even less likely to do so.

Finally, the chapter also noted local political opposition to the Neighbourhood Planning process. In doing so we identified a clientelism through which, as communities conduct their own Plan-making process, they become less reliant on local authority-provided services while simultaneously diluting one of the chief sources of local authority power: planning decisions. Ultimately, the chapter argued that while there is undoubted good to be found in the Neighbourhood Planning system, there are clear signs that both local and central government are reluctant to loosen their control over communities.

Synthesis

In this section we look across our chapters, and consequently across the different tiers of government or governance we have discussed, to identify common themes and issues.

Interactions and overlaps between levels of devolution

A recurring theme at every scale has been that, perhaps because of the 'competitive' approach emphasised by the UK government, different tiers of governance are overlapping in ways that are having negative effects on the success of localism. This is witnessed at a range of scales, including that of the city region vs the city – as discussed in Chapter 4 – exemplified when both Liverpool City Council and the Liverpool City Region LEP both bid for Regional Growth Fund monies in 2012. The 'spare mayors' (Thorp, 2018) duplication of leadership in Bristol and Liverpool is another example, also illustrating the rapidity of policy experimentation we discuss shortly.

Perhaps surprisingly, the city region scale is also having an impact on the community scale. One of the interviews we undertook for

Chapter 6 was revealing about how the Greater Manchester Spatial Framework (GMSF) was all-consuming for the local authorities within Greater Manchester, such that they were unable to devote resources to other aspects of their service: "It was quite difficult to find any neighbourhood level data on quite important things like housing affordability, like quality and condition of housing. It doesn't exist, and they said they didn't have the money to make it exist, to go out and do that work, or pay somebody to go out and do that work … they and the other local authorities are not doing [It …] because they are all thinking about the GMSF."

Too much Brexit and not enough anything else

Across the period since 2010 there are two distinct phases to devolution and localism agenda with a distinct point that marks the change between those phases: 23 June 2016, and the beginning of the Brexit process.

Between 2010 and 2016 the government's reform agenda developed at a rapid pace. After the EU referendum, Cameron's resignation and May's installation as Prime Minister, this rate of change slowed down markedly. Some of this could be ascribed to May's wish to move away from Cameron's agenda – epitomised by her sacking of George Osborne, the chief architect of much of the city-regional agenda. However, May's tenure as Prime Minister will not be known for any overwhelming domestic reform but rather, one that was (ultimately terminally) consumed by the Brexit process.

Across this period, and in dogged pursuit of this agenda, historians will likely point to a number of self-inflicted wounds that made May's task more difficult. Somewhere near the top of this will surely be the decision to call the 2017 General Election. Ostensibly framed as a vehicle to strengthen May's parliamentary majority, and buoyed by both early polling and local election results some six weeks before, the election was a disaster, with May losing her majority, leaving her government unable to pass legislation on its own. Thus, so as to avoid embarrassing defeats, the rate at which new policy was brought forward slowed.

Austerity trumps everything else

Without doubt, one of the major thematic issues across all of the chapters has been the period of fiscal austerity instigated by the UK coalition government in response to rising public borrowing in the aftermath of the 2008 financial crisis and the 'austerity urbanism' (Peck, 2012) that followed. There is a convincing argument that local government – heavily reliant on central government for its funding – was disproportionately negatively affected, and wherever you look in the post-2010 devolution agenda, it is impossible to miss the effects of these cuts.

As discussed in Chapters 5 and 6, austerity had profound effects on the funding choices and priorities made by local authorities, with many forced to pare back services to the point that only statutory services remained. Here, there is evidence which suggests that, in doing so, these cuts more heavily affected the places that were already more deprived, and thus were more adversely affected by the loss of essential services. At the neighbourhood scale, Chapter 6 also suggested that these cuts have also affected the ability of communities to bring forward Neighbourhood Plans – effectively giving credence to Hall's (2011) prediction that neighbourhood planning would be the preserve of those living in 'nice places'.

Chapters 3 and 4 revealed a sub-national space that is no less affected by this austerity – not least as new institutions such as the metro mayors find themselves tasked with delivery of 'local' services such as policing, fire and some planning functions. In some cases, such as Greater Manchester, the metro mayor also has power over health allocations – leading to questions as to the motivations of central government in devolving political 'hot potatoes', themselves beleaguered by austerity at the national level, to already cash-strapped areas. In the emergence of city-regional devolution, there is a fundamental irony at play in that, after heavily cutting local funding to the point where local authorities would struggle to function, the same person, George Osborne, would then release funding to city regions as a means to close the UK's growth gap. This funding, in the first instance amounting to only £30 million per year across a city region, would barely touch the gap left by the broader local government funding cuts. Therefore, between 2010 and his eventual sacking in 2016, Osborne can be observed taking away with one hand, while modestly giving back with the other.

Poorer are people losing out, and are (seemingly) unhappy with our democracy as they find it

However differently phrased – that is, devolution, localism, decentralisation, and so on – the post-2010 agenda has been principally framed by the government around one thing: an increase in the control that citizens have in the issues that affect them. As state spending, particularly through local government, has been reduced, in some instances citizens have been forced to step in to run services such as libraries (Goulding, 2013). So David Cameron's 'Big Society' is taking root in some places – but this appears to be out of necessity rather than any great desire on the part of citizens to run their own services.

Since 2010 greater levels of democratic control have been a fairly persistent characteristic of government reform – from independence in Scotland, to metro mayors in city regions, to referenda on Neighbourhood Plans. However, across this book we have charted a persistent public disengagement and dissatisfaction with those machinations. In many cases this took the form of a rejection of proposals of democratic reform or naked apathy in cases where this reform was thrust upon them (for example, in PCC elections). This is something we have seen before. However, usually such apathy tends to revert, or defer, back to the status quo. In other words, for the most part there is little appetite for change.

Therefore, the vote to leave the EU stands out because of its rejection of the status quo. The reasons behind this vote are multitudinous and contested, but there is a broad consensus which suggests at least one root cause can be found in dissatisfaction on the part of the UK's poorer citizens and their increased disconnection from broader growth agendas in a post-industrial and increasingly globalised world. It would be unfair to say that the Conservative-led post-2010 agenda is the sole cause of this phenomena – indeed, these patterns can be seen well into 'New' Labour's term over a decade earlier. However, with the nature of some Conservative policy activity (that is, austerity) making swingeing cuts in those areas, this agenda is, equally, not without blame.

International lessons

Across the chapters of this book, and following the traditions of learning from others that dates back to the very origins of planning discussion (Abercrombie, 1910), we have drawn on international examples from across the world including Europe, the Americas and Asia. Across these examples we have seen that sub-national policy in the UK is not being developed in a vacuum. Indeed, we can observe elsewhere that other countries (for example, France and South Korea) are beginning to push back against the overwhelming centralisation of their global capitals. Here we have also seen that, in light of the emergence of a new economic orthodoxy which extols the benefits of agglomeration (Pike et al, 2016), these countries are also (re)turning to metropolitan thinking as part of this pushback.

Although there is much we have learned from those international examples, one of the most persistent themes is that all that glitters is not gold. Much of this 'good practice' is often beset with similar issues to those faced in the UK's policy agenda. In other words, our issues are far from unique. If there are common denominators for where policy broadly works well, they take a few forms. The first is relative stability. What characterises most of the European examples, in particular, is the longevity of local programmes where, unfettered by persistent top-down change to the same extent as in the UK, they have had the time to establish, flourish and develop solutions to their strategic issues. The second is that where good practice emerges, it does so through clear and ambitious leadership in those scenarios. In the book we make much of the entrepreneurial turn – but we also discuss policy entrepreneurship (Kingdon, 1984), in which leaders are not afraid to deploy their own political capital in pursuit of a worthwhile goal. Against the backdrop of austerity, local leaders are faced with a choice between either retreating into the preservation of existing activity or seeking out ways to innovate under those conditions. This is what Hambleton and Howard (2012) term 'place-based leadership'. In the case of this place-based leadership, and policy entrepreneurship, a degree of risk-taking is required, and it is where this happens that policy makes its largest, and most worthwhile, leaps. The third is that a confrontational or conflictual relationship between different tiers of government tends not to lead to good outcomes for people. This might appear to be stating the obvious, but it is worth being explicit that the adversarial approach to local authorities from the UK government that has characterised the period since 2010 is both profoundly unhelpful and, in our experience, not typical of other countries. Phrases being used by senior ministers and the Prime Minister such as local authority planners being 'the last bastions of communism' (*Birmingham Post*, 2010) and 'enemies of enterprise' (Watt, 2011) do not suggest an approach that is open to collaboration. Similarly, the tendency to treat the relationship between the local state and civil society as a 'zero-sum' game (Lowndes and Pratchett, 2012, p 32) is both demonstrably false and not mirrored in other places. Accepting that elected local authorities must play a significant part in the governance of our cities, and can do so at the same time as communities, would be a significant step forward.

It is perhaps harder to identify lessons *for* other places from the UK experience. As much of our discussion in this book makes clear, our analysis of the 'localism experiment' that the UK has been running since 2010 has reached far from positive conclusions. In contrast to the high-blown rhetoric that accompanied the introduction of the localism reforms, from the 2010 'Coalition Agreement' onwards, those reforms have not, in general, helped 'people come together to make life better' or built a more 'free, fair and responsible society' (HM Government, 2010a, p 7). It is hard to identify lessons that others might wish to adopt from the sub-national, city-regional or local authority scales – although amidst the broader adversarial environment there are innovative examples of how some cities are engaging with their core–periphery relationship in a positive way. The community scale is where there may be some scope for learning, despite the flaws in Neighbourhood Planning that we discuss in Chapter 6. In principle, it cannot be a bad thing to give communities more say over their future. There is some evidence that introducing statutory plans at the neighbourhood scale, which carry real weight in decision-making, *does* empower people and build capacity for further action. A lesson both for the UK and elsewhere, however, is that trying to do this 'on the cheap', without significant resources to support communities, both financial and professional, does not work – and as others have found, without such support, Neighbourhood Plans simply do not happen (cf Parker et al, 2015).

Rescaling urban governance: A problem-solving panacea?

The book brings together in one place analysis of recent reforms to city governance from the national to the community scale, analysing for the first time the effects of these reforms in an overarching way, explicitly considering whether they can be said to be progressive in nature. Above all, the central theme of this book has been that from neighbourhoods through to supra-regions, while the government has talked about closing divides, often we have seen those divides being widened. In short, places that are richer are tending to do well, and places that are poorer are tending to do badly. It would be unfair to declare the entire period as either a 'success' or 'failure', but it is certain the reforms have not succeeded on their own terms.

There are two broad themes that characterise the nature of this growing gap across all the scales we discuss in this book. The first is that collaboration and coherent governance is important – and anywhere that can demonstrate greater levels of coherent working within, and between, its institutions is better placed to capitalise on reform. This can be seen in Neighbourhood Planning, where centuries-old parish councils are better placed to instigate their own Neighbourhood Plan, through to city regions where places such as Greater Manchester, which has a long history of collaborative governance, is able to steal a march on its competitors. The second is that within this, personalities and leadership counts for a great deal. The period since 2010 has been one of negotiation and deal-making, and we have seen that effective leadership can be vital in extracting the most from those processes. Moreover, in an era that encourages collaboration across different scales, being able to manage competing expectations and outcomes is vital. Those who have failed to rise to this challenge have seen their efforts wither – often taken away by a government with little appetite to act as peacemaker.

Across this period, austerity has been a near-overbearing influence. Reflecting the theme of growing gaps, it is often those most affected by the UK's urban challenges that have been hardest hit. The result has been that all the policy 'frills' have been cut away in favour of core function. The irony of this is that, in a decade of rapid-fire policy experimentation, often those places have had little time to deal with, let alone maximise the opportunities from, the changes that have been thrust on them.

While we have seen devolution and localism as rhetorical weapons across this period, much of this has lacked one key element: fiscal autonomy. Thus, while local areas have enjoyed new powers, they often lack the freedom to make full use of them as their finances are so heavily constrained. This is not an issue that is isolated to England; it is something that is also observed in the devolved nations over a reasonably sustained period of time (since 1998).

In the latter half of this period there has been an elephant in the room: *Brexit*. Its effects have the potential to touch everything we discuss in this book, and both the short- and long-term consequences remain, as yet, unclear. However, since 2016 it has had the effect of paralysing government. This, in a country that is largely still run through top-down policy-making, has caused reform to slow down to the point that it has effectively stopped – for example, the borrowing powers for the Greater Manchester Combined Authority included in primary legislation have yet to be brought into force. The vote itself emphasises some of the fundamental challenges we discuss in this book: not least the growing gap between the 'haves' and 'have-nots'. As we conclude this book, the way forward remains unclear, and it remains to be seen who will govern the post-Brexit space.

What we can say is that there are plenty of challenges for them to deal with, and that those challenges will, if anything, become more profound. If the UK leaves the EU, the so-called 'left-behind' places are likely to suffer the most from the consequent damage to the economy and loss of EU structural funds; if Brexit is avoided, it seems likely, as many have warned, that the people living in those places will feel betrayed and thus even more left-behind.

The situation in the UK may therefore be particularly acute, but urban areas around the world are facing unprecedented challenges as we move towards the middle of the 21st century. The pressures of climate change, migration, an ageing society, resource shortages, and so on demand new approaches to how cities are governed. The UK, specifically England, is at the cutting edge of experimentation with regard to new models of governance. This book presents for the first time an analysis of the last 10 years of this experimentation from 'top to bottom', that is, from the national to the community scales. It has explored how the governance framework for and of cities has changed in recent years, and what effect this has had on the distribution of power and resources within cities. It has concluded that the 'localism' reforms have had, in aggregate, regressive outcomes, making the rich richer and the poor poorer.

Our findings are therefore of relevance anywhere where populist politicians propose taking power away from elites and 'redistributing' it – an increasingly common phenomenon, and as we have pointed out several times, one that is hard to argue with. Indeed, we, of course, agree with the notion of empowerment, and giving people more control over the places where they live. We have throughout this book sought to find evidence that localism works in that way, and have found some glimmers of hope – but we have repeatedly seen that hope snuffed out by the old bugbears of power and money. We remain steadfast in our belief that localism *can* be a progressive force, but not if accompanied by the extreme programme of deregulation and cuts in public spending we have witnessed in the UK. Without strong control and support from the state, less wealthy individuals, communities, towns, cities and regions are less able to take advantage of the tools that are available to them. In such an atmosphere, the most powerful almost inevitably consolidate their position.

Epilogue

One of the persistent themes of this book is that, despite being written during a period of enormous political change for the UK, the issues that have characterised urban governance have remained remarkably static across three successive Conservative-led governments. As we were preparing the final manuscript for the publishers, Boris Johnson's success in the Conservative Party leadership election meant that his would be the fourth administration to govern the UK since 2010.

Johnson's inaugural speech as Prime Minister on the steps of Downing Street gave little clue as to his plans in relation to urban governance – but four days later, a speech in Manchester's Museum of Science and Industry gave us an idea of what the UK's towns and cities might expect under his administration. In his speech Johnson re-affirmed his support for 'HS3', promising a high-speed rail line to link Manchester and Leeds. For towns and cities, Johnson promised more 'self-governing'. If this sounds familiar, then it should. It is no coincidence that this speech was delivered in the same building as George Osborne launched his vision for the Northern Powerhouse five years earlier. Amidst the political obsession with, and paralysis caused by, Brexit, electoral politics moves apace and during the course of concluding and proofing this book we have seen Theresa May ousted as Prime Minister and replaced by Boris Johnson. The calling of a general election for December 2019 means we may well see another new Prime Minister by the time it is published.

British politics is running in overdrive, and at a pace which is hard to keep up with. However, despite this frenetic environment we can conclude knowing that the relevance of the issues we discuss throughout this book are not diminished. Rather, the opposite – whatever the outcome of the imminent general election, and subsequently of Brexit, the long-term questions regarding localism and power are not going away.

References

Abercrombie, P. (1910) 'VIENNA: PARTS I AND II: "Illustrated"', *Town Planning Review*, 1(3): 220.

Abercrombie, P. (1944) *Greater London Plan*, London: University of London Press.

ACRE (Action with Communities in Rural England) (2014) *Community Planning*, Cirencester: ACRE.

Aghion, P., Besley, T., Browne, J., Caselli, F., et al (2013) *Investing for Prosperity: Skills, Infrastructure and Innovation. Report of the LSE Growth Commission*, London: London School of Economics and Political Science.

Aldred, R. (2012) 'Governing transport from welfare state to hollow state', *Transport Policy*, 23: 95–102.

Alexander, A. (2009) *Britain's New Towns: Garden Cities to Sustainable Communities*, London and New York: Routledge.

Allmendinger, P. and Haughton, G. (2007) 'The fluid scales and scope of UK spatial planning', *Environment and Planning A*, 39: 1478–96.

Amin, A. and Thrift, N. (1995) 'Institutional issues for the European Regions: From markets and plans to socioeconomics and powers of association', *Economy and Society*, 24(1): 41–66.

Amsden, A.H. (1992) *Asia's Next Giant: South Korea and Late Industrialization*, Oxford: Oxford University Press [On Demand].

Anderson, G. and Gallagher, J. (2018) 'Intergovernmental Relations in Canada and the United Kingdom', in M. Keating and G. Laforest (eds) *Constitutional Politics and the Territorial Question in Canada and the United Kingdom*, Cham, Switzerland: Palgrave Macmillan, pp 19–46.

Anderson, J. (2018) 'Why I resigned from the Northern Powerhouse Partnership', CityMetric [Online], Available from: www.citymetric.com/transport/joe-anderson-why-i-resigned-northern-powerhouse-partnership-4387 (Accessed 11 January 2019).

Arnstein, S.R. (1969) 'A ladder of citizen participation', *Journal of the American Planning Association*, 35(4): 216–24.

Ashcroft, E. (2018) 'Bristol Arena will not be in the city centre after Marvin Rees confirms decision', BristolLive [Online], Available from: www.bristolpost.co.uk/news/bristol-news/bristol-arena-not-city-centre-1968999 (Accessed 24 December 2018).

Ashkanasy, N.M., Trevor-Roberts, E. and Earnshaw, L. (2002) 'The Anglo cluster: Legacy of the British Empire', *Journal of World Business*, 37(1): 28–39.

Bache, I. and Flinders, M. (2004) 'Multi-level governance and the study of the British state', *Public Policy and Administration*, 19(1): 31–51.

Bailey, N. (2003) 'Local strategic partnerships in England', *Planning Theory and Practice*, 4(4): 443–557.

Bale, T. (2016) '"Banging on about Europe": How the Eurosceptics got their referendum' [Online], Available from: http://blogs.lse.ac.uk/politicsandpolicy/banging-on-about-europe-how-the-eurosceptics-got-their-referendum/ (Accessed 21 January 2019).

Banting, K. and McEwen, N. (2018) 'Inequality, Redistribution and Decentralization in Canada and the United Kingdom', in M. Keating and G. Laforest (eds) *Constitutional Politics and the Territorial Question in Canada and the United Kingdom*, Cham, Switzerland: Palgrave Macmillan, pp 105–34.

Barber, B.R. (2013) *If Mayors Ruled the World: Dysfunctional Nations, Rising Cities*, New Haven, CT: Yale University Press.

Barlow, M., Sir (1940) *Report [of the] Royal Commission on the Distribution of the Industrial Population*, London: HMSO.

Bartels, L.M. (2008) *Unequal Democracy: The Political Economy of the New Gilded Age*, Princeton, NJ: Princeton University Press.

Bartlett, D. (2012a) 'Liverpool Council passes motion to adopt elected mayor system – Re-read David Bartlett's updates from the vote', *Liverpool Daily Post* [Online], Available from: www.liverpoolecho.co.uk/news/liverpool-news/liverpool-council-passes-motion-adopt-3352161 (Accessed 21 January 2019).

Bartlett, D. (2012b) 'Government snub for Liverpool Mayor Joe Anderson's £52m economic development plans', *Liverpool Echo*, 15 November [Online], Available from: www.liverpoolecho.co.uk/news/liverpool-news/government-snub-liverpool-mayor-joe-3329778 (Accessed 21 January 2019).

Barton, H., Grant, M. and Guise, R. (2010) *Shaping Neighbourhoods: For Local Health and Global Sustainability* (2nd edn), Abingdon: Routledge.

BBC News (2013) 'Bristol hosts last car-free Sunday' [Online], Available from: www.bbc.co.uk/news/uk-england-bristol-24600872 (Accessed 24 December 2018).

BBC News (2018) 'Ministers propose reducing number of councils from 22 to 10' [Online], Available from: www.bbc.co.uk/news/uk-wales-politics-43472521 (Accessed 30 November 2018).

Beatty, C. and Fothergill, S. (2016) *The Uneven Impact of Welfare Reform: The Financial Losses to Places and People*, Sheffield, York and London: Sheffield Hallam University, Joseph Rowntree Foundation and Oxfam.

Beaverstock, J.V., Smith, R.G. and Taylor, P.J. (2000) 'World-city network: A new metageography?', *Annals of the Association of American Geographers*, 90(1): 123–34.

Beel, D., Jones, M. and Rees Jones, I. (2018) 'Elite city-deals for economic growth', *Space and Polity*, 22(3): 307–27.

Belfield, C., Cribb, J., Hood, A. and Joyce, R. (2016) *Living Standards, Poverty and Inequality in the UK: 2016*, London: Institute for Fiscal Studies.

Bell, D. and Vaillancourt, F. (2018) 'Canadian and Scottish Fiscal Federal Arrangements: Taxation and Welfare Spending', in M. Keating and G. Laforest (eds) *Constitutional Politics and the Territorial Question in Canada and the United Kingdom*, Cham, Switzerland: Palgrave Macmillan, pp 79–104.

Bennett, L. (2017) 'The Many Lives of Neighbourhood Planning in the US', in S. Brownill and Q. Bradley (eds) *Localism and Neighbourhood Planning: Power to the People?*, Bristol: Policy Press, pp 231–48.

Bentley, G., Bailey, D. and Shutt, J. (2010) 'From RDAs to LEPs: A new localism? Case examples of West Midland and Yorkshire', *Local Economy*, 25(7): 535–57.

Bergsman, J., Greenston, P. and Healy, R. (1972) 'The agglomeration process in urban growth', *Urban Studies*, 9(3): 263–88.

Birch, J. (2018) 'England could learn a few things from Scotland when it comes to affordable housing', *Inside Housing* [Online], Available from: www.insidehousing.co.uk/home/home/england-could-learn-a-few-things-from-scotland-when-it-comes-to-affordable-housing-54978 (Accessed 30 November 2018).

Birmingham Post (2010) 'Eric Pickles labels council planners as stubborn communists' [Online], Available from: www.birminghampost.co.uk/news/local-news/eric-pickles-labels-council-planners-3926761 (Accessed 17 January 2019).

Birrell, D. (2009) *The Impact of Devolution on Social Policy*, Bristol: Bristol University Press.

Blotevogel, H.H. (1998) 'The Rhine-Ruhr metropolitan region: Reality and discourse', *European Planning Studies*, 6(4): 395–410.

Blunden, M. (2012) '"EASYCOUNCIL" offloads services in £1bn deal', *Evening Standard*, 12 May, p 30.

Bogdanor, V. (2010) 'The West Lothian question', *Parliamentary Affairs*, 63(1): 156–72.

Boughton, J. (2018) *Municipal Dreams: The Rise and Fall of Council Housing*, London: Verso.

Bounds, A. (2017) 'Local councils to see central funding fall 77% by 2020', *Financial Times* [Online], Available from: www.ft.com/content/9c6b5284-6000-11e7-91a7-502f7ee26895 (Accessed 22 November 2018).

Bourdieu, P. (1973) 'Cultural Reproduction and Social Reproduction', in R. Brown (ed) *Knowledge, Education and Social Change*, London: Tavistock, pp 71–84.

Bourdieu, P. (1977) *Outline of a Theory of Practice*, Cambridge: Cambridge University Press.

Bourdieu, P. (2005) *The Social Structure of the Economy*, Cambridge: Polity Press.

Bowers, P. (2012) 'The West Lothian question', House of Commons Library [Online], Available from: https://researchbriefings.parliament.uk/ResearchBriefing/Summary/SN02586 (Accessed 21 January 2019).

Bradbury, S. (2014) 'How much will the Giants visit cost Liverpool?', *Liverpool Echo*, 24 July [Online], Available from: www.liverpoolecho.co.uk/whats-on/arts-culture-news/liverpool-giants-2014-how-much-7497422 (Accessed 26 November 2018).

Bradley, Q. (2015) 'The political identities of Neighbourhood Planning in England', *Space and Polity*, 19(2): 97–109.

Bradley, Q. (2017a) 'Neighbourhoods, Communities and the Local Scale', in S. Brownill and Q. Bradley (eds) *Localism and Neighbourhood Planning: Power to the People?*, Bristol: Policy Press, pp 39–56.

Bradley, Q. (2017b) 'A Passion for Place', in S. Brownill and Q. Bradley (eds) *Localism and Neighbourhood Planning: Power to the People?*, Bristol: Policy Press, pp 163–80.

Bradley, Q. and Brownill, S. (2017) 'Reflections on Neighbourhood Planning', in S. Brownill and Q. Bradley (eds) *Localism and Neighbourhood Planning: Power to the People?*, Bristol: Policy Press, pp 251–68.

Bradley, Q. and Sparling, W. (2016) 'The impact of Neighbourhood Planning and localism on house-building in England', *Housing, Theory and Society*, 34(1): 1–13.

Brenner, N. (2004) *New State Spaces: Urban Governance and the Rescaling of Statehood*, Oxford: Oxford University Press.

Bristol City Council (2012) 'Mayoral referendum result' [Online], Available from: www.bristol.gov.uk/voting-elections/mayoral-referendum-result (Accessed 11 January 2019).

Brouillet, E. and Mullen, T. (2018) 'Constitutional Jurisprudence on Federalism and Devolution in UK and Canada', in M. Keating and G. Laforest (eds) *Constitutional Politics and the Territorial Question in Canada and the United Kingdom*, Cham, Switzerland: Palgrave Macmillan, pp 47–78.

Brown, G. and Chin, S.Y.W. (2013) 'Assessing the effectiveness of public participation in Neighbourhood Planning', *Planning Practice & Research*, 28(5): 563–88.

Brown, M. (2015) 'Newcastle should be the capital of a breakaway North and Scotland', *Evening Chronicle* [Online], Available from: www.chroniclelive.co.uk/news/north-east-news/newcastle-should-capital-breakaway-north-9258756 (Accessed 21 January 2019).

Brownill, S. (2017) 'Neighbourhood Planning and the Purposes and Practices of Localism', in S. Brownill and Q. Bradley (eds) *Localism and Neighbourhood Planning: Power to the People?*, Bristol: Policy Press, pp 19–38.

Brownill, S. and Bradley, Q. (eds) (2017) *Localism and Neighbourhood Planning: Power to the People?*, Bristol: Policy Press.

Burnham for Mayor (2016) *Our Manifesto for Greater Manchester*, Manchester: The Labour Party.

Burton, P. (2017) 'Localism and Neighbourhood Planning in Australian Public Policy and Governance', in S. Brownill and Q. Bradley (eds) *Localism and Neighbourhood Planning: Power to the People?*, Bristol: Policy Press, pp 215–30.

Butler, P. (2012) 'Local government cuts: The "Jaws of Doom" are ready to bite', *The Guardian*, 18 December [Online], Available from: www.theguardian.com/society/2012/dec/18/local-government-cuts-jaws-doom-bite (Accessed 1 July 2019).

Butler, P. (2018) 'Northamptonshire forced to pay the price of a reckless half-decade', *The Guardian*, 1 August [Online], Available from: www.theguardian.com/society/2018/aug/01/northamptonshire-council-forced-pay-price-reckless-half-decade (Accessed 26 November 2018).

Cable, V. and Pickles, E. (2010) *Letter to Local Authority Leaders and Business Leaders*, London: Department for Business, Innovation & Skills and Department for Communities & Local Government.

Cambridgeshire and Peterborough Combined Authority (2018) *Combined Authority Invests in Plans to Bring Jobs and Prosperity to Market Towns*, Huntingdon: Cambridgeshire and Peterborough Combined Authority.

Cameron, D. (2010) 'This is a government that will give power back to the people', *The Observer*, 11 September, p 17.

Cameron, D. (2015) 'The Prime Minister's Party Conference Speech in full', ConservativeHome [Online], Available from: www.conservativehome.com/parliament/2015/10/david-camerons-party-conference-speech-in-full-2.html (Accessed 15 January 2019).

Carpenter, J. (2011) 'Planning "isn't brain surgery", says communities minister' [Online], Available from: www.planningresource.co.uk/Development_Control/article/1093322/planning-isnt-brain-surgery-says-communities-minister/ (Accessed 23 July 2012).

Catney, P., MacGregor, S., Dobson, A., Hall, S.M., et al (2014) 'Big society, little justice?', *Local Environment*, 19(7): 715–30.

Chakrabortty, A. (2018) 'In 2011 Preston hit rock bottom. Then it took back control', *The Guardian*, 31 January [Online], Available from: www.theguardian.com/commentisfree/2018/jan/31/preston-hit-rock-bottom-took-back-control (Accessed 24 December 2018).

Chandler, J.A. (2007) *Explaining Local Government: Local Government in Britain since 1800*, Manchester: Manchester University Press.

Church, A. (1988) 'Urban regeneration in London Docklands: A five-year policy review', *Environment & Planning C: Government & Policy*, 6(1): 187–208.

Clapp, J.A. (1971) *New Towns and Urban Policy – Planning Metropolitan Growth*, New York and London: Dunellen.

Clifford, B. and Henneberry, J. (2018) 'Planning regulation, development flexibility and the extension of PD rights', *Town and Country Planning*, 87(10): 383–7.

Clifford, B., Ferm, J., Livingstone, N. and Canelas, P. (2018) *Assessing the Impacts of Extending Permitted Development Rights to Office-to-Residential Change of Use in England*, London: Royal Institute of Chartered Surveyors.

Clifford, M.L. (2016) *Troubled Tiger: Businessmen, Bureaucrats and Generals in South Korea*, Abingdon: Routledge.

Cobbett, W. (1885) *Rural Rides*, vol 1, London: Reeves and Turner.

Coelho, M. (2015) 'Critical Perspectives on Devolved Governance – Lessons from Housing Policy in England', in J. Kilroy (ed) *Critical Perspectives on Devolved Governance*, London: Royal Town Planning Institute, pp 2–4.

Coffee Jr, J.C. (2009) 'What went wrong? An initial inquiry into the causes of the 2008 financial crisis', *Journal of Corporate Law Studies*, 9(1): 1–22.

Collins, D. (2019) 'North of England should set own tax rates, says minister Jake Berry', *The Sunday Times*, 13 January [Online], Available from: www.thetimes.co.uk/article/north-of-england-should-set-own-tax-rates-says-minister-55l9jpbq3 (Accessed 21 January 2019).

Collinson, P. (2017) 'Help to buy has mostly helped housebuilders boost profits', *The Guardian*, 21 October [Online], Available from: www.theguardian.com/money/blog/2017/oct/21/help-to-buy-property-new-build-price-rise (Accessed 4 December 2018).

Colomb, C. and Tomaney, J. (2016) 'Territorial politics, devolution and spatial planning in the UK: Results, prospects, lessons', *Planning Practice & Research*, 31(1): 1–22.

ConservativeHome (2010) 'George Osborne confirms intention to eliminate deficit by 2015 in first Commons clash with Alan Johnson' [Online], Available from: www.conservativehome.com/parliament/2010/10/george-osborne-confirms-intention-to-eliminate-deficit-by-2015-in-first-commons-clash-with-alan-john.html (Accessed 1 July 2019).

Conservative Party, The (2010a) *Invitation to Join the Government of Britain: The Conservative Manifesto 2010*, London: The Conservative Party.

Conservative Party, The (2010b) *Open Source Planning*, Green Paper, London: The Conservative Party.

Conservative Party, The (2015) *Conservative Party Manifesto 2015*, London: The Conservative Party.

Copus, C. (2004) 'Directly elected mayors: A tonic for local governance or old wine in new bottles?', *Local Government Studies*, 30(4): 576–88.

Copus, C. (2009) 'English Elected Mayors', in H. Reynaert, K. Steyvers, J.-B. Pilet and P. Delwit (eds) *Local Political Leadership in Europe: Town Chief, City Boss or Loco President?*, Bruges: Vanden Broele Publishers, pp 29–57.

Couch, C. (2016) *Urban Planning: An Introduction*, Basingstoke: Palgrave.

Coulson, A. (2009) 'Targets and terror: Government by performance indicators', *Local Government Studies*, 35(2): 9–19.

Cox, E. (2016) 'Devolution in England – Is the genie out of the lamp?', *The Political Quarterly*, 87(4): 565–71.

Cox, K.R. (2013) 'Territory, scale and why capitalism matters', *Territory, Politics, Governance*, 1(1): 46–61.

Crisp, R. (2015) 'Work clubs and the Big Society', *People, Place and Policy*, 9(1): 1–16.

Cromarty, H. (2018) *Starter Homes for First-Time Buyers (England): Briefing Paper Number 07643*, London: House of Commons Library.

Cullingworth, B. and Nadin, V. (2006) *Town and Country Planning in the UK* (14th edn), London and New York: Routledge.

Cullingworth, B., Nadin, V., Hart, T., Davoudi, S., et al (2015) *Town and Country Planning in the UK* (15th edn), London: Routledge.

Curtice, J. (2013) 'Politicians, voters and democracy: The 2011 UK referendum on the Alternative Vote', *Electoral Studies*, 32(2): 215–23.

Curtis, P. (2010) 'Government scraps 192 quangos', *The Guardian*, 14 October [Online], Available from: www.theguardian.com/politics/2010/oct/14/government-to-reveal-which-quangos-will-be-scrapped (Accessed 22 November 2018).

Cutts, D. and Russell, A. (2015) 'From coalition to catastrophe: The electoral meltdown of the Liberal Democrats', *Parliamentary Affairs*, 68(suppl_1): 70–87.

Dahl, R. (1961) *Who Governs? Democracy and Power in an American City*, New Haven, CT: Yale University Press.

Damer, S. and Hague, C. (1971) 'Public participation in planning: A review', *Town Planning Review*, 42(3): 217–32.

Dandekar, H. and Main, K. (2014) 'Small-Town Comprehensive Planning in California: Medial Pathways to Community-Based Participation', in N. Gallent and D. Ciaffi (eds) *Community Action and Planning: Context, Drivers and Outcomes*, Bristol: Bristol University Press, pp 157–76.

Dasgupta, R. (2018) 'The demise of the nation state', *The Guardian*, 5 April [Online], Available from: www.theguardian.com/news/2018/apr/05/demise-of-the-nation-state-rana-dasgupta (Accessed 21 January 2019).

David, J. and Hammond, R. (2011) *High Line: The Inside Story of New York City's Park in the Sky*, New York: Farrar, Straus & Giroux.

Davies, A. (2001) 'Hidden or hiding? Public perceptions of participation in the planning system', *Town Planning Review*, 72(2): 193–216.

Davies, J.S. and Imbroscio, D. (2009) *Theories of Urban Politics* (2nd edn), London: Sage.

Davies, J.S. (2012) 'Active citizenship: Navigating the Conservative heartlands of the New Labour project', *Policy & Politics*, 40(1): 3–19.

Davis, A.L. and Tapp, A. (2017) 'The UK transport policy menu: Roads, roads, and a dash of multimodalism', *Social Business*, 7(3–4): 313–32.

Davoudi, S. and Cowie, P. (2013) 'Are English neighbourhood forums democratically legitimate?', *Planning Theory & Practice*, 14(4): 562–6.

Davoudi, S., Crawford, J., Raynor, R., Reid, B., Sykes, O. and Shaw, D. (2018) 'Spatial imaginaries: Tyrannies or transformations?', *Town Planning Review*, 89(2): 97–124.

DCLG (Department for Communities and Local Government) (2009) *Strengthening Local Democracy – Consultation*, London: DCLG.

DCLG (2010a) 'Eric Pickles puts stop to flawed Regional Strategies today' [Online], Available from: https://webarchive.nationalarchives.gov.uk/20120919160104/http://www.communities.gov.uk/news/planningandbuilding/1632278 (Accessed 22 November 2018).

DCLG (2010b) 'Eric Pickles to disband Audit Commission in new era of town hall' transparency [Online], Available from: www.gov.uk/government/news/eric-pickles-to-disband-audit-commission-in-new-era-of-town-hall-transparency (Accessed 22 November 2018).

DCLG (2010c) 'Planning power from town halls and Whitehall to local people' [Online], Available from: www.gov.uk/government/news/planning-power-from-town-halls-and-whitehall-to-local-people (Accessed 3 October 2018).

DCLG (2011a) 'Pickles and Hammond to end the war on motorists' [Online], Available from: www.communities.gov.uk/news/newsroom/1809347 (Accessed 4 December 2018).

DCLG (2011b) *A Plain English Guide to the Localism Act*, London: DCLG.

DCLG (2011c) *Unlocking Growth in Cities*, London: DCLG.

DCLG (2012a) 'Localism Act: Power shift to communities charges on' [Online], Available from: www.communities.gov.uk/news/communities/2126308 (Accessed 9 July 2012).

DCLG (2012b) *National Planning Policy Framework*, London: DCLG.

DCLG (2012c) *Neighbourhood Planning Regulations: Consultation. Summary of Responses*, London: DCLG.

DCLG (2012d) *Unlocking Growth in Cities: City Deals – Wave 1*, London: DCLG.

DCLG (2013) *Extending Permitted Development Rights for Homeowners and Businesses: Impact Assessment*, London: DCLG.

DCLG and Lewis, B. (2015) 'Neighbourhood Planning powers boosting plans for housebuilding by more than 10%' [Online], Available from: www.gov.uk/government/news/neighbourhood-planning-powers-boosting-plans-for-housebuilding-by-more-than-10 (Accessed 14 November 2017).

De Boeck, S., Bassens, D. and Ryckewaert, M. (2017) 'Easing spatial inequalities? An analysis of the anticipated effects of Urban Enterprise Zones in Brussels', *European Planning Studies*, 25(10): 1876–95.

de Magalhaes, C.S., Healey, P., Madanipour, A. and Pendlebury, J. (2003) 'Place, Identity and Local Politics', in M. Hajer and H. Wagenaar (eds) *Deliberative Policy Analysis: Understanding Governance in the Network Society*, Cambridge: Cambridge University Press, pp 60–87.

Dearlove, J. (1979) *The Reorganization of British Local Government: Old Orthodoxies and a Political Perspective*, Cambridge: Cambridge University Press.

Deas, I. (2014) 'The search for territorial fixes in subnational governance', *Urban Studies*, 51(11): 2285–314.

Deas, I., Hincks, S. and Headlam, N. (2013) 'Explicitly permissive?', *Local Economy*, 28(7–8): 718–37.

DEFRA (Department for Environment, Food & Rural Affairs) (2011) '2011 Rural urban classification' [Online], Available from: www.gov. uk/government/statistics/2011-rural-urban-classification (Accessed 21 January 2019).

Dembski, S. (2015) 'Structure and imagination of changing cities: Manchester, Liverpool and the spatial in-between', *Urban Studies*, 52(9): 1647–64.

Dembski, S., Schulze Bäing, A. and Sykes, O. (2017) 'What about the urban periphery? The effects of the urban renaissance in the Mersey Belt', *Comparative Population Studies-Zeitschrift für Bevölkerungswissenschaft*, 42: 219–44.

Dempsey, N. (2017) *Turnout at Elections*, London: House of Commons Library.

Dempsey, N., Burton, M. and Selin, J. (2016) 'Contracting out parks and roads maintenance in England', *International Journal of Public Sector Management*, 29(5): 441–56.

Departamento De Desenvolvimento Local (2017) 'Good Practice Summary: Lisbon Local Development Strategy for Neighbourhoods or Areas of Priority Intervention', URBACT [Online], Available from: http://urbact.eu/sites/default/files/397_Lisbon_GPsummary. pdf (Accessed 14 August 2018).

DETR (Department of the Environment, Transport and the Regions) (1998) *Modern Local Government: In Touch with the People*, White Paper, London: HMSO.

Dewar, D. (2018a) 'Delegating decisions to a town council', *Planning*, 23 November, pp 26–7.

Dewar, D. (2018b) 'The implications of a Hertfordshire local plan holding direction', *Planning*, 28 September, p 12.

DfT (Department for Transport) (2017) *Transport Investment Strategy: Moving Britain Ahead*, Cm 9472, London: HMSO.

DfT (2018) 'Transport Secretary welcomes next step in £1.7 billion fund to transform local journeys', News story, 13 March, London: DfT.

Dieleman, F.M., Dijst, M.J. and Spit, T. (1999) 'Planning the compact city: The Randstad Holland experience', *European Planning Studies*, 7(5): 605–21.

Doak, J. and Parker, G. (2005) 'Networked space? The challenge of meaningful participation and the new spatial planning in England', *Planning Practice and Research*, 20(1): 23–40.

Docherty, I., Goodlad, R. and Paddison, R. (2001) 'Civic culture, community and citizen participation in contrasting neighbourhoods', *Urban Studies*, 38(12): 2225–50.

Dominiczak, P. (2013) 'Minister admits UK transport infrastructure is "poor" but pledges more money to road and rail projects', *The Telegraph*, 8 January [Online], Available from: www.telegraph. co.uk/news/politics/9788252/Minister-admits-UK-transport-infrastructure-is-poor-but-pledges-more-money-to-road-and-rail-projects.html (Accessed 4 December 2018).

Donnelly, M. (2017) 'New secretary of state and county council plan-making powers to come into effect in January', *Planning*, 13 December [Online], Available from: www.planningresource. co.uk/article/1452808/new-secretary-state-county-council-plan-making-powers-effect-january?bulletin=planning-daily%E2%80%A6 (Accessed 9 November 2018).

Dorling, D. (2010) 'Persistent North–South Divides', in N.M. Coe and A. Jones (eds) *The Economic Geography of the UK*, London: Sage, pp 12–28.

Dorling, D. (2017) 'Turning the tide on inequality', *Social Europe* [Online], Available from: www.socialeurope.eu/turning-tide-inequality (Accessed 23 July 2019).

Dorling, D. (2018) *Peak Inequality: Britain's Ticking Time Bomb*, Bristol: Policy Press.

Dorling, D. and Thomas, B. (2004) *People and Places 2001: A Census Atlas*, Bristol: Policy Press.

DWP (Department for Work and Pensions) (2018) 'Unemployment down by over 1.1 million since 2010' [Online], Available from: www.gov.uk/government/news/unemployment-down-by-over-11-million-since-2010 (Accessed 4 December 2018).

Eddington, R. (2006) *The Eddington Transport Study. The Case for Action: Sir Rod Eddington's Advice to Government*, London: The Stationery Office.

Edgar, L. (2018) 'The county role in delivering housing', *The Planner*, August, pp 6–7.

Elcock, H. and Fenwick, J. (2007) 'Comparing elected mayors', *International Journal of Public Sector Management*, 20(3): 226–38.

Engelen, E., Froud, J., Johal, S., Salento, A. and Williams, K. (2017) 'The grounded city: From competitivity to the foundational economy', *Cambridge Journal of Regions, Economy and Society*, 10(3): 407–23.

Evans, M., Marsh, D. and Stoker, G. (2013) 'Understanding localism', *Policy Studies*, 34(4): 401–7.

Featherstone, D., Ince, A., Mackinnon, D., Strauss, K. and Cumbers, A. (2012) 'Progressive localism and the construction of political alternatives', *Transactions of the Institute of British Geographers*, 37(2): 177–82.

Feenstra, R.C. (1998) 'Integration of trade and disintegration of production in the global economy', *Journal of Economic Perspectives*, 12(4): 31–50.

Ferry, L., Eckersley, P. and van Dooren, W. (2015) 'Local taxation and spending as a share of GDP in large Western European countries', *Environment & planning A*, 47(9): 1779–80.

Fischer, F. (2017) *Climate Crisis and the Democratic Prospect: Participatory Governance in Sustainable Communities*, Oxford: Oxford University Press.

Fisher, S.D. and Lewis-Beck, M.S. (2016) 'Forecasting the 2015 British general election: The 1992 debacle all over again?', *Electoral Studies*, 41: 225–9.

Fishman, R. (1994) 'Urbanity and suburbanity: Rethinking the 'burbs', *American Quarterly*, 46(1): 35–9.

Fitzgerald, T. (2017) 'Greater Manchester's mayoral candidates row over region's housing masterplan', *Manchester Evening News* [Online], Available from: www.manchestereveningnews.co.uk/news/greater-manchester-news/greater-manchesters-mayoral-candidates-row-12445676 (Accessed 21 January 2019).

Flynn, N., Leach, S. and Vielba, C.A. (1985) *Abolition or Reform? The GLC and the Metropolitan County Councils*, London: HarperCollins.

Flyvbjerg, B. (1998) *Rationality and Power: Democracy in Practice*, Chicago, IL: The University of Chicago Press.

Flyvbjerg, B. (2002) 'Bringing power to planning research', *Journal of Planning Education & Research*, 21: 353–66.

Foderaro, L.W. (2011) 'As city plants trees, some say a million are too many', *New York Times*, 19 October.

Forbes, N., Anderson, J. and Dore, J. (2012) 'Spending cuts will create social unrest in our cities', Letters, *The Observer*, 29 December [Online], Available from: www.theguardian.com/theobserver/2012/dec/29/letters-coalition-cuts-threaten-cities [Accessed 27 August 2019].

Ford, R. and Goodwin, M. (2017) 'Britain after Brexit: A nation divided', *Journal of Democracy*, 28(1): 17–30.

Forester, J. (1989) *Planning in the Face of Power*, Berkeley, CA: University of California Press.

Foster, J.B. and Magdoff, F. (2009) *The Great Financial Crisis: Causes and Consequences*, New York: NYU Press.

Frost, D. and North, P. (2013) *Militant Liverpool: A City on the Edge*, Liverpool: Liverpool University Press.

Gallagher, J. (2012) *England and the Union: How and Why to Answer the West Lothian Question*, London: Institute for Public Policy Research.

Gallent, N. (2013) 'Re-connecting "people and planning": Parish plans and the English localism agenda', *Town Planning Review*, 84(3): 371–96.

Gallent, N. and Robinson, S. (2012) *Neighbourhood Planning – Communities, Networks and Governance*, Bristol: Policy Press.

Gamble, A. (2012) 'Better off out? Britain and Europe', *The Political Quarterly*, 83(3): 468–77.

Garcia, B. (2017) '"If everyone says so…" Press narratives and image change in major event host cities', *Urban Studies*, 54(14): 3178–98.

Garcia, B., Melville, R. and Cox, T. (2010) *Creating an Impact: Liverpool's Experience as European Capital of Culture*, Liverpool: Impacts 08.

Gardesse, C. and Zetlaoui-Leger, J. (2017) 'Citizen Participation: An Essential Lever for Urban Transformation in France?', in S. Brownill and Q. Bradley (eds) *Localism and Neighbourhood Planning: Power to the People?*, Bristol: Policy Press, pp 199–214.

Gash, T. and Sims, S. (2012) *What Can Elected Mayors Do for Our Cities?*, London: Institute for Government.

Geddes, M. and Davies, J. (2007) 'Evaluating Local Strategic Partnerships: Theory and practice of change', *Local Government Studies*, 33(1): 97–116.

Gehrke, J.P. (2016) 'A radical endeavor: Joseph Chamberlain and the emergence of municipal socialism in Birmingham', *American Journal of Economics and Sociology*, 75(1): 23–57.

Geoghegan, J. (2018a) 'Ten things we learned at the Conservative Party conference', *Planning*, 12 October, p 9.

Geoghegan, J. (2018b) 'Why government has gone quiet on special measures designations', PlanningResource, 5 July [Online], Available from: www.planningresource.co.uk/article/1486983/why-government-gone-quiet-special-measures-designations (Accessed 22 November 2018).

Gerber, E.R. and Kollman, K. (2004) 'Authority migration: Defining an emerging research agenda', *Political Science*, 37(3): 397–401.

Giddens, A. (2003) *Runaway World: How Globalization Is Reshaping Our Lives*, London: Taylor & Francis.

Giovannini, A. (2016) 'Towards a "new English regionalism" in the North? The case of Yorkshire First', *The Political Quarterly*, 87(4): 590–600.

GMCA (Greater Manchester Combined Authority) (2016) *Draft Greater Manchester Spatial Framework*, Manchester: GMCA.

GMElects (2017) 'GMCA Mayoral election results' [Online], Available from: www.gmelects.org.uk/homepage/9/results_may_2017 (Accessed 20 September 2018).

Golding, N. (2010) 'Can the easyCouncil swing it in Barnet?', *Community Care*, 18(15): 14–15.

González, S. (2006) *The Northern Way: A Celebration or a Victim of the New City-Regional Government Policy?*, CiteSeer.

Goodchild, B. and Hickman, P. (2006) 'Towards a regional strategy for the North of England? An assessment of "The Northern Way"', *Regional Studies*, 40(1): 121–33.

Goodwin, M., Jones, M. and Jones, R. (2006) 'Devolution and economic governance in the UK: Rescaling territories and organisations', *European Planning Studies*, 14(7): 979–95.

Goulding, A. (2013) 'The Big Society and English public libraries: Where are we now?', *New Library World*, 114(11/12): 478–93.

Green, J. and Chapman, A. (1992) 'The British Community Development Project: Lessons for today', *Community Development Journal*, 27(3): 242–58.

Green, J. and Prosser, C. (2016) 'Party system fragmentation and single-party government: The British general election of 2015', *West European Politics*, 39(6): 1299–310.

Greene, J.A. (1999) 'Zero tolerance: A case study of police policies and practices in New York City', *Crime & Delinquency*, 45(2): 171–87.

Griffiths, L. (2017) 'Written Statement – Invitation to prepare Joint Local Development Plans and Strategic Development Plans', Welsh Government [Online], Available from: https://gov.wales/about/cabinet/cabinetstatements/2017/jointlocalandstrategicdevelopmentplans/?lang=en (Accessed 30 November 2018).

Groothuis, P.A. and Rotthoff, K.W. (2016) 'The economic impact and civic pride effects of sports teams and mega-events: Do the public and the professionals agree?', *Economic Affairs (Institute of Economic Affairs)*, 36(1): 21–32.

Guardian, The (2018) '*The Guardian* view on record employment: Not the whole picture' [Online], Available from: www.theguardian. com/commentisfree/2018/aug/14/the-guardian-view-on-record-unemployment-not-the-whole-picture (Accessed 4 December 2018).

Hall, P. (1999) 'The Regional Dimension', in B. Cullingworth (ed) *British Planning: 50 Years of Urban and Regional Policy*, London: Bloomsbury, pp 76–90.

Hall, P. (2011) 'The Big Society and the evolution of ideas', *Town and Country Planning*, 80(2): 59–60.

Hall, P. and Pain, K. (eds) (2006) *The Polycentric Metropolis: Learning from Mega-City Regions in Europe*, London: Earthscan.

Halliday, J. (2016) 'Sajid Javid: Devolution deal "off the table" for north-east of England', *The Guardian*, 8 September [Online], Available from: www.theguardian.com/politics/2016/sep/08/north-east-england-devolution-deal-off-the-table-sajid-javid (Accessed 21 January 2019).

Halliday, J. (2017) 'Commonwealth Games: Birmingham beats Liverpool for 2022 endorsement', *The Guardian*, 7 September [Online], Available from: www.theguardian.com/sport/2017/sep/07/ commonwealth-games-brimingham-liverpool-recommendation (Accessed 26 November 2018).

Hambleton, R. (2015) 'Place-Based Leadership and Social Innovation', in J. Kilroy (ed) *Critical Perspectives on Devolved Governance*, London: Royal Town Planning Institute, pp 18–20.

Hambleton, R. (2017) 'The super-centralisation of the English state – Why we need to move beyond the devolution deception', *Local Economy*, 32(1): 3–13.

Hambleton, R. and Howard, J. (2012) 'Place-based leadership and public service innovation', *Local Economy*, 39(1): 1–24.

Hanna, T.M., Guinan, J. and Bilsborough, J. (2018) 'The "Preston Model" and the modern politics of municipal socialism', Open Democracy [Online], Available from: www.opendemocracy. net/neweconomics/preston-model-modern-politics-municipal-socialism/ (Accessed 9 November 2018).

Hansard (2016) vol 604, col 845.

Harris, N. and Hooper, A. (2006) 'Redefining "the space that is Wales"', in M. Tewdwr-Jones and P. Allmendinger (eds) *Territory, Identity and Spatial Planning: Spatial Governance in a Fragmented Nation*, Abingdon: Routledge, pp 139–52.

Harrison, J. and Heley, J. (2015) 'Governing beyond the metropolis', *Urban Studies*, 52(6): 1113–33.

Hart, J. (2017) 'It's still the economy, stupid', Forbes, 27 December [Online], Available from: www.forbes.com/sites/johnhart/2017/12/27/its-still-the-economy-stupid/#444909022c9a (Accessed 4 December 2018).

Harvey, D. (1989) 'From managerialism to entrepreneurialism: The transformation in urban governance in late capitalism', *Geografiska Annaler. Series B, Human Geography*, 71(1): 3–17.

Hastings, A. and Matthews, P. (2015) 'Bourdieu and the Big Society: Empowering the powerful in public service provision?', *Policy & Politics*, 43(4): 545–60.

Hastings, A., Bailey, N., Bramley, G., Gannon, M. and Watkins, D. (2015) *The Cost of the Cuts: The Impact on Local Government and Poorer Communities*, York: Joseph Rowntree Foundation.

Haughton, G., Allmendinger, P. and Oosterlynck, S. (2013) 'Spaces of neoliberal experimentation', *Environment and Planning A*, 45(1): 217–34.

Haughton, G., Allmendinger, P., Counsell, D. and Vigar, G. (2010) *The New Spatial Planning – Territorial Management with Soft Spaces and Fuzzy Boundaries*, Abingdon: Routledge.

Haughton, G., Deas, I., Hincks, S. and Ward, K. (2016) 'Mythic Manchester: Devo Manc, the Northern Powerhouse and rebalancing the English economy', *Cambridge Journal of Regions, Economy and Society*, 9: 355–70.

Hayton, R. (2014) 'Conservative Party statecraft and the politics of coalition', *Parliamentary Affairs*, 67(1): 6–24.

Hazell, R. (2006) 'The English question', *Publius: The Journal of Federalism*, 36(1): 37–56.

Headlam, N. (2014) 'Liverchester/Manpool? The Curious Case of the Lack of Intra-Urban Leadership in the Twin Cities of the North-West', in J. Diamond and J. Liddle (eds) *European Public Leadership in Crisis?*, vol 3, Bingley: Emerald Group Publishing Limited, pp 47–61.

Headlam, N. and Hepburn, P. (2017) 'Directly Elected Mayors: Necessary but not Sufficient to Transform Places? The Case of Liverpool', in D. Sweeting (ed) *Directly Elected Mayors in Urban Governance: Impact and Practice*, Bristol: Policy Press, pp 69–84.

Healey, P. (2006) *Collaborative Planning*, Basingstoke and New York: Palgrave Macmillan.

Healey, P. (2015) 'Civil society enterprise and local development', *Planning Theory and Practice*, 16(1): 11–27.

Heath, O. and Goodwin, M. (2017) 'The 2017 general election, Brexit and the return to two-party politics', *The Political Quarterly*, 88(3): 345–58.

Henderson, A., Jeffery, C. and Liñeira, R. (2015) 'National identity or national interest? Scottish, English and Welsh attitudes to the constitutional debate', *The Political Quarterly*, 86(2): 265–74.

Heppell, T. (2013) 'Cameron and Liberal Conservatism: Attitudes within the parliamentary Conservative Party and Conservative ministers', *The British Journal of Politics & International Relations*, 15(3): 340–61.

Hickson, K. (2013) 'The localist turn in British politics and its critics', *Policy Studies*, 34(4): 408–21.

HM Government (2010a) *The Coalition: Our Programme for Government*, London: HM Government Cabinet Office.

HM Government (2010b) *Decentralisation and the Localism Bill: An Essential Guide*, London: Department for Communities and Local Government.

HM Government (2017) *Industrial Strategy: Building a Britain Fit for the Future*, London: The Stationery Office.

HM Treasury (2010) *Spending Review 2010*, London: HM Treasury.

HM Treasury (2017) *Spring Budget*, London: HMSO.

Hodson, D. and Mabbett, D. (2009) 'UK economic policy and the global financial crisis', *JCMS: Journal of Common Market Studies*, 47(5): 1041–61.

Hopkins, R. (2008) *The Transition Handbook: From Oil Dependency to Local Resilience*, Totnes: Green Books.

Houghton, A. (2017) 'Thousands of tax office workers WILL be moving into city centre India Buildings', *Liverpool Echo*, 17 August [Online], Available from: www.liverpoolecho.co.uk/news/liverpool-news/thousands-tax-office-workers-moving-13490568 (Accessed 26 November 2018).

Houghton, A. (2018) '£5m fund to save our town centres as high street crisis bites', *Liverpool Echo*, 7 July [Online], Available from: www.liverpoolecho.co.uk/news/business/5m-fund-save-town-centres-14860429 (Accessed 21 January 2019).

International Association of Public Participation (2014) 'IAP2's Public Participation Spectrum' [Online], Available from: https://cdn.ymaws.com/www.iap2.org/resource/resmgr/foundations_course/IAP2_P2_Spectrum_FINAL.pdf (Accessed 24 August 2018).

IPPR (Institute for Public Policy Research) North (2017a) *England's New Leaders: How Mayors Can Transform their Cities*, Manchester: IPPR North.

IPPR North (2017b) *Taking Back Control in the North: A Council of the North and Other Ideas*, Manchester: IPPR North.

Ipsos MORI (2017) 'May 2017 Economist/IPSOS Mori Issues Index' [Online], Available from: www.ipsos.com/sites/default/files/2017-06/Issues%20Index_May2017.pdf (Accessed 21 January 2019).

Jacobs, A.J. (2003) 'Devolving authority and expanding autonomy in Japanese prefectures and municipalities', *Governance*, 16(4): 601–23.

Jacobs, J. (1961) *The Death and Life of Great American Cities*, Harmondsworth: Penguin.

Jacobs, K. and Manzi, T. (2013) 'New localism, old retrenchment: The "Big Society", housing policy and the politics of welfare reform', *Housing, Theory & Society*, 30(1): 29–45.

Jeffery, C. (2015) 'Constitutional change – Without end?', *The Political Quarterly*, 86(2): 275–8.

Jennings, W., Brett, W., Bua, A. and Laurence, R. (2017) *Cities and Towns: The 2017 General Election and the Social Divisions of Place*, London: New Economics Foundation.

Jessop, B. (1990) *State Theory: Putting the Capitalist State in its Place*, Cambridge: Polity Press.

John, P. (2014) 'The great survivor: The persistence and resilience of English local government', *Local Government Studies*, 40(5): 687–704.

Johnston, B. (2017) 'How Sajid Javid has ignored inspectors' advice in Tory seats', PlanningResource, 13 October [Online], Available from: www.planningresource.co.uk/article/1447298/sajid-javid-ignored-inspectors-advice-tory-seats (Accessed 22 November 2018).

Johnston, B. (2018) 'Why a city council is bringing outsourced service back in-house', *Planning*, 15 June, p 8.

Johnstone, R. (2015) 'DCLG agrees 30% cuts package with Treasury', *Public Finance*, 9 November [Online], Available from: www.publicfinance.co.uk/news/2015/11/dclg-agrees-30-cuts-package-treasury (Accessed 21 january 2019).

Jones, G. and Stewart, J. (2012) 'Local government: The past, the present and the future', *Public Policy and Administration*, 27(4): 346–67.

Jones, M. and MacLeod, G. (2004) 'Regional spaces, spaces of regionalism: Territory, insurgent politics and the English question', *Transactions of the Institute of British Geographers*, 29(4): 433–52.

Jones, M.R. (1997) 'Spatial selectivity of the state? The regulationist enigma and local struggles over economic governance', *Environment and Planning A*, 29(5): 831–64.

Jones, P. (2015) 'Modelling urban futures', *City*, 19(4): 463–79.

Jones, P. and Evans, J. (2008) *Urban Regeneration in the UK*, London: Sage.

Jones, T., Newburn, T. and Smith, D. (2012) 'Democracy and Police and Crime Commissioners', in T. Newburn and J. Peay (eds) *Policing: Politics, Culture and Control*, Oxford: Hart Publishing, pp 219–44.

Joyce, P. (2011) 'Police reform: From police authorities to police and crime commissioners', *Safer Communities*, 10(4): 5–13.

Keating, M. and Laforest, G. (2018) 'Federalism and Devolution: The UK and Canada', in M. Keating and G. Laforest (eds) *Constitutional Politics and the Territorial Question in Canada and the United Kingdom*, Cham, Switzerland: Palgrave Macmillan, pp 1–18.

Kelling, G.L. and Bratton, W.J. (1997) 'Declining crime rates: Insiders' views of the New York City story', *Journal of Criminal Law & Criminology*, 88: 1217.

Kenny, M. (2016) 'The genesis of English nationalism', *Political Insight*, 7(2): 8–11.

Kentish, B. (2018) 'Theresa May declares "austerity is over" after eight years of cuts and tax increases', *Independent*, 3 October [Online], Available from: www.independent.co.uk/news/uk/politics/theresa-may-austerity-end-over-speech-conservative-conference-tory-labour-a8566526.html (Accessed 26 November 2018).

King, A. (2007) *The British Constitution*, Oxford: Oxford University Press.

Kingdon, J.W. (1984) *Agendas, Alternatives and Public Policies*, Boston, MA: Little Brown & Co.

Kloosterman, R.C. and Lambregts, B. (2001) 'Clustering of economic activities in polycentric urban regions: The case of the Randstad', *Urban Studies*, 38(4): 717–32.

Knapp, W. (1998) 'The Rhine-Ruhr area in transformation: Towards a European metropolitan region?', *European Planning Studies*, 6(4): 379–93.

Kopel, M. and Löffler, C. (2008) 'Commitment, first-mover-, and second-mover advantage', *Journal of Economics*, 94(2): 143–66.

KRIHS (Korean Institute for Human Settlements) (2013) *KRIHS Annual Report*, Sejong: KRIHS.

Kuhlmann, S. and Bogumil, J. (2018) 'Performance measurement and benchmarking as "reflexive institutions" for local governments', *International Journal of Public Sector Management*, 31(4): 543–62.

Kwon, Y. (2015) 'Sejong Si (City): Are TOD and TND models effective in planning Korea's new capital?', *Cities*, 42: 242–57.

Labour Party (2010) *A Future Fair for All*, London: The Labour Party.

Laforest, G. and Keating, M. (2018) 'The Future of Federalism and Devolution in Canada and the United Kingdom', in M. Keating and G. Laforest (eds) *Constitutional Politics and the Territorial Question in Canada and the United Kingdom*, Cham, Switzerland: Palgrave Macmillan, pp 179–86.

Lauermann, J. (2014) 'Competition through interurban policy making: Bidding to host megaevents as entrepreneurial networking', *Environment & Planning A*, 46: 2638–53.

Leather, P. and Nevin, B. (2013) 'The Housing Market Renewal Programme: Origins, outcomes and the effectiveness of public policy interventions in a volatile market', *Urban Studies*, 50(5): 856–75.

Lee, J.S. (1996) 'The politics of decentralisation in Korea', *Local Government Studies*, 22(3): 60–71.

Lee, Y.-S. (2009) 'Balanced development in globalizing regional development? Unpacking the new regional policy of South Korea', *Regional Studies*, 43(3): 353–67.

Leese, R. (2014) 'New powers to Greater Manchester', Manchester City Council '[Online], Available from: www.manchester.gov.uk/blog/leadersblog/post/707/new-powers-to-greater-manchester (Accessed 27 November 2018).

Levitas, R. (2012) 'The just's umbrella: Austerity and the Big Society in Coalition policy and beyond', *Critical Social Policy*, 32(3): 320–42.

LGA (Local Government Association) (2017) 'Plan making – 5 year housing land supply' [Online], Available from: www.local.gov.uk/plan-making-5-year-housing-land-supply (Accessed 17 November 2017).

Liddle, J. (2009) 'The northern way: A pan-regional associational network', *International Journal of Public Sector Management*, 22(3): 192–202.

Liddle, J. (2012) 'Sustaining Collaborative Leadership in City Regions: An Examination of Local Enterprise Partnerships in England', in M. Sotarauta, L. Horlings and J. Liddle (eds) *Leadership and Change in Sustainable Regional Development*, Abingdon: Routledge, pp 53–75.

Lister, S. (2013) 'The new politics of the police: Police and crime commissioners and the "operational independence" of the police', *Policing*, 7(3): 239–47.

Lister, S. and Rowe, M. (2015) 'Electing police and crime commissioners in England and Wales: Prospecting for the democratisation of policing', *Policing and Society*, 25(4): 358–77.

Liverpool City Region (2016) *Liverpool City Region Statement of Cooperation on Local Planning*, Liverpool: Liverpool City Region Combined Authority.

Liverpool City Region LEP (Local Enterprise Partnership) (2014) *Visitor Economy Strategy and Destination Management Plan*, Liverpool: Liverpool City Region LEP.

Liverpool City Region LEP (2018) 'What's on in Liverpool' [Online], Available from: www.visitliverpool.com/whats-on (Accessed 26 November 2018).

Liverpool Echo (2014) 'Controversial skyscraper project puts Liverpool's World Heritage status in danger', 31 May [Online], Available from: www.liverpoolecho.co.uk/news/liverpool-news/liverpool-world-heritage-status-danger-7198363 (Accessed 26 November 2018).

Liverpool Echo (2018) 'The Giants in Liverpool 2018 – RECAP all the pictures and action from the Royal de Luxe street theatre puppet spectacular' [Online], Available from: www.liverpoolecho.co.uk/whats-on/whats-on-news/live-giants-liverpool-2018-wirral-15235297 (Accessed 26 November 2018).

Lloyd, M.G. and Peel, D. (2009) 'New Labour and the planning system in Scotland: An overview of a decade', *Planning, Practice & Research*, 24(1): 103–18.

Lloyd, M.G. and Peel, D. (2012a) 'Planning reform in Northern Ireland: Planning Act (Northern Ireland) 2011', *Planning Theory & Practice*, 13(1): 177–82.

Lloyd, M.G. and Peel, D. (2012b) 'Soft contractualism? Facilitating institutional change in planning and development relations in Scotland', *Urban Research & Practice*, 5(2): 239–55.

Lord, A. (2012) *The Planning Game*, Oxford: Routledge.

Lord, A., Mair, M., Sturzaker, J. and Jones, P. (2017) '"The planners' dream goes wrong?" Questioning citizen-centred planning', *Local Government Studies*, 43(3): 344–63.

Lord, A., O'Brien, P., Sykes, S. and Sturzaker, J. (2015) *Planning as 'Market Maker': How Planning Is Used to Stimulate Development in Germany, France and the Netherlands*, London: RTPI (Royal Town Planning Institute).

Loughlin, J. (1996) '"Europe of the Regions" and the federalisation of Europe', *Publius: The Journal of Federalism*, 26(4): 141–62.

Lowndes, V. and Gardner, A. (2016) 'Local governance under the Conservatives: Super-austerity, devolution and the "smarter state"', *Local Government Studies*, 42(3): 357–75.

Lowndes, V. and McCaughie, K. (2013) 'Weathering the perfect storm? Austerity and institutional resilience in local government', *Policy & Politics*, 41(4): 533–49.

Lowndes, V. and Pratchett, L. (2012) 'Local governance under the coalition government: Austerity, localism and the "Big Society"', *Local Government Studies*, 38(1): 21–40.

Lowndes, V. and Sullivan, H. (2008) 'How low can you go? Rationales and challenges for neighbourhood governance', *Public Administration*, 86(1): 53–74.

Ludwig, C. and Ludwig, G. (2014) 'Empty gestures? A review of the discourses of "localism" from the practitioner's perspective', *Local Economy*, 29(3): 245–56.

Lukes, S. (2005) *Power: A Radical View* (2nd edn), Basingstoke: Palgrave Macmillan.

Lupton, R., Hughes, C., Peake-Jones, S. and Cooper, K. (2018) *City-Region Devolution in England*, London: London School of Economics and Political Science.

MacKenzie, J.M. and Devine, T.M. (2011) *Scotland and the British Empire*, Oxford: Oxford University Press.

MacLeod, G. and Jones, M. (2011) 'Renewing urban politics', *Urban Studies*, 48(12): 2443–72.

Marlow, D. (2013) 'England's non-metropolitan cities: The long march to unlocking economic growth', *Local Economy*, 28(7–8): 875–83.

Marrs, C. (2018) 'Bradley promises legislation to unblock Northern Ireland major decisions impasse', PlanningResource, 7 September [Online], Available from: www.planningresource.co.uk/article/1492202/bradley-promises-legislation-unblock-northern-ireland-major-decisions-impasse (Accessed 30 November 2018).

Marsh, A. (2012) 'Is it time to put the dream of elected mayors to bed?', *Policy & Politics*, 40(4): 607.

Martin, R. Pike, A. Tyler, P. and Gardiner, B. (2016) 'Spatially rebalancing the UK economy: Towards a new policy model?', *Regional Studies*, 50(2): 342–57.

Matthews, P. and Hastings, A. (2012) 'Middle-class political activism and middle-class advantage in relation to public services: A realist synthesis of the evidence base', *Social Policy & Administration*, 47(1): 72–92.

Matthews, P., Bramley, G. and Hastings, A. (2015) 'Homo economicus in a Big Society: Understanding middle-class activism and NIMBYism towards new housing developments', *Housing, Theory and Society*, 32(1): 54–72.

Mawson, J. (2007) 'Regional governance in England: Past experience, future directions', *International Journal of Public Sector Management*, 20(6): 548–66.

May, T. (2016) 'Statement from the new Prime Minister Theresa May' [Online], Available from: www.gov.uk/government/speeches/statement-from-the-new-prime-minister-theresa-may (Accessed 21 January 2019).

McBane, J. (2008) *The Rebirth of Liverpool: The Eldonian Way*, Liverpool: Liverpool University Press.

McCann, P. (2016) *The UK Regional–National Economic Problem*, London: Routledge.

MHCLG (Ministry of Housing, Communities and Local Government) (2018a) 'Government announces new Northern Powerhouse body', London: MHCLG.

MHCLG (2018b) 'Government proposes shake-up of Local Enterprise Partnership', London: MHCLG.

MHCLG (2018c) 'Local plan intervention: Letters to councils' [Online], Available from: www.gov.uk/government/publications/local-plan-intervention-letters-to-councils (Accessed 22 November 2018).

MHCLG (2018d) 'Make a neighbourhood plan' [Online], Available from: www.gov.uk/government/get-involved/take-part/make-a-neighbourhood-plan (Accessed 26 September 2018).

MHCLG (2018e) *National Planning Policy Framework* (2nd edn), London: MHCLG.

MHCLG (2018f) 'Neighbourhood Planning guidance' [Online], Available from: www.gov.uk/guidance/neighbourhood-planning--2#basic-conditions-for-neighbourhood-plan-to-referendum (Accessed 26 September 2018).

MHCLG (2018g) 'Notes on Neighbourhood Planning: Edition 20, March 2018' [Online], Available from: https://assets.publishing.service.gov.uk/government/uploads/system/uploads/attachment_data/file/691602/Notes_on_Neighbourhood_Planning.pdf (Accessed 26 September 2018).

MHCLG, May, T. and Javid, S. (2018) 'Prime Minister launches new planning rules to get England delivering homes for everyone' [Online], Available from: www.gov.uk/government/news/prime-minister-launches-new-planning-rules-to-get-england-delivering-homes-for-everyone (Accessed 26 September 2018).

Middleton-Pugh, J. (2018) 'More delays for GMSF as tensions come to a head' [Online], Available from: www.placenorthwest.co.uk/news/more-delays-for-gmsf-as-tensions-come-to-a-head/ (Accessed 21 January 2019).

Midwinter, A. (2001) 'New Labour and the modernisation of British local government: A critique', *Financial Accountability & Management*, 17(4): 311–20.

Millward, L. (2005) '"We are announcing your target": Reflections on performative language in the making of English housing policy', *Local Government Studies*, 31(5): 597–614.

Monaghan, P., North, P. and Southern, A. (2016) 'Ecological empowerment and Enterprise Zones: Pain free transitions to sustainable production in cities or fool's gold?', *Journal of Cleaner Production*, 134: 395–405.

Mooney, G. and Fyfe, N. (2006) 'New Labour and community protests: The case of the Govanhill Swimming Pool Campaign, Glasgow', *Local Economy*, 21(2): 136–50.

Moore, R. (2018) 'Preston bus station review – A glorious reprieve', *The Guardian*, 9 June [Online], Available from: www.theguardian.com/artanddesign/2018/jun/09/preston-bus-station-renovation-ove-arup-glorious-reprieve-john-puttick (Accessed 26 November 2018).

Moore, T. (2014) *Affordable Homes for Local Communities: The Effects and Prospects of Community Land Trusts in England*, St Andrews: St Andrews Centre for Housing Research.

Moore, T. and McKee, K. (2012) 'Empowering local communities? An international review of community land trusts', *Housing Studies*, 27(2): 280–90.

Morphet, J. (2011) 'Delivering infrastructure through spatial planning: The multi-scalar approach in the UK', *Local Economy*, 26(4): 285–93.

Morphet, J. (2015) 'The Contribution of Planning to England's Devolutionary Journey', in J. Kilroy (ed) *Critical Perspectives on Devolved Governance*, London: Royal Town Planning Institute, pp 15–17.

Morphet, J. and Clifford, B. (2017) *Local Authority Direct Provision of Housing*, London: National Planning Forum and Royal Town Planning Institute.

Morris, S. (2017) 'Welsh Labour to distance itself from UK party in general election', *The Guardian*, 5 May [Online], Available from: www.theguardian.com/politics/2017/may/05/welsh-labour-distance-itself-uk-party-corbyn-general-election (Accessed 30 November 2018).

Mullen, T. (2014) 'The Scottish independence referendum 2014', *Journal of Law and Society*, 41(4): 627–40.

Newman, J. (2014) 'Landscapes of antagonism: Local governance, neoliberalism and austerity', *Urban Studies*, 51(15): 3290–305.

Newman, P.W.G. and Kenworthy, J.R. (1989) *Cities and Automobile Dependence: An International Sourcebook*, Aldershot: Gower.

Newton Dunn, T. (2017) 'NIMBY NONSENSE: Sajid Javid lashes out at babyboomer home owners who deny housing crisis', thesun.co.uk [Online], Available from: www.thesun.co.uk/news/4932350/sajid-javed-housing-millennials-theresa-may/ (Accessed 17 November 2017).

NIC (National Infrastructure Commission) (2015) *High Speed North*, London: NIC.

NLGN (New Local Government Network) (2009) *Control Shift: Alt, Insert or Delete?*, London: NLGN.

North, P. (2016) 'Money reform and the Eurozone crisis: Panacea, utopia or grassroots alternative?', *Cambridge Journal of Economics*, 40: 1439–53.

North, P., Nurse, A. and Barker, T. (2017) 'The neoliberalisation of climate? Progressing climate policy under austerity urbanism', *Environment & Planning A*, 49(8): 1797–815.

Nurse, A. (2012) *Delivering Effective Local Public Services: The Case of Local Area Agreements*, Liverpool: Liverpool University Press.

Nurse, A. (2015a) 'Bridging the gap? The role of regional governance in delivering effective public services: Evidence from England', *Planning Practice & Research*, 30(1): 69–82.

Nurse, A. (2015b) 'Creating the north from the sum of its parts? Research questions to assess the Northern Powerhouse', *Local Economy*, 30(6): 689–701.

Nurse, A. and Fulton, M. (2017) 'Delivering strategic economic development in a time of urban austerity: European Union structural funds and the English city regions', *Local Economy*, 32(3): 164–82.

Nurse, A. and Pemberton, S. (2010) 'Local area agreements as a tool for addressing deprivation within UK cities', *Journal of Urban Regeneration and Renewal*, 4(2): 158–67.

Nurse, A., Desjardins, X. and Chen, C. (2017) 'The Northern Powerhouse: A comparative perspective", *Town Planning Review*, 88(4): 383–400.

O'Brien, P. and Pike, A. (2015) 'City deals, decentralisation and the governance of local infrastructure funding and financing in the UK', *National Institute Economic Review*, 233(1): R14–R26.

O'Connor, R. (2010) 'Nimbys secure their charter', *The Times*, 26 May.

O'Hara, M. (2015) *Austerity Bites: A Journey to the Sharp End of Cuts in the UK*, Bristol: Policy Press.

ODPM (Office of the Deputy Prime Minister) (1998) *Modern Local Government: In Touch with the People*, London: The Stationery Office.

ODPM (1999) *Local Leadership, Local Choice*, London: The Stationery Office.

OECD (Organisation for Economic Co-operation and Development) (2018) 'Income inequality', Paris: OECD [Online], Available from: https://data.oecd.org/inequality/income-inequality.htm (Accessed 30 November 2018).

ONS (Office for National Statistics) (2018) 'Estimates of the population for the UK, England and Wales, Scotland and Northern Ireland, mid-2017' [Online], Available from: www.ons.gov.uk/peoplepopulationandcommunity/populationandmigration/populationestimates/datasets/populationestimatesforukenglandandwalesscotlandandnorthernireland (Accessed 19 November 2018).

Orme, J. (2010) 'Why are some campaigners calling the Localism Bill a Nimby's charter?', *Independent*, 17 December.

Osborne, G. (2014) 'Chancellor: "We need a Northern powerhouse"' [Online], Available from: www.gov.uk/government/speeches/chancellor-we-need-a-northern-powerhouse (Accessed 21 January 2019).

Osborne, G. and Pickles, E. (2011) 'Planning reforms boost local power and growth', Department for Communities and Local Government [Online], Available from: www.gov.uk/government/speeches/planning-reforms-boost-local-power-and-growth (Accessed 18 September 2019).

Pansardi, P. (2012) 'Power to and power over: Two distinct concepts of power?', *Journal of Political Power*, 5(1): 73–89.

Park, B.G. (2008) 'Uneven development, inter-scalar tensions, and the politics of decentralization in South Korea', *International Journal of Urban and Regional Research*, 32(1): 40–59.

Park, S.J. and Abelmann, N. (2004) 'Class and cosmopolitan striving: Mothers' management of English education in South Korea', *Anthropological Quarterly*, 77(4): 645–72.

Parker, G. and Salter, K. (2016) 'Five years of Neighbourhood Planning – A review of take-up and distribution', *Town and Country Planning*, 85(5): 181–8.

Parker, G., Lynn, T. and Wargent, M. (2015) 'Sticking to the script? The co-production of Neighbourhood Planning in England', *Town Planning Review*, 86(5): 519–36.

Parkinson, M. (1985) *Liverpool on the Brink*, Hermitage: Policy Journals.

Parkinson, M. and Lord, A. (2017) *Albert Dock: What Part in Liverpool's Continuing Renaissance?*, Liverpool: University of Liverpool.

Parkinson, M., Hague, J., Sinclair, C. and Pollitt, I. (2017) *The Liverpool Brand – What Is it and Why Does it Matter So Much Now?*, Liverpool: Marketing Liverpol.

Pautz, H. (2018) 'Think tanks, Tories and the austerity discourse coalition', *Policy and Society*, 37(2): 155–69.

Peck, J. (2001) 'Neoliberalizing states: Thin policies/hard outcomes', *Progress in Human Geography*, 25(3): 445–55.

Peck, J. (2012) 'Austerity urbanism', *City*, 16(6): 626–55.

Peck, J. and Tickell, A. (1994) 'Jungle Law breaks out: Neo-liberalism and global–local disorder', *Area*, 26: 317–26.

Peel, D. (2016) 'Liverpool Waters' [Online], Available from: www.liverpoolwaters.co.uk/about/liverpool-waters (Accessed 5 January 2019).

Peel, D. and Lloyd, M.G. (2012) 'The Edinburgh concordat: Contractual, collaborative positive planning?', *Public Performance & Management Review*, 36(2): 275–89.

Pemberton, S. (2017) 'Community-Based Planning and Localism in the Devolved UK', in S. Brownill and Q. Bradley (eds) *Localism and Neighbourhood Planning: Power to the People?*, Bristol: Policy Press, pp 183–98.

Pemberton, S. and Goodwin, M. (2010) 'Rethinking the changing structure of rural local government – State power, rural politics and local political strategies?', *Journal of Rural Studies*, 26(3): 272–83.

Pemberton, S. and Shaw, D. (2012) 'New forms of sub-regional governance and implications for rural areas: Evidence from England', *Planning Practice & Research*, 27(4): 441–58.

Pemberton, S., Peel, D. and Lloyd, G. (2015) 'The "filling in" of community-based planning in the devolved UK?', *The Geographical Journal*, 181(1): 6–15.

Perraudin, F. (2018a) 'No agreed power, no agreed budget: Dan Jarvis on his fight to be Sheffield mayor', *The Guardian*, 23 April [Online], Available from: www.theguardian.com/politics/2018/apr/23/dan-jarvis-labour-sheffield-city-region-mayor-election (Accessed 21 January 2019).

Perraudin, F. (2018b) '"Yours cynically": Emails show DfT contempt for rail users, says MP', *The Guardian*, 20 June [Online], Available from: www.theguardian.com/politics/2018/jun/20/private-emails-show-dft-contempt-for-rail-users-says-mp (Accessed 21 January 2019).

Pike, A., Marlow, D., McCarthy, A., O'Brien, P. and Tomaney, J. (2015) 'Local institutions and local economic development: The Local Enterprise Partnerships in England, 2010–', *Cambridge Journal of Regions, Economy and Society*, 8(2): 185–204.

Pike, A., Mackinnon, D., Coombes, M., Champion, T., et al (2016) *Uneven Growth: Tackling City Decline*, York: Joseph Rowntree Foundation.

Place North West (2018) 'Liverpool misses out on Channel 4', 23 August [Online], Available from: www.placenorthwest.co.uk/news/liverpool-misses-out-on-channel-4/ (Accessed 26 November 2018).

Planning Portal (2017) 'Draft Belfast Metropolitan Area Plan', Department for Infrastructure [Online], Available from: www.planningni.gov.uk/index/policy/development_plans/devplans_az/dbmap2015.htm (Accessed 30 November 2018).

Plimmer, G. and Pickard, J. (2018) 'Crossrail gains new £2bn rescue from government', *Financial Times* [Online], Available from: www.ft.com/content/c0f41e66-fc7f-11e8-aebf-99e208d3e521 (Accessed 21 January 2019).

Porter, A. and Riddell, M. (2009) 'Gordon Brown warns against new age of austerity', *The Telegraph*, 10 October [Online], Available from: www.telegraph.co.uk/news/politics/gordon-brown/6284662/Gordon-Brown-warns-against-new-age-of-austerity.html (Accessed 1 July 2019).

Press Association (2017) 'Jeremy Corbyn: Next Labour government will tackle housing crisis', MailOnline, 14 August [Online], Available from: www.dailymail.co.uk/wires/pa/article-4788604/Jeremy-Corbyn-Next-Labour-government-tackle-housing-crisis.html (Accessed 17 November 2017).

PSA (Political Studies Association) (2012) *The Local Mayoral Referendums Media Briefing Pack*, London: PSA.

Pugalis, L. (2010) 'Looking back in order to move forward: The politics of evolving sub-national economic policy architecture', *Local Economy*, 25(5–6): 397–405.

Pugalis, L. (2011) 'Look before you LEP', *Journal of Urban Regeneration and Renewal*, 5(1): 7–22.

Pugalis, L. and Bentley, G. (2013) 'Storming or performing? Local Enterprise Partnerships two years on', *Local Economy*, 28(7–8): 863–74.

Pugalis, L., Shutt, J. and Bentley, G. (2012) 'Local Enterprise Partnerships: Living up to the hype', *Critical Issues*, 4: 1–10.

Quinn, B. (2016) 'Theresa May sets out "one-nation Conservative" pitch for leadership', *The Guardian*, 30 June [Online], Available from: www.theguardian.com/politics/2016/jun/30/theresa-may-sets-out-one-nation-conservative-pitch-for-leadership (Accessed 21 January 2019).

Raikes, L. (2018) *Future Transport Investment in the North*, Manchester: IPPR (Institute for Public Policy Research) North.

Rallings, C. and Thrasher, M. (2016) *Local and Police and Crime Commissioner Elections May 2016*, Plymouth: Elections Centre Plymouth University.

RIBA (Royal Institute of British Architects) (2018) *Joining the Dots: A New Approach to Tackling the UK's Infrastructure Challenges*, London: RIBA.

Rittel, H.W.J. and Webber, M.M. (1973) 'Dilemmas in a general theory of planning', *Policy Sciences*, 4(2): 155–69.

Robson, B., Parkinson, M., Boddy, M. and Maclennan, D. (2000) *The State of English Cities*, London: Department of the Environment, Transport and the Regions.

Rodriguez-Pose, A. and Gill, N. (2003) 'The global trend towards devolution and its implications', *Environment and Planning C: Government and Policy*, 21: 333–51.

Rodriguez-Pose, A. and Sandall, R. (2008) 'From identity to the economy: Analysing the evolution of the decentralisation discourse', *Environment and Planning C: Government and Policy*, 26: 54–72.

Rosan, C.D. (2012) 'Can PlaNYC make New York City greener and greater for everyone? Sustainability planning and the promise of environmental justice', *Local Environment*, 17(9): 959–76.

Rotheram, S. (2016) *Our Future Together*, Wirral: Labour Party.

Rotheram, S. and Burnham, A. (2018) *Joint Statement from Metro Mayors on Northern Rail Disruption*, Liverpool and Manchester: Liverpool City Region Combined Authority and Greater Manchester Combined Authority.

RTPI (Royal Town Planning Institute) (2016) *Blueprint for a Great North Plan*, London: RTPI.

Rustin, S. (2016) 'Joe Anderson, Liverpool mayor: "It's not about big hitters, like Andy Burnham"', *The Guardian*, 1 June [Online], Available from: www.theguardian.com/society/2016/jun/01/joe-anderson-liverpool-mayor-big-hitters-andy-burnham (Accessed 21 January 2019).

Ryan, F. (2017) 'In Liverpool, Tory cuts have brought a city and its people to breaking point', *The Guardian*, 23 March [Online], Available from: www.theguardian.com/commentisfree/2017/mar/23/liverpool-tory-cuts-city-benefits-poorest (Accessed 17 August 2017).

Salet, W., Vermeulen, R., Savini, F. and Dembski, S. (2015) 'Planning for the new European metropolis: Functions, politics, and symbols', *Planning Theory & Practice*, 16(2): 251–4.

Sandford, M. (2015) *Community Budgets and City Deals*, London: House of Commons Library.

Sandford, M. (2016) 'Public services and local government: The end of the principle of "funding following duties"', *Local Government Studies*, 42(4): 637–56.

Sandford, M. (2017a) *Assets of Community Value*, London: House of Commons Library.

Sandford, M. (2017b) *Combined Authorities*, London: House of Commons Library.

Sassen, S. (1991) *The Global City*, Princeton, NJ: Princeton University Press.

Sassen, S. (1994) *Cities in a World Economy*, London: Pine Forge.

Sassen, S. (1999) *Globalization and its Discontents: Essays on the New Mobility of People and Money*, New York: The Free Press.

Sassen, S. (2001) 'Global Cities and Global City Regions: A Comparison', in A.J. Scott (ed) *Global City-Regions: Trends Theory, Policy*, Oxford: Oxford University Press, pp 78–95.

Satsangi, M. (2007) 'Land tenure change and rural housing in Scotland', *Scottish Geographical Journal*, 123(1): 33–47.

Saxenian, A. (1994) *Regional Advantage: Culture and Competition in Silicon Valley and Route 128*, Harvard, MA: Harvard University Press.

Seth, M.J. (2002) *Education Fever: Society, Politics, and the Pursuit of Schooling in South Korea*, Honolulu, HI: University of Hawaii Press.

Shaw, D. and Lord, A. (2009) 'From land-use to "spatial planning" – Reflections on the reform of the English planning system', *Town Planning Review*, 80(4): 415–35.

Shaw, K. and Robinson, F. (2007) '"The end of the beginning"? Taking forward local democratic renewal in the post-referendum North East', *Local Economy*, 22(3): 243–60.

Shaw, K. and Tewdwr-Jones, M. (2017) '"Disorganised devolution": Reshaping metropolitan governance in England in a period of austerity', *Raumforschung und Raumordnung | Spatial Research and Planning*, 75(3): 211–24.

Shaw, K., Robinson, F. and Blackie, J. (2014) 'Borderlands: Rescaling economic development in Northern England in the context of greater Scottish autonomy', *Local Economy*, 29(4-5): 412–28.

Sheffield, H. (2017) 'The Preston model: UK takes lessons in recovery from rust-belt Cleveland', *The Guardian*, 11 April [Online], Available from: www.theguardian.com/cities/2017/apr/11/preston-cleveland-model-lessons-recovery-rust-belt (Accessed 9 November 2018).

Shelter (2015) 'How much help is Help to Buy?: Help to Buy and the impact on house prices' [Online], Available from: https://england.shelter.org.uk/__data/assets/pdf_file/0010/1188073/2015_09_how_much_help_is_Help_to_Buy.pdf (Accessed 4 December 2018).

Shipley, R. and Utz, S. (2012) 'Making it count: A review of the value and techniques for public consultation', *Journal of Planning Literature*, 27(1): 22–42.

Short, J.R. (1982) *Housing in Britain – The Post-War Experience*, London and New York: Methuen & Co.

Sim, P. (2018) 'Rates of change: Holyrood and income tax', BBC News [Online], Available from: www.bbc.co.uk/news/uk-scotland-scotland-politics-43115967 (Accessed 31 December 2018).

Singh, A. (2018) 'Leaders meet to discuss One Yorkshire devolution with unity tested by ministers', *The Yorkshire Post*, 11 July [Online], Available from: www.yorkshirepost.co.uk/news/leaders-meet-to-discuss-one-yorkshire-devolution-with-unity-tested-by-ministers-1-9247058 (Accessed 21 January 2019).

Smith, D. and Timberlake, M. (2002) 'Hierarchies of Dominance among World Cities', in S. Sassen (ed) *Global Networks, Linked Cities*, London: Routledge, pp 117–42.

Smith Commission, The (2014) *Report of the Smith Commission for Further Devolution of Powers to the Scottish Parliament*, Edinburgh.

Somerville, P. and Haines, N. (2008) 'Prospects for local co-governance', *Local Government Studies*, 34(1): 61–79.

Sonn, J.W. (2010) 'Contesting state rescaling: An analysis of the South Korean state's discursive strategy against devolution', *Antipode*, 42(5): 1200–24.

Sorensen, C.W. (1994) 'Success and education in South Korea', *Comparative Education Review*, 38(1): 10–35.

Southern, A. (2014) 'Something is stirring in Anfield: Elite Premier League football and localism', *Local Economy*, 29(3): 195–212.

Sparrow, A. (2009) 'Tories want to create "big society", says David Cameron', *The Guardian*, 10 November [Online], Available from: www.theguardian.com/politics/2009/nov/10/david-cameron-hugo-young-lecture (Accessed 1 July 2019).

Squires, G. and Hall, S. (2013) 'Lesson (un)learning in spatially targeted fiscal incentive policy: Enterprise Zones (England) and Empowerment Zones (United States)', *Land Use Policy*, 33: 81–9.

St Neots (2018) *St Neots Masterplan for Growth*, Huntingdon: Cambridgeshire and Peterborough Combined Authority.

Stanton, J. (2015) 'Decentralisation and empowerment under the coalition government: An empirical study of local councils in London', *Journal of Planning and Environment Law*, 9: 978–93.

Stanton, J. (2018) 'Rebalancing the central–local relationship: Achieving a bottom-up approach to localism in England', *Legal Studies – The Journal of the Society of Legal Scholars*, 38(3): 429–49.

Stratton, A. (2010) 'Eric Pickles to scrap "agents of Whitehall" in English regions', *The Guardian*, 22 July [Online], Available from: www.theguardian.com/society/2010/jul/22/government-offices-england-regions (Accessed 21 January 2019).

Sturzaker, J. (2010) 'The exercise of power to limit the development of new housing in the English countryside', *Environment and Planning A*, 42(4): 1001–16.

Sturzaker, J. (2011) 'Can community empowerment reduce opposition to housing? Evidence from rural England', *Planning Practice and Research*, 26(5): 555–70.

Sturzaker, J. and Gordon, M. (2017) 'Democratic tensions in decentralised planning – Rhetoric, legislation and reality in England', *Environment and Planning C: Politics and Space*, 35(7): 1324–39.

Sturzaker, J. and Mell, I.C. (2016) *Green Belts: Past; Present; Future?*, Abingdon: Routledge.

Sturzaker, J. and Shaw, D. (2015) 'Localism in practice – Lessons from a pioneer neighbourhood plan in England', *Town Planning Review*, 86(5): 587–609.

Sturzaker, J. and Shucksmith, M. (2011) 'Planning for housing in rural England: Discursive power and spatial exclusion', *Town Planning Review*, 82(2): 169–93.

Summers, D. (2009) 'David Cameron warns of "new age of austerity"', *The Guardian*, 26 April [Online], Available from: www.theguardian.com/politics/2009/apr/26/david-cameron-conservative-economic-policy1 (Accessed 21 January 2019).

Sutcliffe, R. and Holt, R. (2011) *Who Is Ready for the Big Society?*, Birmingham: Consulting InPlace.

Sweeting, D. and Hambleton, R. (2015) 'Analysing Change in Urban Political Leadership: Does Introducing a Mayoral Form of Governance Make a Difference?', Urban Affairs Association Annual Conference, Miami, FL.

Sykes, O. and Nurse, A. (2017) 'Cities and regional development in England – A festival of scales and regions?', *Pole Sud*, 46(1): 79–96.

Sykes, O., Brown, J., Cocks, M., Shaw, D. and Couch, C. (2013) 'A city profile of Liverpool', *Cities*, 35: 299–318.

Tait, M. and Inch, A. (2016) 'Putting localism in place: Conservative images of the good community and the contradictions of planning reform in England', *Planning Practice and Research*, 31(2): 174–94.

Taylor, P. (2017) 'Brexit – When taking back control means giving up control' [Online], Available from: www.politico.eu/article/brexit-taking-back-control-united-kingdom-giving-up-control/ (Accessed 2 August 2018).

TCPA (Town & Country Planning Association) (1999) *Your Place and Mine: Reinventing Planning*, London: TCPA.

TFGM (Transport for Greater Manchester) (2018) 'Greater Manchester announces plans for "Beelines" – The UK's largest cycling and walking network' [Online], Available from: www.tfgm.com/press-release/beelines (Accessed 21 January 2019).

Thompson, M. (2015) 'Between boundaries: From commoning and guerrilla gardening to community land trust development in Liverpool', *Antipode*, 47(4): 1021–42.

Thornley, A., Rydin, Y., Scanlon, K. and West, K. (2003) 'Business privilege and the strategic planning agenda of the Greater London Authority', *Urban Studies*, 42(11): 1948–67.

Thorp, L. (2018) 'Calls to "abolish" Joe Anderson's Mayoral job', *Liverpool Echo*, 24 May [Online], Available from: www.liverpoolecho.co.uk/news/liverpool-news/calls-abolish-joe-andersons-mayoral-14700350 (Accessed 18 September 2019).

Tierney, S. (2015) 'Reclaiming politics: Popular democracy in Britain after the Scottish referendum', *The Political Quarterly*, 86(2): 226–33.

TMP (The Mersey Partnership) (2009) *Economic Review 2009*, Liverpool: TMP.

Tomaney, J. (2015) 'Assessing the Impact of Decentralisation', in J. Kilroy (ed) *Critical Perspectives on Devolved Governance*, London: Royal Town Planning Institute, pp 5–7.

Tonne, C., Beevers, S., Armstrong, B.G., Kelly, F. and Wilkinson, P. (2008) 'Air pollution and mortality benefits of the London Congestion Charge', *Occupational and Environmental Medicine*, 65(9): 630–7.

Trowler, P., Saunders, M. and Knight, P. (2003) *Change Thinking, Change Practices*, York: LTSN Generic Centre.

Turcu, C. (2012) 'Local experiences of urban sustainability', *Progress in Planning*, 78(3): 101–50.

University of Southampton (2018) 'Next stop, the future: Providing evidence-based solutions for improving rail networks' [Online], Available from: www.southampton.ac.uk/news/2016/04/revolutionising-rail-infrastructure.page (Accessed 4 December 2018).

van Oort, F., Burger, M. and Raspe, O. (2010) 'On the economic foundation of the urban network paradigm: Spatial integration, functional integration and economic complementarities within the Dutch Randstad', *Urban Studies*, 47(4): 725–48.

Vaughan, A. (2016) 'Fracking given UK go-ahead as Lancashire council rejection overturned', *The Guardian*, 6 October [Online], Available from: www.theguardian.com/environment/2016/oct/06/uk-fracking-given-go-ahead-as-lancashire-council-rejection-is-overturned (Accessed 23 November 2018).

Veltz, P. (1996) *Mondialisation, Villes et Territoires. L'econome Archipel*, Paris: Press Universitaries de France.

Vigar, G., Gunn, S. and Brooks, E. (2017) 'Governing our neighbours: Participation and conflict in Neighbourhood Planning', *Town Planning Review*, 88(4): 423–42.

Wainwright, H. (2009) *Reclaim the State: Experiments in Popular Democracy* (2nd edn), Calcutta, India: Seagull.

Wainwright, M. (2010) *True North: In Praise of England's Better Half*, London: Guardian Books.

Walker, A. (2016) 'North West Powerhouse promised as Labour chooses Manchester and Liverpool mayoral candidates', *Infrastructure Intelligence*, 10 August.

Wallis, V. (2018) 'Will the UK's starter homes initiative ever get off the ground?', *The Guardian*, 9 May [Online], Available from: www.theguardian.com/money/2018/may/09/uk-starter-homes-initiative-theresa-may-target (Accessed 4 December 2018).

Ward, M. (2016) *Enterprise Zones*, London: House of Commons Library.

Ward, M. (2018) *City Deals*, London: House of Commons Library.

Waterson, J. (2018) 'Channel 4 chooses Leeds as new national headquarters' [Online], *The Guardian*, 31 October, Available from: www.theguardian.com/media/2018/oct/31/channel-4-chooses-second-headquarters (Accessed 21 January 2019).

Wates, N. and Knevitt, C. (1987) *Community Architecture – How People are Creating Their Own Environment*, London: Penguin.

Watt, N. (2011) 'David Cameron calls civil servants "enemies of enterprise" [Online], *The Guardian*, 6 March, Available from: www.theguardian.com/politics/2011/mar/06/david-cameron-civil-service-enemies (Accessed 8 February 2017).

Watts, J. (2017) 'Theresa May promises to personally solve UK housing crisis', *Independent*, 15 November [Online], Available from: www.independent.co.uk/news/uk/politics/theresa-may-housing-crisis-mission-latest-uk-shortage-crisis-homes-a8057046.html (Accessed 17 November 2017).

Weston, A. (2016) 'Liverpool on collision course with Unesco over development ban', *Liverpool Echo*, 14 July [Online], Available from: www.liverpoolecho.co.uk/news/liverpool-news/liverpool-collision-course-unesco-over-11615492 (Accessed 26 November 2018).

Wilks-Heeg, S. (2003) 'From World City to Pariah City? Liverpool and the Global Economy 1850–2000', in R. Munck (ed) *Reinventing the City? Liverpool in Comparative Perspective*, Liverpool: Liverpool University Press, Chapter 2.

Wilks-Heeg, S. and Clayton, S. (2006) *Whose Town Is it Anyway? The State of Local Democracy In Two Northern Towns*, York: Joseph Roundtree Charitable Trust.

Wilks-Heeg, S., Blick, A. and Crone, S. (2012) *How Democratic Is the UK? The 2012 Audit*, Liverpool: Democratic Audit.

Williams, A., Goodwin, M. and Cloke, P. (2014) 'Neoliberalism, Big Society, and progressive localism', *Environment and Planning A*, 46(12): 2798–815.

Williams, J. (2014) 'Should Greater Manchester follow Scotland's example and strive for independence?', *Manchester Evening News*, 11 September [Online], Available from: www.manchestereveningnews.co.uk/business/business-news/should-greater-manchester-follow-scotlands-7750466 (Accessed 21 January 2019).

Williams, J. (2018a) 'Drivers could be charged to go into Manchester city centre', *Manchester Evening News*, 7 October [Online], Available from: www.manchestereveningnews.co.uk/news/greater-manchester-news/drivers-could-charged-go-manchester-15243941 (Accessed 21 January 2019).

Williams, J. (2018b) 'The extraordinary story behind Manchester and Salford's bitter war over Channel 4', *Manchester Evening News*, 28 December [Online], Available from: www.manchestereveningnews.co.uk/news/greater-manchester-news/channel-4-base-manchester-salford-15594299 (Accessed 21 January 2019).

Wilson, P. (2018) 'Liverpool mayor defends city's £280m loan to Everton for stadium scheme', *The Guardian*, 10 January [Online], Available from: www.theguardian.com/football/2018/jan/10/everton (Accessed 24 December 2018).

Wilson, W. (2018) *Stimulating Housing Supply – Government Initiatives (England)*, London: House of Commons Library.

Wilson, W., Murphy, C. and Barton, C. (2017) *The New Homes Bonus*, London: House of Commons Library.

Winter, G., Smith, L., Cave, S. and Rehfisch, A. (2016) *Comparison of the Planning Systems in the Four UK Countries*, London: House of Commons Library.

Wise, M.J. (1969) 'The future of local government In England: "The Redcliffe Maud Report"', *The Geographical Journal*, 135(4): 583–7.

Woestenburg, A.K., van der Krabben, E. and Spit, T.J.M. (2018) 'Land policy discretion in times of economic downturn', *Land Use Policy*, 77: 801–10.

Wong, C. and Webb, B. (2014) 'Planning for infrastructure: Challenges to northern England', *Town Planning Review*, 85(6): 683–708.

Worthy, B., Bennister, M. and Stafford, M.W. (2018) 'Rebels leading London: The mayoralties of Ken Livingstone and Boris Johnson compared', *British Politics*, 14(1): 23–43.

Index

Johnson, Boris 21, 161
Johnston, B. 115
Jones, G. 7, 120
Jones, M. 6
Jones, P. 5, 110

K
Keating, M. 37
Kingdon, J.W. *78*
Kollman, K. 15
Kuhlmann, S. 107

L
Labour government (1945) 102
Labour government (1997–2010)
    (Blair/Brown)
    and austerity 22–3
    and community-led governance
    126, 129
    and devolution 25–6, 29–30, 33
    and local authorities 103–4, 107
    and neoliberalism 32
    and planning 29
    and regional governance 25–6,
    29–30, 47–8
    Labour councillors 143
Labour Party, mayors 79, 81, 85–6,
    87
Laforest, G. 37
land use planning 108, 109
leadership, impact of 159
Liberal Democrats *see* Coalition
    government (2010–15)
Liddle, J. 52
Liverpool City Council 80, 110–14,
    128–9
Liverpool City Region 49, 53
    governing of 90, 91, 92, 96
    mayors 53, 67, 78, 79–80, 85, 86,
    87, 90, 91, 92, 93, 111, 112–13
Liverpool City Region (continued)
    metro mayor vs city mayor 87,
    93
    tensions within 80, 91
Liverpool Waters 110–11, *111*
Livingstone, Ken 25
Lloyd, M.G. 32
Lloyd, Tony 86, 89
local authorities 7, 99–121, 151–2
    adversarial approach to by central
    government 157

austerity 23–4, 104–5, 120, 152,
    155
autonomy of 100–9
and city regions 101
contracting out 115
in devolved nations 30–1
and direct control 106–7
enterprise zones 115–16
entrepreneurialism 109–16, 120,
    152
and fiscal autonomy 105–6
housing 9, 102, 108, 109, 114
indirect control 107–8
key areas of change 101–4
Liverpool case study 110–14
local currencies 116–17
Localism Act 2011 120
monitoring of 107–8
organisational structure 103–4
planning 102, 106–7, 108–9,
    110–11, 115
Portugal *119–20*
Preston model 118–19, 152
radical alternatives 116–19
resilience of 120, 152
local currencies 116–17
Local Democracy, Economic
    Development and Construction
    Act 2009 47–8
Local Enterprise Partnerships (LEPS)
    48–54, *50–1*, 69, 74, 75, 80, 82,
    150
Local Government Acts (1963, 1972,
    1985) 103
Local Government (Boundaries) Act
    (Northern Ireland) 2008 31
localism (concept)
    and austerity 11–13, 104–5
    critiques of 11–12
    definition 10
    government rhetoric of 158
    and neoliberalism 11, 13
    and power 12–13, 14–15
    as progressive force 160
    in UK 11–13
    see also community-led governance;
    local authorities
Localism Act 2011 10, 12–13, 120,
    129–31
London 7, 25, 43, 47, 76–7
London Assembly 25, 47
Lord, A. 141
Low Carbon Liverpool 117

www.ingramcontent.com/pod-product-compliance
Lightning Source LLC
Chambersburg PA
CBHW070925030426
42336CB00014BA/2540